MY RIVER

A Memoir

Richard Kenneth Stearns

Text set in Arial
Manufactured in the United States of America
First Edition
1 3 5 7 9 10 8 6 4 2

Cover design: Gerry Keller

Library of Congress Control Number: 2008900928
Publisher: BookSurge Publishing
North Charleston, South Carolina

Library of Congress Cataloging-in-Publication Data

Stearns, Richard Kenneth
My River – A Memoir
Autobiography
1. Western Washington - History of Boistfort Valley
2. Atomic Weapons – Training, Deployment - Humor
3. US Spy Satellites - Early Development
4. Fly-fishing - Washington, British Columbia - Humor
5. Title

ISBN-10: 1-4196-8940-1
1SBN-13: 978-1-4196-8940-6

Visit www.booksurge.com to order additional copies.

To Grandpa
He called me Dicky

Author's note

As in most memoirs, there's a bit of fiction here. In this case, there are several reasons: Some names were changed because those involved who might be embarrassed couldn't be contacted. Other details had to be omitted or re-written because of non-disclosure agreements with former employers; and as you read through the technical chapters, I hope you'll appreciate that much was changed during a two-year vetting process.

You'll see that my writing style is that of a technocrat. Sorry about that, but I'm writing this as though I'm telling this story to you. So, if you happen to see a few grammatical errors here—well, that's the way I talk.

Forward

Faced with mortality, my life history suddenly becomes important. If I were drowning, it would flash by in seconds; but I have more time now, so it might be nice to write things down. In that regard, I guess you could say I'm lucky.

I always wanted to write my life experience, if for no other reason than to leave with my two daughters, three granddaughters and grandson something they could someday read and know that perhaps I wasn't really the person they thought they knew.

But as I began to write, it became obvious there might be more here than just a simple life story…

Table of Contents

1   The Boistfort Valley

Your urologist says you have cancer. You ask: "How soon do we need to do something about it?" What you most urgently want to ask is: "How long can I expect to live?" but the question sticks in your throat.

You look to your wife of just seven short years and read in DeVonne's eyes the same question.

From the day Dicky was born, women were in his life. For starters, there were five, if you included Mom.

He was brought into his world kicking and screaming by a midwife, Wilma Bamer. Wilma lived across the road from Rose Roundtree's house where Dicky was born. Rose was there. His sister, Vivian, six years older was there. Emma, his grandmother was there also. Nobody ever said where Dicky's father was.

It was on an unusually wet January that floodwaters from My River had spread across the lower Boistfort Valley and prevented travel to the hospital in Chehalis 12 miles away. No matter. Childbirth by way of impromptu midwives was common in 1936. Dicky's family was poor, so flood or not, he might well have been born under these circumstances anyway.

He could have been born in any other place, I suppose; like Bangladesh, Mongolia, or South Carolina. But he was lucky, he was delivered to a place in this world that enabled him to live the American dream. And, to catch trout in My River.

My River was really the South Fork of the Chehalis. She flowed gracefully through the Boistfort Valley for millennia before Dicky's ancestors and others settled the lush meadows created by her floods. Within her flood plain, flowering camas overwhelmed the millions of seeds sown by fir and hemlock, thereby preserving the meadows for themselves.

It was the meadow's place in nature's scheme to provide an oasis within the overwhelming forest. It allowed the scarce winter sunlight to warm the animals that would otherwise not see the sun through the forest's dense canopy. It provided a resting place for the families of the Chehalis Indian Tribe who harvested the edible camas bulbs and threw trout from My River onto her banks.

My River waited patiently along the meadow for settlers to come and change her forever.

In 1846, shortly after the Oregon Territory ceded from the Hudson Bay Company, Great-Great Grandfather, Henry Noble Stearns arrived at the small river port of Kelso after an arduous journey over the Oregon Trail to the Willamette Valley. He had boated down the Willamette and Columbia rivers, and later continued up the Cowlitz River to Toledo where he hired a wagon to take the first of the family belongings to a site ten miles down My River from Dicky's birthplace. There, Henry claimed a homestead. The Indians, who maintained a cedar long house nearby, had named the site Claquato. It was a splendid setting on an oak-treed hill, gently sloping towards the Chehalis River to the south. Mt Rainier and Mt St Helens dominated the horizon to the east.

Trained as a surveyor, Henry was commissioned to determine section corners within townships in Western Lewis County. He did this for the purpose of securing public school funding pursuant to the Organic Law of 1853 that required two sections of each township be set aside for common schools. Accomplishing this, he then served as county superintendent of schools, then county auditor, postmaster and representative to the 1857 Territorial

Legislature. People remarked that he exceeded in making himself useful as a citizen.

As the rush of settlers came to the Boistfort Valley, it was fortunate that the meadows would be there to serve as the breadbasket to the surrounding communities. Unlike those who came in later years, these early settlers didn't have to carve farms out of the dense forest by undertaking the difficult task of clearing out old-growth fir and removing their huge stumps.

The rich meadows produced more than enough harvest for local settlers, and to quench the thirsts of the gold-rich cities of San Francisco and Sacramento, new crops were introduced: ingredients for making beer. Barley and hops soon replaced the flowering camas and Indians were recruited during their fall salmon harvest to pick hops alongside the settlers.

The celebration of the harvest of salmon and hops took on the semblance of a combined potlatch and county fair. Everyone benefited from the opportunity to exchange ideas, crafts and food. Little animosity sprouted up between natives and settlers in those days. There was still plenty for everyone.

But entrepreneurial competition soon supplanted the simplicity of those early harvests. After all, hops were easy to grow, with harvest possible just three years after planting. Those with necessary capital and cleared land were in a position to gain wealth with only a few harvests; but the growing of hops was relatively obscure and the more lucrative markets were not in Sacramento or even San Francisco, but in Europe.

One farmer, Herman Klaber, had both the necessary farmland and Old World connections to make the Boistfort Valley one of the most productive and profitable hop growing areas in the world. Every September, some 2,000 men, women and children migrated to the valley to harvest his crop. Soon, livery stables, a feed store, barbershop, a general store and houses began to sprout up to support the pickers.

As the harvest grew, the workforce demanded additional lodging until there were more than 400 roofed and floored shanties, each containing a stove for warmth and cooking. In addition, Klaber built warehouses, drying kilns and established a wagon transportation system that could efficiently deliver bales of dried hops to the train depot in Chehalis.

All this was part of the Klaber Investment Company, a commercial enterprise that might have been the core of a larger, thriving community, had not one historic event profoundly altered its destiny:

Because of Klaber's high quality hops, brew masters in Northern Europe and England clamored for more of his product. It was on one of his trips to open further markets that buoyed by his successes he booked first class return sailing on England's premier White Star Line.

Ironically, as a consequence of this voyage, the community and post office that bore his namesake would eventually disappear from maps and addresses, but history books would record for posterity the name Herman Klaber as one of the 1500 passengers who perished on the maiden voyage of the Titanic.

In those early days, the topography of the Boistfort Valley made travel difficult to the larger communities of Chehalis and Centralia. While the prairie that formed the main Boistfort Valley enabled easy passage of wagons, My River, after joining the North Fork, narrowed and carved a deep canyon making road building difficult.

For all practical purposes, the Valley was isolated from the rest of the growing settlements of Lewis County. This isolation would be instrumental in building the close-knit community around the Boistfort School System in the ensuing years.

But in spite of this isolation, the population of the Boistfort Valley was great enough in 1853 to be a township. One month after Washington was declared a territory, the county commissioners delineated boundaries for the townships of Cowlitz, Jackson, Chehalis, Centralia and Boistfort. During the same session, school districts were named for each of these townships. In April of 1853, Boistfort was named the first public school district in the new territory of Washington.

6   My River

2   Grandpa's Bear

It is 1991. You had just returned from a happy fishing vacation in Mexico. Along with several messages on your answering machine was one from your family doctor that you return the next day…

Dicky grew up at a place the Boistfort Valley residents then called Richter Hill, its namesake given in reference to a German family of six who moved from Chehalis in the early 1920's to buy the farm that had been cleared out of the woods sometime around the turn of the century. The farm consisted of 60 acres of cleared fields in the form of a letter "L" with 20 more acres of forested second growth filling in the apex.

The Richter farm buildings and orchard were clustered to the north at the end of a gravel road that led from the Valley. None of the fields were level, the upper one above the barn, rose to the peak of the hill behind the barn, then sloped away to the south before it ended abruptly at an ancient, old-growth forest. The field to the west dropped off precipitously, giving the ranch house a commanding view of the Boistfort Valley, some five hundred feet below, were it not for the towering firs that stood in the way. Similarly, the east field, being the most level, tilted toward Lake Creek, but also ended at the edge of what seemed to be an impenetrable forest.

The ranch house, a two-story bungalow with a large front and back porch, had three bedrooms: two up and one down. A kitchen, dining room and living room rounded out the unremarkable home, which had no internal plumbing or electricity. A party line phone and a battery-powered Kent Atwater radio were the only modern conveniences. Laundry was done by washboard, and baths were taken in the kitchen or on the back porch in a copper washtub. Water from a nearby well could be hand-pumped from the back porch.

In 1938, the lack of even modest medical care was taking its toll on local families. In the winter of 1938, two weeks before Dicky's second birthday, his father Kenneth died of pneumonia. Mom (Doris), unable to support her two children by working in the cannery at Chehalis, moved her family to Richter hill. By then, the depression was over and the New Deal was in full swing. Grandpa Eugene, after working as a Civilian Conservation Corps worker for several years, returned to farming. Mom worked part time at the Klaber store to supplement the family income, the source of which, was provided primarily by dairy products sold to the co-op in Chehalis.

But most of the family support still came through bartering and by living directly off the farm. Neighbors appeared with supplemental equipment and extra hands to harvest and share in the wheat grown on the south and east fields. Sausages made by Eugene were traded for smelt and salmon caught from the Cowlitz River by the Hagen family, their closest neighbors a mile down the hill.

Grandpa Eugene and Uncles Wilbur and Roy were expert marksmen, thus venison and grouse were common table fare. A large garden and orchard provided produce for canning and seasonal barter. From the orchard came Italian prunes, Bartlett pears, Bing cherries, and a large variety of apples.

During the fall, the whole family became engaged in the making of cider. Dicky and sister Viv first made a carpet of apples by climbing through apple-tree branches and knocking down the fruit. Then Grandpa and Uncle Wilber traded off the grinding and pressing chores while Grandma, Viv and Mom carried the apples, strained gallons of the sweet juice into milk cans and delivered the pressed lees to the pigs.   Most of the cider was consumed during the weeks leading up to Thanksgiving, but some remained in jugs in the cellar to ferment into vinegar to be used for sauerkraut.

The cellar, a closet-sized excavation lined with cedar planks under the back porch was the primary food storage. Slabs of Grandpa's cured pork, wheels of cheese and various sausages hung besides shelves loaded with jars of fruits, vegetables and meats canned by Mom and Grandma. A root cellar partition contained boxes of apples and pears next to bins of potatoes, beets and onions.

Up the hill, next to the barn, the smoke house was kept active most of the fall and winter. After the annual fall butchering and the resulting hams, bacon and sausages were finished and stored away in the cellar, the serendipitous products of venison, salmon and smelt occupied its racks for the remainder of the winter.

Suffice to say, the farming, hunting, and culinary skills of the typical German family of those years kept everyone well fed.

Dicky couldn't have been happier on Richter Hill. He was still too young to participate in many of the chores, he didn't have to go to school like Viv and Uncle Wilber, and his doting grandmother let him get away with almost everything.   This proved to be his undoing on several occasions, as he had a penchant for exploring.

The old growth forests that virtually surrounded the farm, and the small, no-name creeks that flowed through them held a particular fascination for Dicky. At first, any entry into the thick forest with its ethereal and foreboding intensity was a fearful passage, but soon he discovered it was relatively easy, even comfortable to walk over the carpeted forest floor and crawl under the deadfalls and devil's club to examine the various fauna and flora. It was with particular curiosity that he watched native cutthroat flitting for cover in small pools of tiny, no-name creeks. He adopted a particularly small one and named it My Creek.

Much to the consternation of Grandma, who had no idea where he was most of the time, she badgered Grandpa into keeping an eye on this would-be naturalist who spent hours deep in the forest at My Creek studying his favorite subject. It became clear that if he moved very slowly, he could almost touch the three inch cutthroat as they lay under the mossy banks, and if he presented a shucked periwinkle in just the right way he could have them practically eating out of his hand.

But not quite. The cutthroat hadn't evaded their natural predators such as mink, kingfisher and heron by being stupid. Over the thousands of years of their existence, their acquired instincts kept them alert to alien intruders into their habitat, small human hands included.

This didn't keep Dicky from trying, however, and the challenge of bringing this beautiful, spotted creature to his hand whenever and wherever he could, remained with him for the rest of his life.

Grandpa must have become tired of watching over Dicky in his tireless study of native trout, because one day he decided to instill in him, a deeper respect for hazards existing in the dense forest.

There had always been a general warning about bears, and although the only time anyone ever saw one, it was in a rapid retreat into the woods, front feet crossing back feet in a comical gallop, Viv and Dicky were taught to go the other way if they encountered a bear. So on one of Dicky's many trips down the west field to get to My Creek, Grandpa hid behind a thicket of blackberries and proceeded to make bear-like growling noises, supposedly to send him screaming back to Grandma who was watching the plot from the front porch.

At first, it appeared Grandpa's scheme had worked. Upon determining that a bear was indeed behind the blackberries, Dicky ran back to the house, not in fear as Grandpa had hoped, but rather to arm himself. Having just acquired a toy gun for his birthday, it appeared it was now time to put it to good use and dispatch that bear for good.

So reconciled of Dicky's persistence to explore, Grandpa and Grandma decided it was time to get a dog to watch over him.

This was his first and favorite dog. It was a black and white mixed-breed, mostly-Border Collie they called Shep. It accompanied him wherever he went. There were times Shep seemed to run out of patience just sitting around— particularly when Dicky spent an inordinate amount of time at My Creek staring into the water, or on his back on the cool moss bed of the forest, gazing at the towering fir trees and imagining he was laying not on the cool and soft moss, but on a cloud high over the firs. But when he decided to get up to search out other interesting things, or if he fell asleep, Shep reappeared to lick his face. So Dicky had the best of both worlds: solitude and companionship whenever either was required.

In all the times Dicky went into the woods to explore, he never seemed to get lost. He seemed to have a built-in compass as there was no way he could get his bearings by sight alone, the forest being too dense and impenetrable. Having a sense of when he had gone far enough beyond previous treks such as to loose track of familiar landmarks, he became uneasy and turned back, only to go farther the next time out.

This sense kept him out of trouble—most of the time.

One day, as he went yet farther down My Creek to discover new landmarks, he came upon a newly built truncheon road.   Built of six-inch thick planks nailed crossways on two sets of logs, truncheon, or plank roads were in those days, the cheapest and fastest way to build temporary roads into the woods. Of least concern to the loggers, they were nonetheless the least disruptive of the fragile ecosystem of the old growth forest, as they used only the few trees that had to be cut down to make way for the road, and easily spanned the small streams and bogs that stood in the way.

So here was a new passage. Dicky was most curious to see where it went. He followed it first to the right as it curved downhill. In a short distance it ended at a freshly graveled landing next to the road from the Valley to the Richter farm. Dicky had seen this landing being built during previous trips to and from the Valley in the family Chevrolet, but now he was excited by the prospect of finding out why it was there. Rather than retrace his steps back up the truncheon road, and since it was nearing suppertime, he went home via the farm road with resolve to satisfy his curiosity the next day.

The weather didn't cooperate the next day, or for the next week, so the curiosity of a young mind soon turned to other things and the reason for the truncheon road became less urgent.

It may have been several more weeks, or months until Shep and Dicky once again came upon the truncheon road, and with a restored sense of curiosity quickly turned left up the road to continue their exploration.

The plank road wound up the hill for about a half-mile before it came upon an abrupt opening in the forest created by a fresh logging operation. The smell of fir needles permeated the air, as though branches had been ground up in a blender. A clear-cut with a jumble of newly felled trees lay beneath a newly strung high lead: cables radiating from a single giant fir, topped and stripped of branches—a spar pole.

In the center of the clearing near the spar pole, a small sawmill was being assembled. A huge circular saw and log carriage were already in place under a large shake roof supported by an open structure of jack fir poles. A small pile of lumber near the exit side of the carriage, and a larger pile of sawdust gave evidence that the mill assembly was near completion. At one end of the sawmill, a huge steam engine stood with a myriad of cables, drums, tanks and machinery mounted on a log sled, all connected to the mill by a huge power belt that spanned at least fifty feet. The whole contraption looked exotic and alien, an object of curiosity that had to be examined closer.

No one appeared to be around so Dicky's curiosity could be satiated without being confronted by strangers, any of whom he had little experience. Cautiously, he continued up the road to the sawdust pile and climbed to its crest where he could survey the mill without feeling he was trespassing; sawdust, like hay with which he had more experience, seemed to be neutral regarding ownership. Shep discovered a nest of mice somewhere under the mill's foundation and was preoccupied, so he had no warning of the stranger who had come from behind one of the trucks which were parked by the lumber pile.

The stranger had been watching Dicky's approach for some time and decided to give him a small lesson on the dangers of sawmills. A loud "What do you think you're doing there?" was sufficient to implant in the young explorer a burning desire to be anywhere but there. Being on top of a sawdust pile allowed little room for a quick retreat, however, so he froze in silence until the stranger, seeing his obvious trauma, mellowed, and, with an invitation to show him around, temporarily eased Dicky's fears of being thrown in jail for trespass.

The stranger explained that he was there not necessarily to guard the mill, but rather to work on its completion. He was dressed in the greasy coveralls of a mechanic and obviously knew about the workings of a steam donkey as he started gathering up his tools that were scattered about the base of the engine. There was something else about the stranger that eased Dicky's fears: he had an almost feminine look about him and except for the stubble that covered most of his face, he could have passed for Uncle Roy's wife: Aunt Lila. Dicky shook off the semblance and returned his attention to the one-way conversation:

The stranger explained that his work for today was finished because the boiler had to be rebuilt. It seemed that the 'sumbitchen' donkey operator didn't put any water in the tank before firing up the boiler and burned out some of its innards. A few more words of praise, many of which Dicky hadn't heard before, were laid upon the operator before the stranger decided they were falling on dumb ears, so he resumed his briefing on the workings of the mill.

It was a simple operation, really, at least as it was explained to a 5 year old: The logs, which had already been felled were dragged or skidded to the mill by the donkey, that same contraption that powered the sawmill by way of the long belt. The mill converted the logs to lumber that would be hauled down the plank road and on to town by the trucks.

What happens to the sawdust? Dicky thought, not concerned so much with the economics of the operation as with the prospect of having an artificial ski slope on which to play. As if reading his mind, the mechanic admonished him to stay away from the sawdust pile in particular, and the mill in general because of the inherent danger.

But the sawdust pile? Surely he was being overly protective, Dicky thought. Just like Grandpa's warnings about the bears, there seemed to be a logic there that he couldn't fathom at the time; so on future Sundays, when the mill was silent, and after ascertaining that no one was around to yell at him, he went to his sawdust pile to play— and maybe to examine the workings of the silent steam donkey just a little more.

Another curious and deliciously dangerous place was Herr Burrie's coal mine. Herr Burrie was a Swiss immigrant who lived by himself on a homestead adjoining the farm to the east. A large deposit of low-grade anthracite coal had been known for years to exist under Richter hill, but it had been determined that its commercial worth was limited.

Herr Burrie, being a pragmatist of sort, but a nonconformist in nature, took on the challenge of proving the experts wrong. On the side of a knoll overlooking his small rustic cabin, he started a lateral mine shaft, complete with a steel-railed coal cart on which to haul out the profits. Most of the neighbors knew of the mine, but discounted it as being a folly by a strange man whose language few understood. Grandpa's rudimentary German and Herr Burrie's Swiss were sufficiently similar, so the Richters knew more about him than most.

Dicky learned about the coal mine on a visit with Grandpa, who had some reservations about taking him along. Grandpa knew full well that Dicky, given the tour, would probably return to the mine unaccompanied as soon as he had the chance.

And Dicky did. Not right away, because the mile-plus journey was longer than the short walk to the sawmill—his other favorite playground—and when the faint whistle of the sawmill's steam donkey echoed through the woods on a clear day, it was as though it was beckoning him to come for another look. With the mill and the logging operation around it, everything was always changing. Moreover, the path to Herr Burrie's farm was not well defined after it left the lane to the lower cow pasture, and it took Dicky several trips to gain enough confidence to hike the last quarter mile through the woods.

In my mind's eye, I can still visualize the lane past the horse trough and down the hill to the lower cow pasture. It was defined not so much by fences, but rather by the thick evergreen blackberry thickets on either side that overgrew the original barbed-wire fences. There was a shallow well partially obscured by thickets in the left side of the lane from which water could be poured into an adjoining horse trough.

Fanny and Babe were the farm's two part-Percheron workhorses. Only Grandpa could manage them, and then, sometimes not too well. Fanny was the more gentle, and he used her to pull a wheel-less, single, mould-board plough while he struggled to keep it within the hardscrabble topsoil. Dicky sometimes followed behind in the furrows to compete with crows and seagulls for worms with which to tempt My Trout. Because some of the furrows had never been turned before, he sometimes found arrowheads.

When both horses were hitched as a team, it didn't take much to make them run away. One time they took off while Grandpa was raking hay, throwing him from his tenuous, metal-seated perch on the rake and breaking his ankle. Another, and more memorable time, Grandpa, Viv and Dicky were hauling hay from the field next to the orchard. Viv's job was to start and stop the wagon between Grandpa's pitchfork tosses of haystacks onto the load. The haystacks, each about three feet high, were spaced about ten feet apart, so all Viv had to do was rap the reins on Fanny's rump a few times to move them forward, then pull back to stop them. Easy enough for a ten-year-old girl who was comfortable around horses anyway. Dicky's job was to tamp the hay down so the load could be even. With the weight of a five-year-old, there was not much tamping, but he enjoyed the ride except when the load became high and unstable. During one such time of instability, a pitchfork of hay, probably laced with omnipresent thistles, fell from the front of the load onto the rumps of Fanny and Babe. They bolted from Grandpa's fruitless attempt at grabbing the reins and galloped directly at one of the blackberry thickets that defined the lane. Viv, collecting her composure, and realizing she hadn't the strength to rein in one, let alone two headstrong Percherons, gave Dicky a command to jump when she counted to three. Dicky was either frozen in fear, or couldn't hear the 'three' over the din, but apparently at the instant Viv jumped, Fanny and Babe, not wishing to run directly into the briar patch, made an abrupt right turn. The wagon flipped, launching Viv high and far into the patch. Dicky, still dumb with fear, stayed with the load and landed softly on half the load, the other half landing on top to cushion him from the wagon.

In the aftermath of the runaway, Viv came out of the briar patch badly scratched, but uninjured. Apparently the heavy blackberry vines let her down gently. Dicky was scratched from thistles as he backed from under his cushion of hay. Grandpa was angry that the doubletree attaching team to wagon was torn from the wagon's tongue as it flipped, and then when the harnesses were torn up when the team raced through the orchard. It took a couple days to restore everything so the haying could be continued.

After a few more trips down the lane past the site of the runaway, the journey to Herr Burrie's place became routine and the mine soon became the center of Dicky's attention. It was a dark and foreboding horizontal shaft carved into the side of a hill at the end of a small canyon, and much like the sawdust pile at the sawmill, it bore a screed of slag that fell down the hillside in an ever increasing pile. As the pile gained in size, another length of rail was added and the small cart bearing the slag required a longer push to deliver its load to the brink.

This part of the operation fascinated him the most, but he never ventured into the mine to see its inner workings, somewhat out of fear of dark places, but certainly because of Herr Burrie's broken English admonition:

"If ever I catch you in dis mine, I vill skin you alive and send you home necket."

Besides, as long as Dicky kept in Herr Burrie's good graces, he got to help push the coal cart to the precipice and watch with glee as the slag went tumbling to the canyon below.

On a subsequent trip to the coal mine, he made a new discovery that diverted his attention: another no-name creek, a tributary to Lake Creek, which contained the same dark spotted cutthroat that inhabited My Creek by the sawmill. These fish were bigger, however, as he later discovered that this creek joined Lake Creek after a short run, and he reasoned, that bigger water had bigger fish.

And he was right in that score, because it was there that he saw his first salmon. Not just one, but dozens, all frothing about in a small riffle in a frantic mating dance he didn't understand. But this fascinated him, and for hours he watched as the larger females dug redds while the males and jacks sparred for position alongside. Below, an entourage of smaller and sleeker fish that he recognized as larger versions of the trout he studied on My Creek darted forth to eat an errant egg that escaped from the redd.

All this turmoil bothered Dicky because he had always assumed the trout to be a gentle creature that someday might accept his hand offering of a shucked periwinkle. Now he was looking at fish fully capable of biting off his hand, and by their actions, it seemed they had the inclination to do so. But it was clear to him also that the larger and more menacing salmon were different from the cutthroat with which he felt comfortable. With their red sides and hooked snouts, they would seem out of place in the placid pools of My Creek, and he never expected to see them there.

But just to be sure, he looked with more concentration on subsequent visits. There were none, so he happily concluded that My Creek was off limits to salmon.

There were still many distractions for Dicky that took him away from his new discoveries. A hutch built against the barn particularly fascinated him. It contained rabbits. It may originally have been for chickens of which he was also interested, but now it held a mixture of brown and white rabbits, all furry and not prone to scratching and squawking. Rather than just looking at them and maybe sticking a small finger through the coarse chicken wire to pet them, he decided instead to crawl in with them. Soon Grandma became aware of what he was doing and admonished him to stay out of the pens or she'd lock the door next time she caught him. Next day, having forgotten Grandma's warning, he was again caught inside playing rabbit, so with a big frown that said 'I told you so', she wired the gate shut from the outside, thus trapping him inside with his friends. Not in the least discouraged, he figured out if he unwound the chicken wire he could easily escape.   Doing so, he hid out in one of his hayloft hidey-holes high in the barn, and watched Grandma chase the rabbits that, taking their clue from Dicky, gratefully escaped their confinement and headed straight for the garden.

The Richter farm held many vivid memories. The pungent smells of the horse stables, the chicken coop, the pigpens, I can still remember. Somehow the smells of cow manure I've blocked out—perhaps because the care and feeding of cows later became too much of a chore. I can remember the derelict Model 'T' outside the garage below the house, where Viv and Dicky sat in its leather back seat on a clear summer night and gazed in wonder at the universe displayed above them. Viv would try to explain the difference between the stars and planets, but to Dicky, they were just all too grand to be explainable.

I also remember Dicky sitting at the kitchen table and having a corn-eating contest with Grandpa. It could never really be told exactly who won, because Grandpa, having false teeth, ate after cutting his off the cob with a knife. Dicky could snitch by missing a few kernels or two as he drooled butter down his chin, but when all was done, a count of empty cobs on each plate usually resulted in a tie according to Mom, Viv or Grandma. Punctuated with a long and satisfying belch, Grandpa would claim he was the winner, saying he ate more corn, empty cobs notwithstanding. Dicky felt if he imitated Grandpa's belch, he could one day be victorious. But to the amusement and appreciation of Mom and Grandma, he never came close.

3   **Uncle Ralph**

"Seems your blood work came back with a positive PSA reading" your doctor casually announces, giving reason to think that it was nothing worse that an elevated cholesterol reading. What you know about PSA? Nothing.

Following its construction in 1918, Boistfort High School became the center of social and cultural activities for not only its students, but also the entire community. It was a model educational institution on par with much larger schools in the state, even though the student body never exceeded a hundred. Among its most notable graduates were Gordon Sweany, founder and CEO of Safeco Insurance, and Scott Crossfield, first man to fly at twice the speed of sound. Academic and athletic successes kept public funding healthy, even through economic hardships of the Great Depression.

It was during the roaring 20's, with athleticism and glamour at their peak, when Dicky's Aunt Emmagene began dating Ralph Blake. They became the couple that would come to epitomize the style of the times: Emmagene, a sophomore with her flapper chic and banjo repertoire, and Ralph, a senior and star pitcher of the county champion baseball team.

After graduation, Ralph contracted tuberculosis and was sent to recover at a clinic in Arizona and attend pharmaceutical school, while Emmagene went to Centralia College. Later they married and settled in Seattle where he became employed as a pharmacist for the Boyle Drug Stores.

I think the most important and lasting quality about Uncle Ralph was that he was an avid outdoorsman. His favorite fishing stream was Lake Creek that flowed conveniently past the Blake farmhouse.

He knew where to find fish and did so whenever he had the opportunity to escape from his demanding job in Seattle. Most of the time he fished with Aunt Emmagene, but sometimes he took Grandpa or Uncle Wilbur. On one memorable occasion he asked Dicky.

Dicky could scarcely contain himself. He was going fishing with Uncle Ralph, and to make the trip even more special, he was to have his very own outfit: a beautiful nine foot telescoping steel rod that weighed at least two pounds, equipped with a single action reel the size of a silver dollar. It didn't matter that the rod was slightly bent at the tip section and it was missing a guide; and no matter that the reel held all of 20 yards of nondescript line that resembled a coiled spring; It must have been once useful to Uncle Ralph, and now it was Dicky's.

Of course they would have to get up at five AM, and of course they would have to get everything ready the night before including the digging of worms, the assemblage of gear, the selection of clothes, boots, the preparation of lunch.

These were the necessary first steps of the fishing trip ritual; steps Dicky would dance a thousand times in the future, but none would be as heady as this, his very first fishing trip!

It goes without saying Dicky didn't sleep much that night. Nor did Uncle Ralph, because against his better judgment, he chose to sleep in the spare bed in Dicky's room instead of staying at his parent's farm at the bottom of the hill as he and Aunt Emmagene usually did on their visits to the Valley. Uncle Wilbur usually occupied this spare bed, but he was away at college, perhaps the reason for Dicky's invitation in the first place, because Uncle Wilbur and Uncle Ralph often fished together whenever they had the opportunity.

But now, much to Dicky's good fortune, Uncle Wilbur was busy. It would also be fortuitous that he would soon be married—a fate Dicky thought would free up Uncle Ralph for even more trips with him.

But he had to be a good fishing partner for this to happen, and tonight he was getting off to a bad start. In his anxiety to make sure they didn't oversleep and miss the morning bite, he probably asked Uncle Ralph at least 20 times:

"Is it time to get up yet?"

Surprisingly, Dicky's misbehavior wasn't mentioned at the breakfast table the next morning. Mom, who would always be up to get breakfast on countless future fishing trips, knew the significance of this trip and also wanted to get it off on the right foot. She appreciated Dicky's need for adult male companionship, and probably was instrumental in convincing Uncle Ralph to take him along.

In retrospect, this proposition was probably discussed at length because of Dicky's relative isolation from male companionship. The only other males around were Grandpa and Uncle Wilbur. Grandpa, being of strict German ideology, was generally too busy to spend much time with a seven year old and seemed to be loath to give guidance or discipline unless it was done within the context of farm work. In any case, praise was unheard of.

Uncle Wilbur was more like a distant older brother who was now away most of the time at college. So Mom and Uncle Ralph probably agreed to occasionally take Dicky out of his little world on Richter Hill, and to learn the ways of his role model from the big city.

This day was not the time to revisit this decision, however, so after eating a hardy breakfast and inspecting gear for the last time, the two anglers headed out in Uncle Ralph's '39 Ford coupe.

Dicky always enjoyed riding with Uncle Ralph because he drove fast. At least faster than grandpa did in the family Chevrolet, which wasn't saying much, but it nevertheless thrilled him to feel the inertia of the corners and hear the gravel scatter as they descended to the valley below.

In a few minutes they arrived at the first fishing hole: a stretch of riffles on My River just below the Klaber Store and on the Ridenouer farm.

Before starting to fish, however, there were some preliminary things Uncle Ralph needed to convey. While he had received standing permission over the years from Mr. Ridenouer and other farmers to trespass through the many acres they owned along the river, he felt Dicky needed his first rules in fishing etiquette: Never cross a farmer's field without permission. Never make his barbwire fence squawk when climbing over or through. And always leave gates the way they were found.

The first rule Dicky found somewhat difficult, being shy around adult males, and found it sometimes impractical to go to farmhouses to seek permission. He would usually access the river at a location convenient to the road or outside the farmer's sight, and would walk or wade within the riverbank until it was close to the road again.

This method of accessing My River put Dicky into difficult wading situations, a habit he sometimes came to regret; but it also allowed him to access areas normally not fished. Uncle Ralph, on the other hand, probably explored the entire river many times as a teenager, and now had little time to fish in what he considered to be non-productive water. So they would fish his way, and of course at this juncture, Dicky knew of no other way.

Once they crossed Mr. Ridenhour's pasture and arrived at the first riffle, Dicky was given a short lesson on hook baiting, line presentation and stealth; but curiously, nothing in the way of landing and unhooking a fish.

Perhaps Uncle Ralph thought too much instruction in one outing would just be confusing, and besides, to catch a fish on his first trip might be expecting too much. He was given one crystal clear instruction, however:

"Don't fall in. But if you do, be sure to yell."

And thus instructed, Dicky was left on the bank to dunk his worm-festooned hook in a lifeless two-foot deep eddy while Uncle Ralph waded across and downriver to fish one of his favorite riffles.

As Uncle Ralph disappeared around the bend of the river, Dicky wondered how a fish was going to find that gob of worms that had now settled to the bottom of his assigned pool. It lay there lifeless. The only thing moving were a few periwinkles or caddis larvae crawling lethargically on the sandy bottom and some water skippers skittering along the waters edge. A water ouzel flitted along the opposite shore and disappeared underwater, probably in search of some nymphs or other goodies.

Dicky's attention span for this place was reaching its limit.   Being acquainted with the feeding habits of the cutthroat of My Creek, it was clear that there were no fish in this place and that he was wasting his time. He needed to see a trout before he could catch one, he reasoned. Moreover, how would he know when to set the hook if he didn't see the take—a quandary whose resolution might have destined his fate as a dry-fly fisherman. It now seemed logical however, that he should be emulating his mentor, and since Uncle Ralph had started fishing just below Dicky's assigned pool in the tail-out of the riffle before moving down river, maybe that's the direction where Dicky felt he should be fishing.

He studied how to get there.   Here was his first challenge in big river strategic wading; a questionable endeavor, however, not having hip boots like his mentor, only barn boots whose tops cleared nine inches at best. Besides, it was early spring and the water was still quite cold, so he decided to get to the riffle by climbing down a small embankment above and to the left of his goal.

Something happened next that ensconced in him a deep respect for moving water. It wasn't so much his clumsiness that caused the next events, but rather because his hook with the now waterlogged worms had caught under a root along the waters edge. As he reached down to extract the hook, an adjacent root he was using for a foothold broke unexpectedly and launched him into the swirling riffle.

He plunged into the shocking water to his armpits and bobbed downstream, rod still in hand, involuntarily paying out line to the stubborn root still attached to his hook. Fortunately the riffle quickly became shallow, and although the water there moved faster, he was able to regain his footing and scramble to shore, gasping and shivering, probably as much from the impending chastising he would receive, as from the cold.

Better get back to my assigned pool, he thought, so as to lessen the consequences of his transgression. With rod still tightly clutched, he carefully wound in the line that had now somehow broken free from the offending root, and returned to the scene of his dunking.   None the worse for wear, save for being wet, Dicky still had his prized rod, the hook attached to the 20# test leader was still there, sans worms. He began to feel confident he wouldn't be too severely chastised.

Then he remembered Uncle Ralph's departing instructions: "If you fall in..."

So to be heard above the noise of the rushing water, he yelled to the top of his lungs:

"Uncle Ralph!" "Uncle Ralph!"

A short time later Uncle Ralph came crashing around the corner of the river, creel bouncing off his hip, rod pointing behind with line strung out haphazardly. *Not a careful wader* Dicky thought, as his hip boots were obviously full and he was struggling to cross the river in a spot clearly deeper than where he had crossed before. As he spilled ashore and sloshed up to where Dicky waited meekly, he asked between gasps:

"What's wrong?" "Why are you all wet?"

To this, Dicky stated the obvious: "I fell in."

4   **Sex Education on the Farm**

What you know about PSA? Nothing. Your family doctor says: "I'll refer you to a urologist I could recommend."

There was a lot of hanky-panky between the farm animals that didn't seem to be particularly unusual to a six year old who didn't think much about his own sexuality. It was always with a giddy voyeurism that Dicky watched the larger animals do it, not knowing why they did it, but it seemed when they did it, they did it to the exclusion of everything else, so he reasoned it was important to them. On one occasion he saw grownup people do it, but at the time he never associated it with barnyard animal behavior.

Dicky shared a small bedroom with Uncle Wilbur when he still lived on Richter Hill. He slept in an army-style cot under the sloping rafters on one side and Uncle Wilbur slept in a double bed pushed against the opposite rafters. A single four-drawer dresser under a window overlooking the west field separated their beds. A coal-oil hurricane lamp on the dresser was their only light source and even when turned up to the point of smoking, it never illuminated the corners of the room. For Dicky, these dark corners always harbored goblins, but whenever he turned up the lamp to see for sure, it smoked and caused its globe to be sooty, making things even darker—and spookier.

When Uncle Wilbur attended college, Dicky had the room to himself, except for those times he had a break from his studies, and for the short time after he graduated and married Aunt Oralee. It must have been shortly after their honeymoon that they visited Richter Hill and spent a night in

Uncle Wilbur's old bed.   Knowing Dicky was a sound sleeper, Uncle Wilbur convinced his bride that it would be OK to continue the consummation of their marriage if they did it quietly, and to make the mood appropriate, leaving the lamp on, but turned down low. Dicky was actually asleep when they came to bed, but a short time later he must have had a dream that someone was softly shaking him, not unlike the time Uncle Ralph woke him to go fishing. As his eyes snapped open, he saw not Uncle Ralph, but a shadow cast by the lamp on the rafters behind the foot of Uncle Wilbur's bed, which curiously moved to the cadence of the shaking. He moved his pillow to get a better view. The shaking stopped so he quickly closed his eyes and faked sleep. Motion resumed within a minute and now he was in position to see. At first he only focused on Uncle Wilbur who appeared to be positioning himself to do push-ups. Then Aunt Oralee's flaming red hair and milk-white skin caught the dim light and his attention simultaneously. Her naked breasts were undulating ever so slightly to the cadence, the nipples almost the color of her hair. Dicky hadn't seen a naked grown woman before, even just the top half. He was fascinated, not so much as to what Uncle Wilbur was doing, but by the image of this beautiful woman. Surreptitiously, Dicky was Uncle Wilber, enjoying her attention as the cadence increased until her arms suddenly surrounded his neck and pulled him down, flattening these objects of his attention. Forgetting his ruse of being asleep, he strained to keep seeing her nudity and immediately caught the attention of the two lovers. They looked at him sheepishly then kissed in a long passionate smooch, after which Uncle Wilbur reached over, cupped his hand behind the lamp chimney and blew the room into darkness.

After seeing Aunt Oralee that way, Dicky should have been embarrassed around her, but somehow never associated her clothed persona with the woman he saw under Uncle Wilbur. Instead, he saw that night an image of the painted mermaid on an antique glass vase in the top shelf of the dining room cupboard.

The painted mermaid even had red hair and nice boobs—like the ones Mrs. Bucklyn had. Mrs. Bucklyn was a substitute teacher when Dicky was in the first grade. When she bent over to help with penmanship drills or get the pupils bundled up to go outdoors, her cleavage demanded his attention. She complimented Dicky on his hair during one of her displays, said he had something every woman wanted: a widow's peak. Then, he had no idea what she was talking about, but interpreted the compliment as a sexual come on. Later, he found the widow's peak to be an early indicator of male pattern baldness, a malady that came too early in his life; and although he was constantly reminded by women that baldness was a sign of virility, the extra hormones that lay beneath was something he had trouble dealing with later in life. Even in his adolescence, however, Dicky quickly learned to appreciate the sexual attention and compliments like those favored on him by Mrs. Bucklyn.

5   Seattle

The words of your family doctor set in motion a set of events that forever changes your life. At the time, you have no information that would concern you one way or another...

Seattle and Boistfort seemed thousands of miles apart in the 40's, so travel to this metropolis from the Richter's Lilliputian community was a special treat indeed. The family didn't have adequate transportation to make long trips by car, so outside of the Valley, trains were most commonly used.

Trains in fact were everywhere in the '40's. The local train, the Chehalis Western, made bi-weekly trips from South Bend, stopping at communities such as Lebam, Francis, PeEll, Meskil and Adna to move passengers, livestock and produce to the markets of the twin cities of Chehalis and Centralia. On the way, a whistle stop at Ruth served passengers from the Boistfort Valley. Although Ruth was only a few miles from Richter Hill, grandpa generally drove the Chevrolet in order to take farm produce directly to the grocery store owned by his sister, Lou and brother-in-law Meinert. This usually meant an overnight stay at Great Grandpa Richter's place just a few miles south of Chehalis. Riding the Chevrolet usually came at a price, however. Passengers usually had to get out and walk up the steeper hills because there wasn't enough horsepower to haul everyone. Because Dicky was the smallest, he usually stayed aboard with Grandpa and encouraged the walkers trudging along behind. Trips such as these, whether by train or car, were enjoyed immensely by the whole family, some members more than others.

Dicky's first trip to Uncle Ralph and Aunt Emmagene's place in Seattle occurred during the height of WWII. Uncle Ralph had a draft deferment because of his history of TB. He had just opened a new drug store on 5th and Seneca, across from Seattle's largest and most prestigious hotel: The Olympic.

Mom, Viv and Dicky were invited up to visit for a week and see Uncle Ralph's new store. It was *the* classic drugstore of the era, complete with soda fountain, newssland and pharmacy. Being the quasi-social center of the block, it attracted dignitaries who were guests at the Olympic.

Uncle Ralph soon acquired a reputation for being the local authority for fishing in the area, so it was common for hotel guests to be referred to him by the Olympic staff. Autographed pictures of sportsmen like Bing Crosby and Ted Trueblood were hung proudly in the store along with framed articles from the *Post Intelligencer* and the *Seattle Times* extolling his fishing expertise. These were heady times and Uncle Ralph was in his element.

It was on this train trip to Seattle that Dicky saw his first military uniform. He was fascinated, not so much by the uniforms worn by fellow military travelers, of which there were many, but by those on the sentries posted on either end of each passenger car. Because the trains traveled by and through sensitive war effort areas, the windows were blacked out and sentries were posted to keep casual viewers from the platforms between cars. They looked menacing with their guns and helmets, but in a curious way, none of the passengers seemed to mind, travel being a luxury that had been severely restricted by gasoline rationing.

Dicky's fascination with the army uniform must have been observed by Mom, because during a visit to the Bon

Marche, Seattle's premier department store, he was fitted to a kid-sized uniform of an officer of the U.S. Army Air Corps, complete with brass buttons, garrison cap, lieutenant's insignia and leather belt. Who was more pleased was hard to tell, given all the attention received from soldiers as they walked down the busy streets of Seattle. Mom, in her early thirties, single, pretty and stylish, was probably the real focus of their attention, but Dicky relished all their salutes and quickly learned to return them.

Uncle Ralph and Aunt Emmagene's home in the Roosevelt District of Seattle's north end was a modest two-bedroom structure over a full basement. Sited on a small lot just off the trolley route to Bothell, it was typical of many of the homes built during the early 20's. At the end of two tracks of concrete that defined the driveway, stood a small one-car garage containing Uncle Ralph's shiny '39 Ford coupe. Beneath the garage rafters a boat hung on pulleys such that it could be lowered along with its attached rack to the car below at a moment's notice, and whenever the fish might be biting.

The basement consisted of three rooms: a combined workshop-laundry room, a furnace room with an octopus-looking oil fired behemoth, and the den.

This den was more than just a room. To Dicky, it was a place of wonder. A bear rug growling at a brick fireplace dominated the center of a large room paneled in knotty pine. To the right of the fireplace a large cabinet with four glass doors contained several rifles, half dozen shotguns and three bamboo fly rods. In one corner stood several more rods, mostly spinning and casting, and an assortment of level wind and fixed spool reels. On one wall, deer and antelope heads stared across to a set of headless elk horns. Various pictures of fishing and hunting scenes and a matched leather sofa and chair completed the decor. The knotty pine coffee table sported the latest issues of

Outdoor Life, Sports Afield, and *Grey's Sporting Journal.* Dicky had never seen a room like this before. Even the menacing bear rug seemed urbane. *Someday I will have a room like this*, Dicky promised himself.

6   WWII

You learn normal PSA levels should be between zero and four. Yours is 9.2. Not too far out of tolerance, you think, but after learning that PSA has something to do with prostate problems, you schedule a visit to the urologist.

As a family, the Richters were relatively unaffected by the war. Except for the daily huddles around the Kent Atwater radio to listen to the news at noon and six in the evening, life on Richter Hill remained pretty much unchanged. None of the uncles donned uniforms, no one really sacrificed much, save for the embarrassment of being German in a society that too often didn't bother to separate the good guys from the bad.

Grandpa and Uncle Wilbur worked extra hours in order to increase farm production required of everyone in the war effort. There was little capacity to increase the output of dairy products, so crops were changed to provide extra food. More potatoes were sacked and delivered to the Lewis-Pacific Dairyman's Association, a co-op organized early in the 20th century to funnel farm goods to the larger markets of the east. The LPDA became a conduit to the chow halls of the many camps and forts around the region. Another crop was ship knees.

Ship knees were carved from fir and hemlock trees to be used in the production of boats, usually smaller than 100 feet in length. It was known for millennia that the bend of the tree where the roots joined its trunk was very strong. Strong enough to keep the tree from toppling in a windstorm, and strong enough to make a skeleton of a boat without the extra bracing that otherwise took up valuable hull space. Making ship knees was hard work as the roots had to be dug up and the stumps split to enable the bend, or 'knee to be exposed for subsequent carving. There were lots of stumps, however, as the 40 acres below the upper field had yet to be cleared, and its collection of old growth fir stumps from a clear-cut of years previous would be sufficient to build several ships. Because ships were now being built in yards throughout Puget Sound, there was plenty of work for Grandpa and Uncle Wilbur. It was their contribution to the war effort, and they felt good about it.

Being on the coast during the war meant the taking of certain necessary precautions. At least they were made to appear necessary by the various media. War posters in the school, the *Daily Advocate* and *KELA* radio all warned about the 'yellow peril' and exhorted everyone to practice blackout conditions, should they ever be required. And although there was hardly enough light in the farmhouse by which to read, Mom and Grandma nevertheless made blackened curtains for the windows and made blinders for the Chevrolet's headlights. The only occasion they ever thought necessary to fear for an invasion, however, was a time, that in retaliation for the Doolittle Raid on Tokyo, a Japanese submarine lobbed several shells harmlessly toward the Oregon coast.

The episode was unnecessarily inflated by the news service, which caused a mild panic. The central switchboard located in the Hobbs home near the Curtis store sounded an emergency phone alert. The phone alert was a series of short rings, usually to alert neighbors in case of fire, and typical of the party line phone system where almost immediately everybody knew anything unusual and most things mundane, the impending danger of an invasion rippled throughout the Valley.

Fog lay heavily over Richter Hill that day, so when several planes roared overhead, the worse was feared, no one knowing whether they were Zeros or Hellcats. But rather than retreat to the cellar as instructed, everyone ran outside to see the invading craft. They seemed to be flying extremely low, but never appeared, and the thick fog soon engulfed the noise of their single engines as they droned off to the north.

This was a memorable day when most everyone stayed indoors with the windows blackened and the radio tuned to the news until the batteries became too weak to pick up any station other than *KELA,* sited halfway between Chehalis and Centralia. It soon became apparent that no invasion was imminent and the 'all clear' was sounded on the party line, after which personal stories were relayed for the rest of the week on how each neighbor perceived and reacted to the impending danger.

Later in the war when victory became widely anticipated, the vehicles and aircraft of the military became less of a mystery, and every plane that flew over was viewed with familiarity and pride. Every fighter was known by sight, often by sound. P-38s were the favorite. Neil Thomas, Class of '39, flew one of those. The Bell Aero Cobra, the fastest prop job ever, was Scott Crossfield's plane, although he didn't show up flying it until long after the war. Usually when a plane buzzed a particular farm, neighbors excitedly called neighbors to confirm that another son or nephew had returned from overseas or from flying school to show off his flying skills.

But whenever a single olive drab sedan appeared in the valley, it and its occupants, were accepted with apprehension, knowing that sometimes the reasons for their visits were to inform families of the loss or injury of a loved one.

Military maneuvers were sometimes conducted in the area, often overhead in the form of mock dogfights, delighting all who watched, except for the farm animals.

One such episode occurred when a flight of three B29s flew low over Hamilton's turkey farm and stampeded over two thousand birds into My River, drowning most of them. The army later paid for each dead bird, as they would have anyway, since Mr. Hamilton's turkeys were under contract to become K-rations.

Viv and Dicky were treated one day by the visit of a dozen or so tanks, halftracks and jeeps to Richter Hill, obviously on maneuvers from Fort Lewis. It happened as they were waiting for the school bus about a quarter mile down the hill from the farm, and they couldn't believe their eyes. Just like in the movies, they thought, each tank being bigger than they imagined, and each occupant being a hero of Audie Murphy proportions. They watched in delight, hoping the school bus would be late. And often it was.

As the last jeep disappeared into the woods, surely on its way to a secret rendezvous with a much larger force, it was all Viv and Dicky could do to keep from following, forgetting all about school. But they had mixed feelings about that, wanting in the worst way to see more, but also having so much to tell the rest of the kids, they would be heroes. And indeed they were, as the subject would reverberate through the school for days. Sketches of tanks and jeeps soon became objects of art classes. The army was on Richter Hill. Maybe they're still there, waiting for secret orders from Ike himself.

Such as these were the war stories of the Boistfort Valley, embellished by those touches of reality of which the residents had only fleeting glimpses.

The end of the war brought few changes to the Valley. Some were inevitable products of a wartime mentality, but many were futile attempts to return to the past, to pick up where they left off five years earlier. The '39 Chevy stored under canvas in the barn along with memories of courtships no longer possible; the baseball team, whose '44 county championship could have been inevitable, except for the absence of its star pitcher who fell at Guadalcanal; the simplicity of life on Richter Hill not encumbered by the need for electricity or indoor plumbing. All these would become bittersweet memories, but in the autumn of 1945 it was more important to get on with life.

In the few years before the war, and after Dicky's father died of pneumonia, Mom had been courted by Elmer Ellingson, the eldest son of Norwegian immigrants who lived on the road to Lost Valley. Dicky's earliest recollection of Elmer was during his rounds as a road grader driver for the county. Elmer would toss a stick of his favorite 'Black Jack" chewing gum to Viv and Dicky as they watched him turn the grader around at the end of Richter Road. They later learned he was authorized to grade only to the end of the county road, a quarter mile down the hill, but courtship is often blind to rules, so he ventured to the top of Richter Hill in hopes of seeing the object of his affection, and maybe to court her kids, also.

I never recalled Elmer coming to call on Mom, but he must have. It was likely a very proper courtship that might have developed had it not been for the war. But as with many courtships, the war took its toll as Elmer went to Pearl Harbor to work for the Navy as a welder, and Mom continued to work at the Klaber store.

Their relationship continued via correspondence, and when Elmer returned on the troop ship that autumn of '45, they were married in a simple civil ceremony in Seattle.

Along with the marriage came the necessity to move off of Richter Hill to a place more suitable for a young family. By that time, Viv was a teenager and fully involved in school, and Dicky was an adolescent of nine years. Elmer, being the eldest of seven siblings, had first rights to purchase the Ellingson homestead after the family matriarch moved to a nursing home in Chehalis. With meticulous savings from his four years of work in Pearl Harbor, Elmer presented a generous down payment to the Ellingson estate, and he and Mom began to realize a bit of the American dream.

To call it a ranch could be a stretch, but as with many farms of the '40s, Lost Valley Ranch provided minimal support to a family if everyone worked at it. It had all the rudiments of a farm: a three-bedroom ranch house with indoor plumbing, a large attached woodshed with fruit room and upstairs bedroom, a barn with 10 cow stanchions and two horse stalls, a small chicken coop and assorted outbuildings, all sitting on eighty acres.

Farming had never really been Elmer's forte, and he missed the steady, good-paying work that came with his service in Pearl Harbor. So when Weyerhaeuser needed a welder in its maintenance shop at Camp McDonald, he welcomed the guaranteed income. This was Elmer's occupation and the sole source of the family support for the next 25 years. Mom, after having to scrape by on meager earnings at the Klaber store, was particularly thrilled. Now Elmer represented a father for her children and a family provider that enabled her to live the life she must have sorely missed.

On the other hand, Lost Valley Ranch was to be Dicky's home for the next eight years and he wasn't totally happy with this situation. On Richter Hill, his domain was supreme. He had three women to watch over him: Mom, Grandma and Viv. Dicky never found a father figure in Grandpa who was a strict German authoritarian, who criticized and never praised. Now, with his mother's remarriage, Dicky was getting the father figure and whole new set of circumstances that upset his entire world. For reasons he could never understand, Shep, his closest companion, was sold to a farmer who had a small place across the Chehalis Western tracks on the way to town. He was never told why, but he blamed Elmer for wanting to be rid of Shep, and Mom for not standing up for him. This devastated Dicky, and for years, every time they drove to town, he strained to see if Shep was there.

Elmer could have been more of a source of conflict to Dicky, but Viv got in the way. For the first year of living in the same house, they were at each other's throats. Most of their arguments were about differences of opinion on a myriad of subjects, and occasionally Mom took sides. To Elmer's credit, he never raised his voice or became physical, but Dicky never knew what to expect and forever kept his distance. This meant of course, that he and Elmer would never be the father and son that sometimes both yearned to be.

Farming the Lost Valley Ranch was the source of Dicky's work ethic. Throughout his teen years it was his job to milk the cows, clean the barn, and feed the chickens. For this, he was allowed to keep any extra money from the sale of surplus eggs and milk his efforts might produce.

In theory, being a farm entrepreneur was to be Dicky's guiding principle. But if Mom and Elmer thought that this would be an incentive for him to work solely for the benefit of his financial bottom line and the ultimate betterment of the farm, they were mistaken. Thanks to Uncle Ralph, Dicky had already been hooked on fishing, and now the ultimate distraction was right at his doorstep; the wonderful, free flowing, fish laden, South Fork of the Chehalis—My River.

7 My River

You enter the urologist's office not knowing what to expect. Other patients in the large waiting room seemed healthy enough. Did they all have prostate problems? How many with cancer? How many were sterile, impotent, or incontinent? You had studied prostate related illnesses over the weekend and had many questions, afraid of the answers.

While My Creek on Richter Hill had been the source of Dicky's pre-adolescent entomological and piscatorial education; My River, as it flowed fewer than 200 feet from the front porch of his new home on Lost Valley Road, would be his university.

It contained all the elements of a fisheries laboratory: native and searun cutthroat, rainbow and steelhead, four runs of salmon—spring and fall Chinook, silvers and chum—and an assortment of chub, sucker, eel and shiner. The gravel shoals and riffles were dotted with pebbles of soapstone eroded from large seams of riparian limestone that formed underwater ledges and drop-offs. Competing for a place in the bottom of riffles and drifts were hoards of caddis larva, mayfly nymphs and fresh water mussels. Along the shoreline crayfish scooted under clumps of waterlogged wood, and dried shucks of huge stonefly nymphs could be found stuck to boulders.

Just downstream from Dicky's home, the Lost Valley Bridge provided a means to reach either side of the river, whose depth made it otherwise difficult to cross by wading. The bridge provided more than just a crossing, however. It was there Dicky spent many hours a day, lying with his head and shoulders under the railing, staring down into the large pool formed below a submerged soapstone ledge. The clarity of the water and the shadow of the bridge afforded an unobstructed view of the inhabitants of the Bridge Pool.

Always there were the suckers: large scaled, carp-like, non aggressive bottom feeders, whose place in the food chain seemed just right for the otter and mink who caught them easily. They huddled under the drop-off of the soapstone ledge, sometimes flushed out by an aggressive cutthroat seeking its calm and shelter.

From his bridge vantage, Dicky could easily distinguish the native cutthroat—My trout—from the rainbow trout and salmon smolts.   The cutthroat were more speckled, larger, darker and more aggressive than their cousins the rainbow trout that stayed in the faster water and were more difficult to observe. They incessantly competed for any and all food that drifted down the chute from the riffle some fifty feet upstream. As for the rainbow trout, most were juvenile steelhead, the largest achieving six to eight inches before they returned to the ocean's bounty sixty miles downstream. When they returned as full-size steelhead it was generally in the winter, so a study of these magnificent trout was not as easy as were his favorite, the cutthroat.

Farther downstream from the Bridge Pool was a larger, deeper pool that served as the community swimming hole. It was formed at the end of another large limestone deposit that must have been subterranean to Lost Valley Ranch. The clear water moved through slowly in the summer months and with large, overhanging alders and a 10-foot-high bank on one side, it was the ideal spot for a refreshing dip. The first swimmers of the season commandeered a plank from a pile of lumber in the

Ellingson barn for a diving board, and hung a cable trapeze across the river between two of the tallest alders.

The presence of a dozen swimmers on any given afternoon flushed upriver, the few chubs and suckers that preferred still water. Knowing that trout preferred the faster running water of the Bridge Pool, Dicky hadn't considered the possibility that the swimming hole held anything worth fishing for. But on one exceptionally bright and warm summer day he made a startling discovery. Upon climbing to the cable trapeze platform to make his first screaming plunge into the still water; he spied large, spotted forms circling in the depths of the pool some 50 feet below. Scaling one of the overhanging alders for a better view revealed a sight to excite even the most veteran fisherman, let alone an adolescent just learning to fish.

Salmon!

There were dozens of huge spotted shapes, just like the cutthroat of My Creek on Richter Hill, except these were a hundred times bigger. And there were more: dozens of smaller precocious males or jacks darting into the formation to be chased by the larger males. Completing the attendant entourage, were schools of immature steelhead; and to Dicky's delight, the unmistakable dark-spotted and golden-sided cutthroat. Some had to be 20 inches long.

Swimming was no longer a priority that hot summer day.

8   Spring Salmon

"First we need to take some tests," Dr. Rand said after asking a few introductory questions of his own. "We need to find out what is causing the elevated PSA, so we will schedule an ultrasound scan of your pelvic area and take a few tissue samples of your prostate. We'll have a pathologist examine the tissue for cancer and go from there."

The person or committee responsible for buying books for the Boistfort School District had to be in Dicky's deepest gratitude. Given the small budget and the smaller space reserved for the grade school library, the selection had indeed to be—well, selective.

Why he chose this particular book for his first book report didn't seem important at the time. Perhaps his 5th grade teacher, Mrs. Godwin, had read it, and knowing of his interest in fishing, but lack of the same in reading, saw the advantage. Or maybe in browsing for covers or titles of interest, Dicky detected the small, embossed fish under the book's title: *Return to the River*, by Roderick Haig-brown.

The passages in this book, about the life of the largest of the pacific salmon, the Chinook, captivated, inspired and held Dicky's interest then, as they did throughout his life. It was through the keen observations of this naturalist-poet from Canada who painted a picture so vividly to a farm boy of ten; and as Dicky watched the majestic salmon from his alder tree perch high above the Swimming Hole, he could imagine himself in the Master's persona.

It would be twenty-nine years later when Dicky had the opportunity to meet the author during a book signing at a dinner meeting of the Washington Fly Fishing Club in Seattle. When he told the author the book he was signing that night was the first serious book he had read as a youth, and how it had so influenced his attitude towards the environment, the Poet-Laureate of British Columbia appeared to be genuinely moved.

A few months later Roderick Haig-Brown died of a heart attack at his home in Campbell River, BC. Needless to say, this book occupied a place of honor in Dicky's fishing library for many years.

Dicky's study of the Spring Salmon continued at Lost Valley Ranch. By the second or third week of each May he routinely climbed to his alder tree observation post over the Swimming Hole in anticipation of their arrival. As expected, they appeared after the last freshet of the spring and often revealed themselves by jumping high out of the water in an apparent act of ecstasy at arriving at their nuptial home.

Like a parade of monarchs, the Spring Salmon commanded the attention of all the other river creatures when they arrived to take over for the summer. Chubs and suckers left for the Bridge Hole upriver, followed by the mink and otter that changed their hunting area accordingly. Human predators or poachers took note also, but usually kept their distance because of their proximity to the Ellingson house and the well-traveled bridge.

Dicky learned the adult salmon didn't readily feed while in the river, but the jacks did. In fact, a gob of worms cast strategically from his limb-perch often provoked a take that required all his faculties to keep from falling out of his tree. Most attempts of setting the hook resulted in hook, line and worms jerked into an overhanging branch, with the ensuing gnashing of teeth and spooking of fish. On the rare occasion a fish was hooked, it was always a frantic scramble to get out of the tree without falling in.

His first successful catch, a fine jack of about four pounds, was delivered at a dead run, still flopping, to Mom as she stood at her kitchen door wondering what all the commotion was about. This fish was easily ten times larger than the biggest trout he had caught before. The whole family was truly impressed. Pictures were taken and the word was spread of his fishing prowess—particularly to Uncle Ralph, whose praise was less than enthusiastic

Curiously, Uncle Ralph was never complimentary of fish that Dicky caught outside of trips they made together. But it wasn't until he so enthusiastically helped beach a 37 pound Chinook on the Toutle River, that Dicky may have understood why: In some ways Uncle Ralph probably thought of him as the son he never had, so anything he did outside of his tutelage was less a reflection on him than on Mom or Elmer.

As Dicky became more adept at catching jack salmon from the Swimming Hole, his technique also became more sophisticated. Instead of swinging a worm-festooned offering from overhanging trees, he graduated to hardware. A flatfish or Colorado spinner became lures of choice because a newly acquired, second hand spinning reel, again from Uncle Ralph, allowed casts from shore. No longer did he have to keep his tree-climbing movements stealthy, and knowing the routes of the salmon as they cruised the Swimming Hole, he could strategically place offerings without spooking them.

His luck improved to an occasional hookup on an adult salmon, but no matter the strength of his leader, he was never able to bring one to shore. His telescoping steel rod was no match for twenty-plus pounds of angry salmon, and he soon learned of the futility of hooking one.

With the coming of the first rains of autumn, the salmon became increasingly restless, and almost totally oblivious to his lures. Then as suddenly as they appeared in the spring, they were gone. The entire entourage of jacks, searun cutthroat and immature steelhead moved out with their benefactors: the egg-laden Chinook hens and their hook-nosed mates.

The Swimming Hole now seemed so empty, except for an occasional chub or sucker that returned to reclaim their domain. But Dicky learned that with the departure of the salmon to their spawning riffles upstream, came another opportunity to catch My Trout. A size twelve hook garnished with a single salmon egg drifted through a riffle below the spawning salmon almost always produced a fat and feisty cutthroat of twelve to fifteen inches.

Dicky came to appreciate the salmon in the Swimming Hole in ways that he probably never would, had it not been for *Return to the River*. The dead carcasses of the giant, spawned out salmon would have been just another smelly wading inconvenience, had he not read in the Master's prose that they were nature's way of perpetuating the food chain so vital to the growth of cutthroat and other creatures that he enjoyed so much in My River.

His only wish was that he might have better articulated this appreciation to the Poet that evening at the book signing.

9   Trap Line

You return the next week for the pathologist's test results. They were positive, meaning cancer cells were found in three of your five tissue samples.

Up to the time of moving from Richter Hill, and outside of school, Dicky had little contact with boys his age, so he played mainly by himself. Now, downriver from Lost Valley Ranch, the Klaber Store stood alone on the riverbank and across the road from the remnants of the hop yard established fifty years before by Herman Klaber. It served as the trading center for the Valley. Complete with a butcher shop, it sold dry goods, hardware, fishing tackle, produce, ice cream and Dicky's favorite: licorice cigars. It was also the post office, gas station and gathering-place for a game of checkers around a pot-bellied stove—a typical country store.

The Ericksons who moved to the Valley from Oregon owned it. They had one son, Gerald, who was Dicky's age, so naturally they started doing things together. They rode their bikes, swam, fished and generally did the kid-type things there existed to do in the country. The river was their playground, and they built trails along its shore to get to and from their respective homes and to its riffles and drifts where they fished.

Gerald, being the son of a merchant, was the source of certain interesting things Dicky hadn't before considered: Fishing and hunting catalogs.

Outdated Herter's catalogs were available for poring over at his leisure and glossy pictures of Wright & McGill fly rods in the Cook's Hardware catalog created fantasies of ownership seemingly unachievable.

"Seventy-five dollars for a bamboo fly rod?"

Even Uncle Ralph seemed incredulous. But the Herter's catalog had more reasonable prices. For fourteen dollars and fifty cents, plus shipping, a two-piece fiberglass fly rod kit, complete with cardboard rod tube could be ordered by mail. Also a fly tying vice was available for about six dollars. For twenty dollars, Dicky reasoned, he could have an outfit similar to Uncle Ralph's and be able to tie his own flies besides. Considering the typical flies Gerald's dad was selling at the Klaber Store: a Parmachenie Belle, size six, on a snelled 20# leader for fifteen cents, he figured he could make and sell enough flies to buy that Wright and McGill rod.

The Herter's catalog was Dicky's fantasy window to a world of hunting and fishing he had not imagined. Over an inch and a half thick, it had gadgets and paraphernalia mostly unheard of by a farm boy, but on a practical level, large selections of hooks, lines, leaders, fly tying materials and camping supplies were described, all accompanied with exaltations by Jacques Herter himself on the merits and advantages of using each particular item.

Toward the back of Herter's catalog, just before a chapter on beer and winemaking, a section on trapping captured Dicky's attention. He remembered another catalog at the Klaber Store: a Sears and Roebuck flier advertising for muskrat and mink pelts. Cash was paid for any that were mailed, parcel post, to an address in Chicago. Included were instructions on skin preparation and shipping.

Being aware of the many fur-bearing animals that dwelt along My River, the thought of yet another way of living off the land other than milking cows excited Dicky. An order to Herter's for a *"How to Trap Your Own Furs"* *manual, and* a scrounging through the woodshed to yield a dozen #2 rusty Victor traps put him into the fur trapping business.

There were two small creeks that emptied into My River within a mile of Lost Valley Ranch: Beaver Creek and Lost Valley Creek. Both slow flowing, they serpentined through pastures and lowland areas, and supported an abundance of muskrat. A couple of test traps set under an apple or carrot on a branch stuck in the shoreline resulted in a drowned critter for almost every trap set.

How easy, Dicky thought. All he had to do is skin them out, stretch their pelt over a split cedar shake and pack them off to market. After thoroughly butchering his first attempt at skinning, he realized there was a lot to learn about trapping and skinning.

Elmer was a tremendous help in skinning. Dicky learned the importance of a sharp knife, on how to completely skin all parts of the animal, and to stretch the pelt over a cedar shake, tapered and sized for each pelt. Trapping was harder than he had imagined, but having committed to at least give it a try, he set up his trap line between Lost Valley Ranch and the Boistfort School, two miles upriver.

On the two or three days a week that he wanted to run the trap line, he donned barn boots and set his traps on the way to school. After arriving at school, he would change into school clothes from his gym locker, and at the end of school the next day, he would reverse the process by changing back to his trapping clothes and 'harvest' his trap line on the way home.

How much money he made on those winters of his school-route trap line, was open to conjecture, depending on his overhead costs of preparing and shipping the furs. Because he had to divert time from his first preoccupation: fishing, he soon tired of the job and sold his traps to Gerald, who had more of a business sense.

He did save a muskrat pelt for fly tying materials, though.

10   Speeders, Lokies and Trestles

A follow up bone scan test proves negative, meaning the cancer hadn't spread outside the prostate area, so your survival chances look better.

Lost Valley Ranch not only had My River running nearby, it also had a railroad to capture Dicky's attention. The Chehalis Western Railroad maintained a spur running from the confluence of the South and North Fork of the Chehalis River to Weyerhaeuser Timber Company's Camp McDonald Operations on Mill Creek, a major tributary of My River. It cut through Lost Valley Ranch and separated it midway, leaving about thirty-five acres on either side. It was used mainly to haul logs to market, but also to transport equipment and supplies necessary to sustain the huge logging operations that the WTCo managed around the Boistfort Valley and into the Willapa Hills to the west.

Where the Chehalis Western spur ended at Camp McDonald, a large network of WTCo rails extended far into the hills to move logs to a marshalling yard across Mill Creek from Camp McDonald. Once the cars of logs were sorted, they were coupled together, often as many as 100 cars, for the long trip to the log dump on Puget Sound, near Olympia, then rafted to WTCo's mill in Everett. It was a big operation, employing dozens of locomotives, hundreds of railroad cars, assorted speeders, rail mounted skidders and donkeys, all operating on hundreds of miles of rail.

Dicky was fascinated, of course. Not only by the parade of trains that chugged through Lost Valley Ranch, but also by the myriad of equipment they hauled.

Sometimes there were rail-born bunkhouses for the remote camps high in the hills. There were huge cranes large enough to lift a locomotive back onto its tracks after a not infrequent derailment. Speeders or 'crummys' of different sizes and configurations went by with their loads of men and equipment. There was a myriad of different locomotives whose identification numbers Dicky soon learned, both by sight and the sound of their whistles. Number 200, the main work horse of WTCo's fleet was a huge 180 ton Mallet which could pull up to 100 loaded cars. A smaller Mallet, number 202, served as backup and sometimes helped Number 200 when an unusually long train was assembled. The lokie that went by most frequently was Number 104, a small, forty ton Porter. It was used to move equipment and specialty loads up and down the tracks in support of maintenance activities. This 'lokie was most fascinating. Instead of water tender immediately behind, it was built with a saddle tank over the boiler thus giving it a short, fat appearance. Elmer named it 'Spunky'.

One day, Spunky was employed in the laying of crushed rock on the tracks running through Lost Valley Ranch, and as usual, Dicky was there to observe from his observation platform: the top rail of one of two heavy gates Elmer built to separate trains from livestock. The crews of most of the lokies knew Dicky by sight, and would wave or give a short whistle toot as they went by. This day, however, Spunky stopped directly in front of the gate and the engineer, whom everyone knew as Jake, beckoned for him to come over.

"We're going to make one more trip up to the gravel pit today," Jake yelled down from above Spunkie's wheezing wheel pistons. "Would you like to ride along with us?"

Dicky couldn't believe his ears. Ride in a locomotive? Previously he hadn't even been this close to one, and now he was being asked to climb up, inside, and ride along with the crew. He could hardly contain his enthusiasm as he simultaneously nodded and said most emphatically that he would.   Unlike the engineers of Numbers 200 and 202 who worked for the Chehalis Western Railroad, Jake was a WTCo employee, somewhat older and less concerned about railroad regulations. But before Dicky could come aboard he had to meet two criteria: First he had to get permission, and second, he had to wear an engineer's cap.

No problem on finding an engineer's cap, Dicky thought excitedly. He knew exactly where one was: hanging from a nail on the back porch, it was one of many assorted hats Elmer collected from who knows where.

Dicky spun on his heel running faster than he had ever before, covering the distance from gate to back porch in record time; giving Mom some concern that something was drastically wrong, and as she met him on the porch, he was breathless, adding to her fears.

"Mom! Mom! They asked me to ride on the train with them," he blurted after catching his breath. "Can I go? They'll bring me back before dark," he added, thinking the clincher might be in her knowing he wouldn't be riding around on the tracks at night, like some hobo.

Of course, Dicky was allowed to go. How could a mother not give permission to a kid who was as excited as anyone could get? Before he could dash back to claim his ride, however, he was ordered to wear a jacket and a hat, as it would probably get cold. Good thing she reminded about the hat. In his excitement, he'd forgotten it for sure, but he grabbed the stripped, dusty and shopworn fedora hanging limply from its nail and raced back to his waiting adventure.

"You look just like one of us!" Jake said, as Dicky climbed the last rung of the steel ladder to the cab and cautiously peered inside at the dazzling array of valves, switches, wheels and gauges.   Besides Jake, there were two others in the cab: Vic, the brakeman and Bob, the conductor, who, absent a caboose, got to ride up front.

"Here, you can have my seat," Vic said, patting the smooth and shiny leather seat on the left side of the cab.

"No, he should have my seat," corrected Jake. "After all he's going to be the engineer, so he needs to be here," he said, pointing to the even smoother leather of his chair.

Jake sported quite a few more pounds than Vic, as was evidenced by the depression of his chair. Over thirty years with the WTCo, he was comfortable with his job and relished showing off his "office" as he called it. Standing behind, as Dicky craned to see over the accumulated clutter on the window shelf, he proceeded to show the controls to run the lokie, and most important, the lanyard that actuated the steam whistle. He explained that one short whistle meant stop, two longs: go ahead, three shorts: back up. Then as if to test the young engineer, he said:

"OK, give the signal to back up and we'll get another load of gravel."

Dicky reached for the lanyard and hung a little long on the first 'toot', making instead one long and two shorts. Nervously, he looked at Jake to see if he signaled something forbidden, whereas Jake grinned, reached for the lanyard and signaled with two shorts.

"Two shorts means forget the previous signal and highball, or let's go," he said as he pushed the throttle forward after moving another lever to a position marked 'reverse'.

The lokie lurched backward against its now empty three gravel cars and started picking up speed as it passed the gate where Mom stood waving. Jake told Dicky to give her three toots, which he did, correctly this time, to which Mom laughed and waved again. Waving back, Dicky felt like he had died and gone to heaven.

They started up the grade towards Camp McDonald, crossing first the Lost Valley Road, then a farm road to Edgar Pier's place. At each crossing Dicky was instructed to give the crossing signal: two longs, two shorts; which he did without making a mistake. Vic and Bob both approved with their thumbs up. Dicky didn't look back, but by Jake's hand on his shoulder, it was easy to tell he approved also. As they came to Camp McDonald, the tracks on ether side increased in numbers until they entered the marshalling yard where scores of cars loaded with logs stood, ready for the long journey to Olympia. Jake slowed Spunky almost to a crawl whereupon Bob walked forward on the catwalk, climbed down to a small platform over the cattle guard and released the coupling to the first gravel car. Jake applied the brakes and they slowed even more, but not before Bob stepped off, walked forward and threw a switch on the track that enabled Spunky to move past the siding where the three gravel cars, now under their own momentum, moved to be reconnected. Bob re-boarded, this time to the rear and Jake pushed the throttle forward to pass the siding where the gravel cars were coasting along. Slowing down again, Bob jumped off, threw another switch and re-boarded, almost as in one motion. Jake expertly slowed Spunky almost to a stop, whereupon the gravel cars overtook and jolted against its coupling. They were a train once again, this time with the cars behind.

"It's better we pull the cars up the steeper grade going to the gravel pit," said Jake as he pulled on the lanyard to give the go ahead signal.

Dicky could appreciate the complexity of maneuvering inside the marshalling yard and was relieved that Jake took over the signaling duties. Besides, he was preoccupied by the switching operation and appreciated the way Bob orchestrated his train. Not once had the entire train stopped, but now Spunky was pulling, not pushing; and as they picked up speed once again, Dicky was excited to see some familiar landmarks. They first crossed the bridge over Mill Creek whose still water beneath revealed several large suckers seemingly unconcerned about the rumbling overhead. Dicky couldn't see into the riffles, but knew My Trout swimming therein wouldn't be so lackadaisical. Next they crossed Slide Creek over which the trestle bridge made of hundreds of logs and timbers snaked gracefully along the contour of its canyon. Other trestles were crossed, some higher, many lower; all with rushing streams beneath that commanded Dicky's interest almost as much as the train.

They finally reached the gravel pit, a huge scar blasted from the side of BawFaw Peak, the highest in the Willapa Hills. A fire lookout tower less than a quarter-mile away stood alone over the scrub fir and huckleberry around its base. Like the trestles, it was made of logs and timbers and rose majestically above the Noble fir and cedar that grew tenaciously on the windblown terrain.

Another place I needed to visit someday, Dicky thought.

The gravel cars were filled by an operation where Bob manned a large dozer and pushed gravel into a chute under which the cars were moved until each was full. That completed, Jake maneuvered the train to another siding and the process of reversing the position of cars to lokie was repeated, this time it being necessary to keep Spunky in front to prevent runaways. They returned to the Lost Valley Ranch late in the afternoon. Dicky was still elated at his good fortune and anxious to tell Mom, Elmer and Vivian of his experiences. He bade goodbye to Jake, Vic and Bob who each shook his hand. As he climbed down from the lokie, and waved to his new friends, he felt uplifted, indeed confident that he could meet and talk with adult men, something previously he had difficulty doing.

So in the future, as Dicky hiked along the Mainline on the way up Mill Creek to go fishing, whenever a speeder approached, instead of jumping into the bushes to hide, he confidently put out his thumb.

11   Mill Creek

You learn of two options for getting rid of the cancer: surgery or radiation. It was time for a second opinion, and doctors at the Swedish Tumor Institute, after looking over your now growing medical file, graciously declined to offer their services.

Everyone called it Mill Creek, even though on the maps it was shown as Stillman Creek. Named after Henry Stillman who was possibly the first American settler to claim property in the Boistfort Valley, it branched off My River a little more than a mile above Lost Valley Ranch and drained most of the headwaters of BawFaw Peak. Lesser creeks were its main tributaries: Slide, Keller, Little Mill, Lost Valley and Halfway. The main body above Little Mill Creek was most sought for it's fishing, and was the least accessible. Totally within WTCo's boundaries, it could only be accessed via logging railroads. Later when the rail operations were phased out, logging roads proved to be the undoing of good fishing along Mill Creek because they made waters easily accessible, but also because of runoff and slides caused by hasty and improper road building. During a torrential rain, one such slide damned a canyon tributary before it burst and released millions of tons of mud, water and debris, scouring the entire streambed, and for years voiding it of any habitat for trout.

Before the roads were built, however, trout reigned supreme, their domain protected by the inaccessibility of their habitat. The railroad up Mill Creek followed the main stream for about five miles, then crossed over a low bridge, switched back several times to gain altitude, only to cross again, this time over a high trestle some six miles farther upstream on its way to Camp Seven. Camp Seven was one of two remote logging communities on WTCo's McDonald Operation, the other being Camp Six. Speeders went to both regularly to transport workers and supplies. Knowing this, Dicky's fishing trips took on a new dimension. If a speeder came along and he could ride, he enjoyed the option of getting off at the first bridge, fishing up stream or down, or going the next crossing and fishing the upper creek. Either option gave plenty opportunity to catch many trout—not large, the biggest seldom exceeded fourteen inches—but all eager to attack any offering. Most riffles terminated under logs criss-crossed over and within the stream, so Dicky's technique was to weight his fly, usually garnished with a periwinkle, and drift it under the log until he felt a strike. Often there might be several strikes on the same drift and he learned to be patient until a larger trout set the hook by itself. On trips like these, he never returned without a limit and was proud to show his full creel of twenty fish to the speeder occupants on the way home. To them, Dicky became known as the champion fisher kid of Mill Creek. To Mom, he was the provider of the evening menu, and Mom loved fried trout.

One trip up to the second crossing proved almost to be Dicky's undoing.

Mom packed extra sandwiches into his creel, knowing he intended to spend all day fishing. He intended to cover the six miles down to the low bridge, where he might be picked up and transported back to his bicycle at Camp McDonald. It was an ambitious undertaking as he had never explored some of the creek and was uncertain of its terrain.

He was lucky to catch an early speeder out of Camp McDonald on its way to Camp 7, and was scrambling down the canyon under the high trestle before the first rays of sun reached the giant firs sheltering the creek far below.

Knowing he had a lot of water to cover, he decided this trip should be one of exploration. If an exceptionally good-looking riffle became accessible, he would fish, but would save the last few miles to get his limit before it got dark. He set off walking along the shoreline strewn with large boulders and logs—easy enough to traverse—jumping from one to the other as he made his way downstream. He was making good time, and by the time the sun was overhead, he estimated he was halfway to the low bridge.

He reached into his creel for one of several sandwiches Mom packed the previous night. The paper bag and waxed paper were damp from the two trout he couldn't resist keeping. He looked at them again as he unwrapped his first sandwich. They were both fourteen inches with the characteristic markings of native cutthroat that had seen little sunlight: dark, almost black backs fading to sides of dark green and stomachs of pale yellow. The leading edges of their fins were white and under their chins two red slashes almost glowed from their brilliance. Dominating all these markings were the dark spots spreading from the tip of their noses to the ends of their tails. Dicky sat on his log perch; legs hanging down towards a deep pool below and watched others, equal in size, as they darted about in their feeding activity. He never tired of watching My Trout, but now it was getting past noon, and he still had miles to go.

Downstream, the terrain was receding steeply and he could hear cascading water of increasing intensity. As he proceeded, the canyon walls became steeper, dropping perilously toward the creek. No longer could he find logs and boulders on which to proceed, but instead found it necessary to stay higher in the canyon until the creek fell away hundreds of feet below. Now to figure out which route to go: he could attempt to rejoin the creek by scrambling down the canyon walls, but being so steep made that risky. He didn't want to break anything, particularly his rod, and it became increasingly difficult to traverse the sides of the canyon while keeping it out of harm's way. It was a fiberglass pack rod of three pieces, four if one considered the reversible handle so it could be converted from a fly rod to a spinning rod. He decided to disassemble it to make it easier to climb around the obstacles and trees hugging the canyon walls, which, in spite of him staying high on their sides, became steeper and steeper. Finally he gave up all hope of getting back to Mill Creek, but instead concentrated on finding an easier way to proceed.

He climbed up the ridge that overlooked the creek until he reached its crest. To his surprise the other side was freshly logged. Far across the next canyon within whose trees were now prone, lying like jackstraws, a single tree remained: a spar pole, with cables radiating in all directions from its truncated top. One cable reached back to his side of the canyon, the end of which was secured to several large stumps. This was a scene he hadn't expected. *How much longer before the logging reached Mill Creek,* he wondered. His thoughts turned to how to get out before it got dark. Fortunately, it was mid summer and twilight wouldn't come for another four or five hours, but now the going was more complicated. He could attempt to cross the canyon to the spar pole; but having no idea where the rail spur might go, discarded that notion. Proceeding on the ridge, he assumed the stream within the logged-off canyon would eventually join Mill Creek. This would be his route back to the lower bridge. He continued down the ridge, now dropping precipitously toward both canyons. Soon, he needed to make a choice as to which side of the ridge to traverse: the logged off side, or the Mill Creek side. Choosing the Mill Creek side, he proceeded to work his way down its steep slope until again the sound of rushing water far below greeted him.

But now the canyon wall was becoming vertical. He looked for an animal trail that might provide passage to the water, but there were none. Even deer had better sense than to try what he was attempting. He proceeded down the ridge, but again found it necessary to stay parallel to the water, indeed getting farther away until it could no longer be heard. Refusing to backtrack, he found himself on a cliff overlooking the conjunction of Mill Creek and the creek from the freshly logged canyon. His quandary was evident: he needed to get down to either creek, each now flowing gently in their respective valleys, but in so proceeding, he had scaled down a path he wasn't sure he could retrace. In other words: he was stuck.

He was starting to be concerned. Not so much about having to spend the night in the woods, he had done that before on camping trips with Uncle Ralph. One trip was with Mom and Elmer when the bear riffled the garbage can next to the floorless tent where they were sleeping, and he could see its paw less than a foot from his head.

He thought: *Yes, I could stay overnight in the woods by myself. Yes, it would probably get cold, but I have matches and I could make a fire. I wouldn't even get hungry because I had two trout I could cook on a forked stick. I had done that before too.*

To bolster his confidence, he felt in his pocket the round waterproof container of matches he always carried when fishing. No, his problem wouldn't be in staying out all night. It would be in worrying Mom. He remembered one evening when Jacky Borne didn't show up for dinner. Jacky was a few years younger, so even though the Bornes lived just up the road from Lost Valley Ranch, they didn't play together. At first Jacky's parents weren't concerned, but after they called around to see if anyone had seen him and no one had, they organized a search party. All the neighbors showed up and went around yelling "Jacky...Jacky!" Knowing he liked to play near and in Lost Valley Creek, the search party concentrated in finding his body somewhere there. Finding no body, they regrouped at the Borne ranch at which time his dad Jack decided to go to Jacky's bedroom to get an article of clothing for one of the neighbors dogs who purportedly had some bloodhound lineage. Shortly after, a whoop came from upstairs, then some cusswords. Seems during all this commotion, Jacky had been safely asleep in his bed.

So to avoid the embarrassment of a search party, Dicky needed to escape from his predicament—from the cliff overlooking his destination, so close, but now so unobtainable. He worked his way back toward Mill Creek and looked for any possible way to get down. As he stood over another ledge some thirty feet below, he could see a possible avenue of escape.

But how to get to that next ledge, he wondered. *If only I had thirty feet of rope—no make that sixty feet—I could loop it around this tree and retrieve it for the next possible descent.*

He made a mental note to have one next time. *Fifty feet should do.* His mind snapped back to the problem at hand. Above, several dead jack firs lay strewn down the bank, one of which had a large root jutting at right angles from its trunk. Reaching up, he could grasp its tip, so he carefully pulled it down until the root could be hooked around the tree to which he was clinging tenaciously. Now his predicament was partially solved. He could shinny down the jack fir to the next ledge if the root held its position. If not, while a fall wouldn't kill him, a broken leg might make things difficult. He looked in his creel for a solution. His two trout stared back. No help from them. Beneath one of the sword ferns he placed in the creel to keep them fresh, a spool of leader material appeared. He had just purchased it from the Klaber Store for this trip. The store had a few fishing items in the glass door cabinet behind the pot bellied stove: Eagle Claw snelled hooks, split shot sinkers,

Colorado and Indiana spinners, and, fortunately for Dicky, leader material.   He un-spooled the leader, and, taking about twenty turns around the root and tree, secured the trunk of the jack fir so it wouldn't slip from its hooked position. He mentally calculated the breaking strength of the leader: six-pound test times twenty turns equals one hundred twenty pounds.

Good for my weight, but I better take a few more turns for the jack fir, he thought.

Using the remainder of the leader would provide the necessary margin of error, he calculated mentally, so, sticking the disassembled pack rod in his belt, he carefully shinnied down to the next ledge, and, to the ultimate safety of the Mill Creek Valley.

It took another hour to reach the low bridge. By then, it was dark and it was still three miles to the closest phone; five miles beyond that to his bicycle, then another three miles home. *This is not going to be my best day fishing*, he said to himself, as his eyes adjusted to the shiny rails disappearing into the darkness.

He had not walked more than a few hundred feet when the unmistakable click-clack of speeder wheels telegraphed down the tracks. Behind him, around the bend by the low bridge, came the lights of the Last Run from Camp Seven.

"What in tarnation are you doing out here in the dark?" yelled Frank, as he slid open the speeder door.

In addition to Frank, the speeder operator with whom Dicky had become acquainted on previous rides up Mill Creek, six loggers were on their way to town and had already started celebrating. One in particular decided to take on Dicky's case.

"How many fish did you catch?" he slurred.

He wore red suspenders over a striped shirt and black jeans. In his haste to shave for his big night on the town, patches of toilet tissue still stuck to bloody spots on his chin and neck. His breath smelled of Vitalis, or maybe it was his hair.

"Two," Dicky answered, trying not to make eye contact.

"Two!" he retorted. "You mean to tell me you fished until dark and only caught two? What kind of fisherman *are* you anyway?"

"I don't know," Dicky responded in a low voice, wishing the logger would just drop the subject. But of course he didn't and went on:

"We'll let's see the two that you caught anyway."

Dicky sheepishly opened the creel and to his horror, there remained only the sword ferns. When he scaled down the jack fir he remembered the creel snagging on one of the limbs. Apparently when he removed the leader he hadn't buckled the flap tightly and the trout had slipped out. Now he had nothing to show for his ordeal. Dicky's ears burned as the logger peered into his creel.

"They're so small I can't see them for the ferns," he roared. Laughter from the other loggers echoed through the speeder and Dicky wished he had arrived at the low bridge a few minutes later.

Walking home was preferable to this, he thought. Finally, Frank intervened:

"Why don't you leave the kid alone?" he shouted from his seat at the speeder controls. "Can't you see he's had a rough day?"

Dicky's appearance was indeed disheveled: Wet and torn jeans, tennis shoes with the soles loose and flopping, shirt and coat coated with pitch, face and hands scraped from clinging tenaciously to his jack fir ladder. Somewhere he lost his hat, probably during his harrowing escape down the cliff. Dicky had little time or inclination to make himself presentable, and started to worry more about how Mom would react to his coming home at this time, in this condition. The loggers continued their banter. Dicky tried to ignore their comments about his appearance and was relieved when the speeder finally pulled into Camp McDonald.

"Where do you want to get off?" Frank shouted to no one in particular.

Thinking he was addressing the loggers, Dicky didn't respond. Frank asked again, this time looking at him.

"My bike is down in the shop," Dicky responded. He had parked his bike in the back of Elmer's welding booth, knowing there it would be safe while he was fishing. He had intended to bike the three miles home via the railroad, but was not looking forward to doing so in the dark. It was hard enough navigating over the railroad ties in the daylight, and the tires on his bike would surely take a beating from the coarse gravel he now couldn't see.

"Get your bike and I'll meet you at the end of the shop after I drop off the rest of my passengers, Frank said.

Dicky didn't understand at first, but then realized that Frank, feeling sorry for his plight and embarrassment, was offering to give him a ride home.

Shortly after ten thirty, the speeder rolled to a stop at Lost Valley Ranch. Dicky thanked Frank and wearily pushed his bike through the rail gate and pedaled the remaining quarter mile to the house. Mom was waiting up with dinner. For once, he couldn't provide any fresh trout for the main course, but somehow she wasn't disappointed.

12   Keller

"Your youth favors surgery" opined the chief radiologist at the Swedish Tumor Institute. If, after surgery, you require radiation, it can be accomplished, and we'd be happy to accommodate you, but if we radiate first, the resulting scar tissue will preclude surgery".

The boyhood friend Dicky was most destined to grow up with was not the farm kid next door, nor the classmate a mile down My River, but rather the eldest son of high school friends of Uncle Ralph and Aunt Emmagene. By virtue of this relationship alone, Dicky and Gerry's would be a lifetime of friendship.

Even though the Kellers lived over 10 miles away from Richter Hill and Lost Valley Ranch, Gerry and Dicky met and played on the occasion when their families played cards or socialized. School and fishing were their common interests. Gerry was a year Dicky's junior, but they had a lot in common: their families were pioneers to the Valley, of German decent, and enjoyed the outdoors above anything else. Camping was their family's favorite pastime, and many weekends they traveled to the beach or the mountains where fishing, clamming or hunting were their common pastimes.

Gerry's dad, Oscar John, was known by all his friends as Sparky. This name was given to him early in school because of his effervescent humor. Then, everyone was given a nickname, and his was Spark Plug or 'Sparky' for short. He was known to most of the Valley residences as a hard working, hard drinking logger who enjoyed and appreciated his family and friends, yet kept a private life that most of his detractors felt was seedy at best and illegal at worst.

Rumors abounded regarding Sparky's moonshine still, operated and craftily hidden somewhere in the back '40 of the old homestead. Active and profitable during prohibition, its secret was maintained long after the 30s. Even in the 40s and 50s, there always seemed to be a pint of its product available during special occasions, and to Sparky, most occasions were special: Saturday night dances, hunting trips, fishing trips, any man-type gathering where, hunting, campfires, sawmills, bulldozers, trucks or tractors were involved.

On one late afternoon bullshit session at the Keller homestead, Sparky, several of his cronies, Gerry, and Dicky were gathered around someone's pickup truck. A good quarter mile away from any likely container of booze, Sparky strolled over to a fence line, jiggled a fence post loose from the soft ground, pulled it out, thrust his arm down the fencepost hole and produced a gallon jug. It was passed around to all participants.

Gerry and Dicky never attempted to find any of Sparky's stashes. The idea never entered their minds, being more than content to indulge in high school sports, any and all things related to the outdoors, and comedy.

They loved funny movies and saw all the Bob Hope-Bing Crosby road shows. Afterward they reenacted the catchy lines and kept themselves in stitches. Classmates more often than not would find them giggling over something spontaneous. They had a knack of seeing humor in almost anything and were known as the Dean Martin and Jerry Lewis comedy team of Boistfort School.

In addition to enjoying each other's humor, they were competitive. Or at least Gerry was, and enjoyed beating

Dicky in most one-on-one sporting activities. Whether it was basketball hoops, shooting cans off fence posts, catching the most trout, anything physical, Gerry was usually the winner. There was neither gloating on his part, nor animosity on Dicky's, so they got along, and in fact, constantly invented new things in which to compete.

Anything relating to fishing intensely interested them. From the Herter's Catalog they purchased fly tying and rod building stuff and, of course Gerry always tied more and better flies, and built the neater fly rod.

Much later Gerry's craftsman skills extended to building beautiful wooden fly boxes and fly tying bobbins. He made enough for Dicky and gave them unselfishly to anyone else who appreciated them.

And they went on fishing trips. Some were of the type: "Let's go fishing." "OK, wheredoyawannago?" "I don't care, let's decide when we get there." But the best trips were those that took lots of planning, and much anticipation—the type of trip that involved camping, or at least leaving at around three AM.

Most of the good places to fish had to be behind closed gates or where there were no roads. There had to be an element of difficulty, of secrecy—known only to a few—to be really worthwhile. The streams and creeks flowing within the woods belonging to Weyerhaeuser met these criteria almost completely.

The Weyerhaeuser Timber Company owned almost all the land around the Boistfort Valley. Its holdings in fact, extended all the way to the Grays and Willapa River drainages, scores of miles to the west, and contained streams rarely fished. The inaccessibility of these streams added to their mystique and excitement. For Gerry and Dicky, they were the inspiration for long range fishing plans.

In the 40's and 50's the WTCo drove the economy of the Valley. New clear cuts became evident on the slopes of BawFaw Peak which dominated the Valley to the west, and the constant flow of logs out of the Valley by way of the Chehalis Western Railway reminded all who lived there that timber was king. Anyone who didn't have a large farm or their own holdings of timber soon came to the realization that working in the 'woods', for the WTCo, was a reasonable and respectable job. Also, the pay was good.

The woods provided a myriad of jobs: from tree fellers, to bull cooks, from choker setters to welders, from locomotive engineers to carpenters—woodworkers or loggers they were called. And camps were built to house feed and support them. The main camp, McDonald, was constructed at the terminus of several railroad spurs that wound up the slopes of the BawFaw to smaller, more temporary camps.

These smaller camps, usually built on railroad cars, were sited convenient to the logging operations such that the distance from job to bed could be minimized. During the week the loggers worked a dawn to dusk shift, punctuated by two enormous meals and a multi-sandwiched lunch prepared by a dedicated cooking staff.

On Friday night, the loggers, bathed and ready for action, rode the long trip down the BawFaw on railroad passenger cars to Camp McDonald to be greeted by wives or girlfriends, or they would speed off to town on their own to spend their wages.

Eventually these camps weren't economical for the WTCo to maintain. With the introduction of more efficient and faster transportation for the loggers, the camps were phased out, leaving only their supporting infrastructure as evidence there had once been a community of over 200 men living there. One important part of this infrastructure was the water reservoir, or watershed—really just a hastily dammed up creek from which water was piped to the camp a few hundred feet below. This watershed took on the appearance of a small lake, a few acres in size, but large enough to supply water for the steam locomotives, the needs of the camp, and, perish the thought, for firefighting.

Some of the loggers took to fishing the many streams around the camps and decided that the reservoirs would be a good place to protect some of the cutthroat they caught. The small streams containing many of these native fish were being systematically destroyed by the indiscriminant slashing and dragging of logs through their midst, and although most of the loggers either didn't care, or see the long range consequences, some could see that by saving a few trout from this destruction, there might be some left to catch later.

Several years after the closure of Camps Six and Seven, Gerry and Dicky learned of these trout rescue efforts, and decided they should explore their reservoirs to see if any trout survived.

The closest reservoir was the Camp Six watershed. Nestled between BawFaw Peak and a smaller peak appropriately named Little BawFaw, it quickly became part of the natural landscape with hemlock and cedars sprouting from huge nurse logs that rimmed its shoreline. Beavers immediately moved in and added to the dam's height until the scrub alders and willow brush occupying the headwaters became inundated. The rail spur that once carried materials for the dam's construction became overgrown with alder brush. Similarly, a trail from the slowly decaying Camp Six all but disappeared.

The Explorer's assault on the Camp Six watershed was planned via a direct route up Slide Creek. The Mainline rail spur to Camp Six had been converted to a logging road, which now bypassed many of the tall railroad trestles. It should be only five or six miles from the gate, they reasoned.

The WTCo had a long-standing policy of not allowing trespassers into its woods, unless of course, it served its own purposes.   A case in point was the deer-hunting season:

Since deer tended to feast on the tender shoots of small fir trees that were replanted on newly logged areas, they were considered pests. Before logging, deer were scarce in the largely old growth forested areas, and they weren't a problem. Now there were large deforested areas, and their population exploded. Used to grazing on the small evergreens heretofore only found in naturally burned areas, the large expanse of newly planted firs was, to the deer, like manna.

Hunters by the hundreds were transported from Camp McDonald to these cleared areas on railroad flat cars, and the shooting began. At the end of each hunting day, the same cars moved back down the hills, stacked with deer, one or two for each hunter. This was the WTCo's first successful public relations program. The rest of the time, for the public, the woods were closed.

Covertly then, the watershed at Camp Six was Gerry and Dicky's goal. Their plan included sneaking in under cover of dark so as not to be caught by any of the Weyerhaeuser bosses and unceremoniously escorted back to the main gate, or worse: delivered to the County sheriff for trespassing.

To avoid being caught, they would take their camping gear, leave at dusk and walk up the mainline logging road in the moonlight until about midnight, then bed down until dawn and hike the rest of the way to where they could get off the traveled roads and set up camp at their destination. They would fish for a couple of days, pack their catch in some of the snow that still lingered in shaded areas, and, as they had ascended, make their way back down to the valley when it was dark.

Equipment lists, food items and fishing tackle were revised tenfold over the winter as their plans gained in stature and importance. The size of their inventory became so great that they decided upon, and then abandoned the idea of using a bicycle trailer that they designed, to be towed up the hill like a rickshaw.

"Too heavy," Gerry said. "Besides, if we have to jump in the ditch to hide from a truck coming up or down the hill, we won't be able to hide the trailer. To me, it's more important that we don't get caught, than it is to have that camp stove."

"Yeah, I guess you're right," Dicky agreed reluctantly. "We probably don't need that ice chest either. Maybe we could smoke the fish we catch and bring them out that way."

It would be decades before they adapted the idea of catch and release, a concept that would greatly simplify their logistics.

After school was closed for summer vacation, their day of departure finally arrived. The weather had been typically wet that spring, so the woods were open for logging. This was good insofar as the severity of their punishment was concerned, should their fears of being caught materialize, but bad because there would be a lot of activity en route to their destination, thereby increasing their chances of being caught. On the other hand, if the woods were closed, except for an occasional fire patrol warden, they'd be the only ones there and their chances of being intercepted by the warden were less—but the severity of their punishment would be unthinkable. The Explorers were therefore glad the weather was wet.

As a means of carrying their gear, they settled on two pack boards from the Yard Birds war surplus store in Chehalis. Merl Henry, one of Gerry's neighbors, and a Korean War veteran, introduced the pack board idea. Their gear, wrapped in pup tent halves and lashed to the pack boards, consisted of forty-five pounds of food, blankets, fishing gear and an old tin frying pan with a two foot long handle that fiendishly conducted rain water into Gerry's pack, soaking everything therein.

"Good thing we found out about that stupid frying pan before we got underway," groused Gerry as he set about to repack his gear.

"You got that right" Dicky observed wryly, "And it was a good thing you left your pack outside last night, and that it rained. We're lucky also that my pack that I wisely kept inside, contained that ten pounds of pancake flour, otherwise we'd really have a mess. I guess lady luck is with us so far."

But lady luck was fickle, and it rained steadily for the next ten days.

They sat about, waiting for it to quit, tied more flies, re-inventoried their gear a couple of times, and played a hundred thirty seven more basketball games of Horse in the Keller barn. Meanwhile, their plans evolved to a more ambitious trek, bypassing their original goal of the Camp Six watershed to venture miles farther to George Creek and the North Fork headwaters of the Chehalis River. This would be a weeklong trek, which traced the river downstream, eventually ending at the town of PeEll where they could call Gerry's mother to drive them home.

Elmer came up with this idea by suggesting they should be able to find an old fire trail he once used when he was a fire lookout on BawFaw Peak. This trail, he assured, would take them down the back slope of BawFaw to George Creek through virgin timber into waters seldom fished by anyone except those hardy and knowledgeable enough to hike the extra five miles. The trailhead was somewhere along a long ridge defining the edge of new clear cuts that the WTCo was in process of starting. The steepness of the ridge, as it descended to George Creek, would keep the WTCo logging operations in abeyance for a few more years, reasoned Elmer, so they could have some assurance that their passage would be undetected.

Their plans became a little more complicated because of some uncertainty as to where the fire trail started and how difficult it would be to find because of all the new logging encroaching on the area. Nevertheless they decided to embark on this, their greatest adventure: a trek that would test their woodsman skills. Gerry and Dicky, in fact, became uncertain of these skills and decided to invite another novice camper so as to be able to redirect blame, should they become lost.

Gerald Erickson was the invitee. He was thrilled to accept, of course, not knowing of devious motivations, and eagerly accepted the heavier and bulkier items they redistributed for his pack. Gerald's mother, being skeptical of the three teenager's collective skills, insisted upon a date to check in from PeEll, before she called for a search party. A week, plus or minus one day, would be the agreed reporting date.

The rains stopped, and the weather forecasts became favorable for their journey to start. Better, the phase of the moon would give them full moonlight by which to hike. They eagerly checked their gear for the umpteenth time and loaded their packs into Sparky's pickup for the trip to WTCo's main gate.

The gate of course was locked, otherwise knowing Sparky; he probably would have driven almost to their destination. Secretly, they were thankful that it *was* locked, because otherwise their plans would have been messed up at the onset, and the element of danger contemplated for so long would no longer be part of their excitement. So as they bade Sparky goodbye at the gate and ducked under its bright yellow bar stretched across the road, their adrenalin started pumping. They were in forbidden territory, it was dark and the moon hadn't come up yet. As eyes became accustomed to the outline of the road bordered by jack firs, they imagined around every bend there was a WTCo boss in his pickup. Waiting for them.

The first few hours seemed like an eternity. To assure the cover of dark, they had to depart after ten PM. The summer solstice had just eclipsed the week before, allowing precious few hours of darkness to get to those woods that wouldn't have a lot of logging activity the next day. Knowing they couldn't dally, an adrenalin-fueled pace put them well up the slopes of BawFaw before the moon came up.

As they ascended, sounds of traffic in the valley below became magnified. Several times a large truck geared down, making them think they were about to be flooded by its headlights as it came around the next corner. The first time they jumped into the ditch in stark terror, only to look at each other sheepishly after realizing it was at least ten miles away. Darkness had a way of magnifying their senses—and imagination.

"What was that!" yelled Gerald, as they simultaneously jumped into the ditch again. By now they all had hair-trigger reflexes.

"Just another truck down in the valley," Dicky responded, heart pounding as they strained to hear gravel under tires.

"No, not that" Gerald said, his voice quivering. "That scream. Didn't you hear it? It sounded like it was coming from up the hill."

A chill crept up Dicky's back. He could feel the sweat under his pack board become cold, imagining some alien creature lurking around the next corner. Stumps became bears.

"I didn't hear any scream," Gerry said without conviction. "You guys are starting to get paranoid."

"Not me," Dicky said, not wanting to seem paranoid. "I didn't hear a scream either."

Just then, the cougar screamed. Not just a little cat like yowl, but a full throated, blood-curdling scream that sent them into the ditch once again, then immediately back on the road in terrified retreat. When they had gone a few hundred yards, they slid into another, well concealed ditch and, short of breath, hearts pounding, contemplated what they had heard.

At this point Dicky wasn't too concerned at what he had heard, but rather how he could discreetly change his shorts.

13 George Creek

Before the date of your surgery, you research the Internet for all the information you can glean from others who had similar symptoms. One of its PC-related websites leads to a support group of thousands of other prostate patients: some who were cured, some still undergoing treatment, and others whose wrenching story was related by surviving relatives or friends.

The WWII Navy F4F Wildcats were on their last leg up the coast from San Pedro Naval Air Station. They had stopped overnight at Treasure Island, refueled and took off early for the Sand Point NAS on the outskirts of Seattle. The forecast for Seattle and Portland was cloudy with winds gusting to 50 knots from the Southwest. Not good flying weather, thought Lt/JG Joe Holmes, but what the heck. This would be his last flight before getting back home to June whom he hadn't seen since shipping out to the South Pacific 6 months ago. "A 50-knot tailwind will put us in Seattle well before dark," thought Joe.

It was 1945. The war was finally over and GIs everywhere were coming home. There was a requirement to ferry some of the war material back to the States, however, and those GIs with pilot's ratings were selected to ferry anything and everything they knew how to fly.

The Wildcat wasn't totally unfamiliar to Joe. He had in fact flown three sorties over hostile waters in the Wildcat before the fighting had ended. And three was enough. He was ready to pick up his life as a student once again, this time as a doctorial candidate in the University of Washington's School of Engineering.

Because of Joe's academic achievements in his undergraduate work at the UofW, he was able to obtain a student deferment—even though many of his fellow students were being drafted, and even though he had completed all his ROTC training for his Navy pilot's wings. In fact, he had flown backseat on some of the latest Navy fighters at Boeing Field as part of this training, and had understudied test pilots who worked for Boeing. Joe was on the fast track to become one of them, they pointed out. The war was winding down, and the prospect of flying as a civilian was exciting.

"Maybe it would be better to get some combat experience first," thought Joe. "I've flown practice strafing runs over the Whidbey target range, but I can see there's a certain advantage of shooting at something live."

This idea didn't go over too big with June, his fiancé of seven months.

"You've got the world at your feet and you want to go and get your rear shot off" wailed June. "You've been lucky to avoid the draft, your grades are in the stratosphere, and Boeing will hire you in a heartbeat after you get over your ROTC commitment. Get your PhD, then the war will be over and you can even come back and fly Boeing planes as a Navy pilot."

But Joe's mind was made up. He had always excelled in academics, athletics and drama. He knew where his advantage would be: experience; and to gain this advantage he studied, scrimmaged, acted, practiced. Now he knew there was no experience like combat. He had to have it.

"Just three or four months and the war in the Pacific will be over" he assured a teary June.   "You can complete your requirements for your pre-med by then, and we can get married next May, just as we've planned."

Joe felt he hadn't been very convincing in furthering his argument, but this was the first time he said the "M" word in several months, so it at least gave him selfish comfort in trying.

Now he was on his way home, and his predictions to June were correct. The war had lasted just a few more months, but some things were not as he had so confidently thought. He had never pictured himself as a pacifist, but the events of his combat sorties made him reevaluate where he wanted to go as an aviator.

Sure, he had strafed a Jap ship, a target of opportunity he was told; and sure, it could have been radioing intelligence information to the Jap High Command; but it looked more like one of the many fishing boats at Neah Bay from which he had fished with his father before the war. His thoughts turned to his dad, a skillful and proud Makah Indian fisherman who sacrificed to send his eldest son off to the university in Seattle, a city so close, but culturally so distant he never visited. Never had the desire.

Joe thought that maybe testing new war machines wasn't such a good idea after all. There are better ways to pay society back his NROTC scholarship.

Joe's thoughts snapped back to his flying.   His wingman came over the radio:

"This weather's closing in Skipper," said Michael. "Maybe we should drop down below this stuff so we can see how thick it is."

Joe was startled both by Mike's urgency and the term 'Skipper'. Only three months his junior, Ensign Mike Steadman had never referred to him as 'Skipper'. He looked at his altimeter. It was fluctuating between eleven and ten thousand feet. "We're indeed getting buffeted around," thought Joe, now concerned about both pilots and their crafts.

"According to our flight plan, the terrain below should be no more than five thousand" Joe replied. "OK, let's go down and see if the flying is any better down there. It can't be much worse, and I don't want to risk icing up if we go higher. Let's close up and drop down to six thousand."

Joe pushed the stick of the Wildcat forward, and in formation, Mike followed, their wingtips only yards apart.

Down, down to sixty-three hundred feet. Still there was under-cast. The buffeting was no less severe. In fact, the side winds were causing alarming yawing of the Wildcats such that they had to widen their formation to the point where visibility between the planes was marginal.

"Skipper!" squawked Mike over the radio, his voice this time laden with terror. This is getting bad! I can't keep from drifting all over the place. This side wind is worse than our tailwind."

Before Joe could punch his radio in reply, Mike's plane was upon him. Mike's wingtip dropped grotesquely onto his prop and, as if in slow motion, both wings, Mikes left and Joe's right, disintegrated in a fury *of fabric and aluminum. Immediately, both cockpits met, as if the hapless aviators needed to shake hands goodbye, then both plummeted the remaining four thousand feet to George Creek flowing peacefully below.*

As Gerry, Gerald and Dicky examined the Pratt & Whitney engine that had been brought to a special landing high above the George Creek drainage, they marveled at its size. Timber surveyors found the remnants of the Wildcats some months earlier. There wasn't much intact to identify, but according to the Government Missing Planes Report, and later, through extensive searching by the authorities, dog tags were found among skeletal remains that hadn't been scattered by animals. No additional investigation as to cause of crash was deemed necessary, so the one engine not destroyed by fire was dragged from the side of the canyon to a landing punched through the old growth timber.

They were on their way to fish George Creek and knew of the gristly find—everyone did—but since they were there illegally, viewing this evidence seemed particularly filled with trepidation.

"We've got to get going," Gerald said nervously. "I can hear the trucks getting closer, and from the tracks in the mud, it looks like they've been here yesterday."

"There's no reason for them to come here," said Gerry, "Unless they're coming back to look at the engine. They won't be logging this area for a long time yet and those are logging trucks coming up the grade past Camp Seven."

"I'd just as soon we got out of here," Dicky said. " Besides, this place is giving me the creeps, and we still haven't found the fire trail down to George Creek"

With renewed determination, they left what would be referred to by all as the *Airplane Canyon*, and circled around the ridge, through tall stands of Western Hemlock, some four feet thick. Thoughts of getting caught eased considerably. Soon they came upon a surveyor's stake with a marker plate and an "X' carved on top.

"Township 34, Range 3 West, Southwest Corner," called out Gerry as though their position were suddenly found, and everyone knew exactly where they were. Actually they did know where they were, but had no reference point as to where they wanted to be. They had a rough map printed within a hunting brochure published by the WTCo, but none of the explorers knew how to find section points on it, so they were no more 'found' than before they made their discovery of the surveyor's stake. They plodded on, however, and soon came upon a blaze on one of the larger hemlocks. Farther down the canyon, another blaze on even a larger hemlock appeared.

"This has to be the trail," Gerald shouted excitedly as he slid down the increasingly steep slope.

There were few small trees or undergrowth in this tall stand of hemlock, so it was easy to see the blazes as they led tantalizingly down the canyon.

"This better be the right trail this time," said Gerry wearily as he shifted his pack board so as to achieve a better balance on the steep grade. "This time I'm not about to climb back up and look for another possibility."

They had spent a good part of the morning going down one false trail after another in their quest to find

George Creek, and their worries about being caught after trekking all night was being replaced by real weariness. They hadn't slept and wanted desperately to find George Creek, even if they had to climb down a sheer cliff to get there.

And the canyon walls did indeed get steeper. So much so they took off their packs and slid them down the slope ahead as they schussed down the hill on their behinds. *Damn the contents of our packs, damn the seats of our pants*; they were tired, and ached to get down to a level spot where they could sleep.

Massive tree trunks hugged the slopes of the canyon and offered some means of slowing their decent. Soon they caught a glimpse of sunlight reflecting off water below and yelled in relief as the steep slope gave way to the valley floor. George Creek had finally been found!

The floor of the valley formed by the eons of George Creek's gentle meanderings was no more than two or three hundred feet wide; flat with little underbrush, save for sword ferns and an occasional bush of devil's club, none of which posed an impediment to hiking. The canopy of massive fir and cedar filtered the sunlight such that it resembled the ethereal rays through stained glass windows of huge cathedrals. The few places where sunlight reached the water, its shimmering reflections on the undersides of the great cedars cast an eerie green light back to the ground. It was as close to a religious environment Dicky had ever experienced, and at the time he attributed this feeling to lack of sleep and weariness of body.

They collapsed on cushions of cool moss and were soon asleep.

Later in the day, they set about making camp. Using ferns, hemlock branches, and deadfall hemlock poles, they constructed a lean-to within one of the many ox-bows formed by banks of the creek as it meandered down the valley.   A fire pit of boulders under a cooking tripod completed the campsite. It was like they had imagined from pictures pored over in *Outdoor Life* or *Field and Stream*. They were proud of themselves. This was the culmination of a year of planning and they felt like true outdoorsmen.

"Let's make sure we only use dry wood for our fire," Dicky cautioned Gerald as he set out to gather firewood for their evening meal. "We don't want our smoke to be seen by the lookout on BawFaw, or anyone else, for that matter."

"There are lots of dead logs about," Gerald replied. "I'll get some pitchy knots. They should burn good and hot without giving off much smoke at all."

"Get some of the dead cedar from the driftwood along the creek bank" added Gerry. "Meanwhile I'm going to catch a few fish for supper"

"Not so fast," Dicky retorted, assuming the role of camp master, knowing full well his authority extended only to his superior age.

"We all start fishing at the same time," he added, eyeing the sparkling drift downstream that he just knew had to contain at least a couple twelve inch cutthroat that had never seen a hook and line before.

Surprisingly, both fishing companions agreed, and together the three explorers hurriedly assembled their fishing rods and set off to experience the second leg of their camping adventure: Fishing virgin waters.

"Life couldn't get much better," Dicky thought aloud.

First casts brought forth a flurry of trout, practically colliding to grab their flies, but disappointedly, all about six inches in size. Under more protective cover, images of larger fish could be seen, only to be sent scurrying away by the commotion of the small, precocious steelhead, all-vying for the same food.

"Juvenile steelhead," Dicky yelled to his partners upstream, shaking off the third six-incher in as many casts. "We need to figure out how to get something bigger to the cutthroat swimming deeper in the holes."

Just then, Gerry shouted: "Got one!" then: "Broke him off—he had to be at least fifteen inches!"

"What's the secret?" Dicky inquired, releasing yet another juvenile steelhead. In his excitement, he had forgotten techniques used previously in fishing similar waters on Mill Creek, to which Gerry now reminded:

"Just leave the fly in the water longer without setting the hook on the first bite. Soon the bigger fish will take it away from the small ones and hook themselves."

Dicky looked about to locate another periwinkle with which to garnish his fly, a McGinty tied on a size ten hook. Finding nothing on the fast flowing riffle, he drifted the bare fly under a log at the end of the drift. He felt the small tugs of the steelhead fry, then nothing.

Hooked the log, he thought as he pointed his rod at the end of the line in preparation for breaking it free. He had tied plenty of flies, so it was more important to tie on a new one than to spook the fish by trying to retrieve a snagged one. Suddenly the log tugged back, and a trout bigger than any seen before thrashed about on the other side of the log. Having rod pointed straight at the fish provided no yielding resistance whatsoever, so the six pound test leader quickly parted.

"What was that?" Gerry shouted, seeing Dicky's short-lived reaction to this huge strike.

"I think it must have been a summer steelhead," Dicky responded. Having seen a few summer runs on the Toutle River, he could only guess at what he had seen, but surely the native cutthroat couldn't be that large. With shaking fingers, he tied on another McGinty and drifted it under the same log.

Finally, after shaking off several more juvenile steelhead, he hooked a respectable cutthroat of about eleven inches and brought it to hand. Its markings were beautiful: greenish gold sides with pale yellow leading edges on the pectoral and ventral fins, dark spots from stomach to its almost translucent tail and adipose fin, and the unmistakable bright red slashes under its chin giving it its namesake.

He studied this beautiful specimen for a few more seconds before breaking its neck and sliding it into his canvas creel lined with sword ferns.

They stayed in Oxbow Camp for two more days, fishing upstream and down, finding it necessary to go only a few hundred yards in either direction to catch all the trout they needed for food. Finding good use of the ten pounds of pancake mix they brought, they dusted the trout first in a mixture of flour, salt and pepper, then fried them in butter. They could each easily consume a half dozen at each meal, which meant their daily bag limit of eighteen fish each were just enough for three meals a day.

But they quickly ran out of pancake flour—something they hadn't expected, and butter quickly gave way to bacon grease, which also gave out after the third day. Now they were relegated to roasting the trout on forked sticks, hence their daily catch diminished accordingly: saving only a few larger cutthroat that roasted easier without burning or falling off the forked sticks. They had grossly underestimated their staple food supplies and regretted being so careless with the bacon grease the first few days.

"Don't we have something to save the bacon grease in?" asked Gerry as Dicky emptied the frying pan into the fire after frying the last of the bacon.

"I don't think so," Dicky replied. "Unless you want to eat that last can of pork and beans for breakfast. Besides, I'm not too keen about carrying around an open can of bacon grease with all these bears around," he added, remembering the fish carcasses and piles of bear scat along the creek.

So the Explorers ate roasted fish for the remainder of their journey. For a special treat, they ate the can of pork and beans, and then, in a fortuitous find, happened upon an elk hunters cabin—an A-frame of long split cedar shakes, that contained a stash of canned beef jerky, and—more pork and beans. They weren't starving, but roasted fish was becoming low on their list of favorite foods, just below pork and beans.

They picked up the pace of finding their planned way down George Creek, down the North Fork of the Chehalis River, and finally to PeEll where they were to call Gerry's mother. But by day three, they had only made it to the mouth of George Creek. Fishing became less important than making headway down river which became more difficult as the river became wider and faster. The gentle flow of George Creek gave a false sense of timing, and now they were faced with following the Chehalis in it's dash to PeEll, some thousand feet below and ten miles away.

Shoes became the first casualty of their trek. Not made for wading over large boulders and sharp rocks, basketball sneakers that served well on the courts last winter started to deteriorate. Tears along the canvas sides exposed feet to the abuse of abrasive sand and small pebbles that filtered in unabated. Cut strips of a spare tee shirt tied around the offending shoe helped until it, like the bacon, butter and pancake flour, also gave out. With miles to go, they were running out of consumables. Next were Dicky's pants. Or more correctly: a leg of his pants.

On night six, they bivouacked along the river which they had traversed—waded—several times in their attempt to make time. Wading became more challenging as the river increased in size, however, and after they reached the confluence of Crim Creek, still five miles above PeEll, wading became more of an ordeal of getting thoroughly wet. That night they built a larger fire than usual in an attempt to dry everything out. They had long stopped worrying about getting caught building fires in WTCo's precious woods and built a large, smoky fire of damp driftwood, took off their clothes to dry them on— forked sticks.

Unfortunately one of the legs of Dicky's only pair of jeans dried faster than estimated, and caught fire. Being not yet into the cutoff style, he chose to wear the jeans as is, wanting to have at least one leg protected from the now present mosquitoes, for which they hadn't brought any repellent. The mental list of items and quantities to include on their next trek kept growing.

Gradually, traces of civilization became evident. Empty salmon egg jars along the river were the first clue, along with a noticeable difference in the size and numbers of trout. Steelhead fry were still present in great numbers, but cutthroat were fewer and less willing to come to their offerings. Just as well, as they were all getting tired of fishing—something heretofore unheard of—but it was time to get home and they hungered for a round meal of chicken, spuds, gravy, and ice cream.

Just then, around a bend of the river, a bridge came into view. Even better: a car was parked on the approach, presenting hope that maybe, just maybe, they could get a ride the last few miles into PeEll. Weary of slipping on rocks, being constantly wet from the waist down and being hungry, they wouldn't be shy at asking for a ride, even if they looked like refugees from the Battle of the Bulge: Dicky with a burned off pant leg, everyone else all grimy and smelling of campfire smoke, shoes flapping and bandaged with rags.

"Who would give us a ride in this condition?" Dicky wondered aloud.

"In this condition, who could refuse to give us a ride?" responded Gerald, looking at Dicky's banged up, chewed up leg protruding from his burned off pant leg. "Not to give us a ride would be really mean."

But fortune smiled, because the person in the car was no one else but Walt Newberry, a farm kid they knew from school that lived up on the South Fork. He decided to come over to the North Fork to do some fishing, he explained.

Walt, or "Snoose" as his distracters, and closest friends called him, was somewhat of a renegade insofar as the student body of BHS was concerned. He came by his nickname honestly: he chewed. Even in grade school he chewed. As long as they knew him he chewed. Plug tobacco mostly, but in more social situations, snuff was his choice. Since most loggers chose snuff, Walt was probably destined to become a logger, and everyone just assumed he was getting an early start on an acceptable habit among loggers.

Walt could also have been a career baseball player, a profession also identified by snoose chewers because he possessed an extraordinary throwing arm. He was BHS's premier pitcher, noted for his fastball mainly, but after he set up his batters, he could throw almost anything over the plate and get called strikes. His setup consisted of a fastball, high and in with such velocity that it could knock a board off the backstop. Any pitch after that would have the batter, often the catcher and umpire, ducking for cover. Anything close to the plate the ump would call strikes just to get the inning over and back to relative safety. When Walt herded cows, all he had to do was pick up a rock and the entire herd would run for the barn.

"You guys want to go fishing?" Walt asked, as he spat a stream of brown liquid out the passenger side window. He was also noted for his spitting accuracy, which he showed off whenever he had the opportunity.

Just then Sam Kaslowski came up from under the bridge, zipping up his pants from an apparent call with nature. Sam was a shirttail relative of Walt who lived in PeEll.

"Sam and I are going up a new logging road up Crim Creek to see if there's any fish in some of the feeder creeks," explained Walt as he cut a huge wad of chew from a plug he carried in his hip pocket and stuffed it into his right cheek. "Weyerhaeuser hasn't put up a gate yet, so we can drive all the way up to the end of the spur. And since it's Sunday, there's probably not going to be anyone up there to run us out."

Fishing was probably one of the last things the Explorers wanted to do at this juncture, but Walt represented a ride back to PeEll, even home, so if they had to detour a bit, it sure beat walking, so they dumped packs and rods in the trunk of his Pontiac and slid into the back seat. And sitting felt wonderful!

"Good thing Sam had to take a shit," said Walt as he steered the Pontiac across the bridge, "or you guys would be still walking. We haven't seen another car up here all morning."

They were grateful, of course, but would have preferred to be heading in the other direction. Knowing of Walt's predisposition at poaching and noting the presence of a 30-30 rifle in the trunk, Dicky for one, felt uneasy about becoming an accessory. Besides, there wasn't room in the trunk for their packs and a deer.

Fortunately deer were not in evidence that day, so they didn't get the chance to test Walt's predisposition. Walt stopped the Pontiac at a culvert and grabbed his rod, a short nondescript switch with two guides and a taped on reel. Walt noticed the critical review of his tackle:

"No sense giving the Game Warden something he can use," rationalized Walt, apparently speaking from the experience of having his tackle confiscated for fishing out of season, in closed waters, taking over limits, keeping undersized, or all of the above. "Wait here while I try this creek," he said as he slid down the screed to a trickle of water flowing from the culvert.

"I'll eat every fish you catch out of that puddle," yelled Sam, still seated in the Pontiac, not seeing any need to join Walt in this folly.

No more had Sam's words stopped echoing when an eight-inch cutthroat came flying up the screed on the end of Walt's line.

"Be sure to unhook him before you eat him," grinned Walt as he ricocheted another stream of snoose off a flat rock in smug satisfaction.

Before Sam could grab his rod and join him, there were two more cutthroat flopping on the bank, each of about eight inches, and each dark sided from just recently being in the cover of the forested canopy. Now there was only the cover of newly fallen trees crisscrossing over the creek. They knew that soon the creek, as a sustainer of cutthroat, would disappear, no longer having trees to hold back the runoff in the winter and to meter out the flow in the summer.

What Walt, Sam and scores of other trespassers were doing, one could reason, was a salvage operation. Before the dozers and skidders came for the logs and totally annihilating this and every other fish-bearing creek like it, why not catch every, and all fish therein?

"They're going to die anyway," grinned Walt, not understanding the full impact of his observation.

Nor did most of the residents see the full impact of what was going on. Behind locked gates, streams were being stripped of cover and inundated with mud and debris. Too soon, there would be precious few fish like these beautiful, dark sided, dark spotted cutthroat that Dicky first discovered on My Creek.

But there wasn't anything anybody could do about it. Logging was King and they were its subjects.

14   Toutle River

You learn that radical surgery would be highly invasive with no guarantee you wouldn't be impotent, incontinent, or both.

Two rivers were Dicky's favorites. My River, running by Lost Valley Ranch was closest and by default, was number one. Except for those winter months when she was out of shape because of runoff from the increasing numbers of clear cuts in her headwaters, she could be approached anytime, and generally gave up her fish. An accommodating, slow-meandering stream, with long, deep holes, she occasionally yielded a trout, less occasionally a smallmouth bass, but more often a chub or a sucker. My River was generous, and Dicky rarely left her without being rewarded.

The Toutle, on the other hand, was a brawling, free flowing stream, borne of Mt St Helens. She was always hospitable to trout and salmon—never slowed down anywhere long enough to accommodate anything else. The riffles flowed swiftly into her deep holes and swept out fish not fit to live there.   In the winter, after the salmon had their way, the steelhead found her to their liking, swimming with deliberate speed from the ocean to rest before proceeding to repeat the spawning dance of the salmon. Also, the cutthroat—Harvest Trout— accompanied the salmon and gorged themselves on eggs that spilled from their redds.

For Northwest rivers, the Toutle was fairly short. Close to the ocean, she had only to flow into the Cowlitz River some twelve miles above the mighty Columbia. Less than twenty more miles upriver, the Toutle separated into three forks, the North, generally flowing clear from Spirit

Lake, the South, often running milky directly from the melting snows of Mt St Helens; and the Green River, originating from springs in the Green Mountain Foothills. The choice of which fork to fish was always easy for Dicky, particularly since the road to Spirit Lake followed the North Fork. He generally found little need to venture far from the road to find good fishing, as the migrating fish all swam by any given spot anyway.

Less than thirty miles distant from Lost Valley Ranch, the Toutle was close enough for a day trip, but he always preferred to overnight in one of its many campgrounds and fish early the next day. Daybreak came late in its deep canyons and the trout, after a night of feeding, could often be found in the shallows and easily caught for breakfast. Fresh trout frying over a campfire: Dicky thought this is the way all fishing trips should be.

Uncle Ralph introduced Dicky to the Toutle. He also was fond of this river even though it was another ninety miles distant from his home in Seattle. He knew of her fabulous runs of salmon and steelhead, but also fished for its cutthroat in the fall. He knew of the large runs of Harvest Trout that followed the salmon in their spawning runs and stayed afterwards, also to spawn in the gravel stirred up by the salmon. Unlike the salmon that died after spawning, however, the cutthroat often went back to sea, only to return to spawn again, sometime as many as three or four times.

And it wasn't unusual for Uncle Ralph and Aunt Emmagene to catch several of the three or four-year returnees. On one memorable trip, Dicky was fishing with Uncle Ralph about a quarter mile downstream from where Mom and Aunt Emmagene were fishing. A scream came from their location and thinking one had fallen in, Uncle Ralph and Dicky both scrambled up the bank, got into the Ford and raced back up the road.

It turned out Mom hooked a large Harvest Trout and had been hanging on to the rod with both hands while Aunt Emmagene stood alongside attempting to reel it in. The trout would have none of it, however, and managed to wind the line around a large boulder. Seeing the futility of their situation, Uncle Ralph finally took the rod, pointed it at the boulder, took a few turns of line around his hand and broke the line. Dicky knew Mom never forgot that disappointment, and for years afterwards wished he could have figured out a way to retrieve her Harvest Trout.

Dicky caught his largest fish on the Toutle. He was eight years old and was fishing with Uncle Ralph, Aunt Emmagene and Mom. It might have been on the same trip that Mom lost her Harvest Trout, I can't remember. I do remember he was fishing for trout using a small F-4 flatfish, orange with black frog spots on the end of a spinning outfit provided by Uncle Ralph. He hooked several small trout of about ten inches, landed two, making his day a blazing success. It was getting late in the afternoon, so after making a few last casts, he intended to make his way up the bank to the Ford and rest.

But just then he must have hooked the bottom because his line became fixed to something not yielding to pressure. As he started to maneuver downstream to try to extricate his flatfish, the bottom started moving upstream, slowly at first, and then lunging viciously as it picked up speed. As line raced off his reel, he knew this was no mere trout. It was a salmon. A Chinook. The largest of the Pacific species, sometimes attaining weights as high as one hundred pounds. This fish felt all of that, as he raced up the rocky shore to keep a few precious turns of line on his reel. Uncle Ralph immediately assessed the situation and reeled in his line to give his expert guidance in preparation to gaff the salmon. Gaffing would not come to pass for the next hour and thirty minutes, however, as the salmon wasn't about to yield any water between shore and the middle where it sulked, obviously insulted at being fooled by such a young neophyte. Grudgingly it held its position on the bottom of the drift, only moving as Dicky applied pressure from below. With only ten-pound test leader, it was impossible to move, except to turn it's head slightly when it attempted to run against the current. Several times it turned downstream to descend the next riffle, but stopped at the last moment as per Uncle Ralph's yelled instructions, Dicky released all pressure.

Unbeknownst to Dicky, Uncle Ralph and the dozens of onlookers who gathered on the road above, the salmon was slowly losing strength——not so much by Dicky's token pressure—but rather because its mouth was held closed by the two sets of size 14 treble hooks attached to the Flatfish. Fatefully, it was slowly suffocating, so by the time night had overtaken the growing shadows of Kid Valley, Dicky could pull it to within a few yards of shore. There, illuminated by a half dozen onlookers' flashlights, it held it's position as if to make its last stand, gasping for the few precious gulps of water it could obtain through involuntarily clenched teeth. Several times Uncle Ralph waded out, gaff in hand, only to retreat when it started to swim back to deeper water. Finally, he was able to sneak behind and strike with the gaff, throwing the salmon toward the bank with such force that he propelled himself into the current and had to struggle ashore, soaked and sputtering. Again, Uncle Ralph had dunked himself on Dicky's behalf.

A cheer went up from the gallery as Mom and Aunt Emmagene did a Brown Bear Act on the flopping salmon and Uncle Ralph dispatched it unceremoniously by a rap to the head with the handle of his gaff. Triumphantly, they hauled it up the bank to the highway where one of the onlookers produced a scale. This magnificent salmon, Dicky's biggest fish ever, weighed in at thirty-seven pounds.

Memories such as these always returned Dicky to the Toutle. Even during his twenty years in the Air Force, I don't think he ever came home on leave without returning at least for one day to fish some of his favorite drifts along the Kid Valley. Hardly ever did he come home fishless, except for those days its waters were un-fishable; often because of runoff from clear cuts the WTCo had unexpectedly started upstream. But the runoffs were predictable for the most part, and after a day or two of no rain, one could expect the fishing, especially for steelhead, to improve.

It was on one of those days Gerry and Dicky ventured for a day trip to Kid Valley. He was home on leave for a week, and it had rained several days, putting most rivers out of shape, the Toutle especially. Deciding to go anyway, they reasoned that to fish, even in muddy water, was better than to not fish at all. So they fished all morning and into the afternoon without so much as a strike. As they grudgingly headed for home, Gerry suggested they stop at the barrier dam on the Cowlitz River to watch the action along the picket line.

The Cowlitz River was once a free flowing stream before the City of Tacoma built two hydroelectric dams, Mayfield and Mossyrock, each blocking migration of salmon and steelhead to the rich spawning grounds availed by upstream tributaries: Rivers Cispis, Tilton, and Ohanapecosh; Creeks Johnson, Iron, and Winston, and scores of smaller streams. Below the first dam they added a barrier dam to divert all migrating fish into a hatchery to be artificially spawned or sorted for further processing, meaning they were either killed for animal food, or sent upstream in tank trucks so they could spawn naturally in many of the tributary streams. The numbers of naturally spawned fish were pitifully small compared to the huge runs before the dams, however, so in mitigation—a word evoking different emotions by fishermen and dam people alike—a long artificial embankment was built below the barrier dam to allow the maximum numbers of fishermen to access the hoards of fish waiting to enter the hatchery. It was sort of like fishing in a barrel.

When Gerry and Dicky arrived at the picket line, it was late in the afternoon and it continued to rain. They found a vacant parking spot so they could watch the action and listen to the Seahawks game from the comfort of Dicky's car. As expected, fishermen, some slinging lures, others bait, occupied every yard of the bank, but all casting in synchronization lest their lines get tangled. It was an amazing sight; such cooperation amongst what would be normally thought of as a rag-tag bunch of rugged individualists, standing in the rain, elbow-to-elbow, ever optimistic, hoping to hook one of many steelhead waiting to enter the hatchery. On the car radio the Seahawks were playing the Chargers and the score was tied, so attention was more on the game than the fishing. It was obvious that there were few fish being caught anyway, as the space between fishermen increased until late in the fourth quarter, a gap of about 30 feet opened up in front of the observers sitting dry in their car. A field goal with the clock running out decided the game for the Seahawks, so with elevated spirits, Dicky turned to Gerry and said:

"I think I'll take a few casts," and slid out the front seat to assemble his rod.

The water was still relatively clear, but the increased flow showed the effects of mud entering the lower reservoir from Winston Creek, the headwaters of which had been mercilessly clear-cut in the past few months. Not optimistic of his chances, Dicky decided to continue using the #2 bright silver spoon that proved to be ineffective on the Toutle, and stepped to the waters edge some twenty feet in front of their car and made his first cast.

As the spoon swung halfway through the drift, it stopped abruptly. Thinking it had probably hung up on one of many wads of lures accumulated by countless other hang-ups, Dicky pointed the rod down the line in preparation to breaking it off.

This lure hadn't been very productive anyway, he thought, concluding this might be a good time to just reel in, throw the rod in the trunk and drive home—tired and fishless.

Just then, the lure wad started pulling back. A bright steelhead cartwheeled off the surface and started downstream in a series of leaps that left no doubt it was on the end of his line. Almost in unison, fishermen upstream and down groaned in disbelief. Not only had they not hooked anything all afternoon, not only had they stood in the rain all day trying, but here's this interloper who sat all this time in the warmth of his stinking Cadillac, gets out, scratches, yawns, and in one cast, hooks a steelhead.

At the sound of cussing and other choice expletives, Gerry woke from his nap and watched the action from the warmth of the car. After about five minutes, the steelhead played out and Dicky worked it to within a foot of shore whereupon Gerry casually strolled to the water, gaffed and dispatched it with a blow to the head. With a smirk, he remarked in a voice so all could hear:

"It's about time you got your limit. Now maybe we can go home."

As the nearest fisherman threw his rod to the gravel in disgust, the interlopers hurriedly deposited rod and fish in the trunk and drove away. In the rear view mirror Dicky could see the gathering of an unruly mob. Before they could retreat to the first bend of the road to safety, they fully expected to endure ricocheting rocks—or worse.

That was the last time they fished the Cowlitz River picket line.

But the Toutle was good to Dicky and he returned many times to reap its bounty. He learned where the early summer run steelhead could be found in the long drifts of the Kid Valley. He knew he could likely find solitude when the Huskies were playing in a Rose Bowl game. He went there when the weather turned cold, knowing there would be drifts just coming into shape that harbored fish fresh from the sea. He fished there often when he wanted solitude, and often he found it. Other times he'd fish with Gerry on those weekends they both needed to get away.

It was on such an occasion on a grey December day they planned to fish for winter steelhead and overnight in a camper borrowed from Carmen's uncle, Chuck. A typical cab-over model mounted on a three quarter ton Ford pickup, it had a stove, heater, refrigerator, two beds and reasonable space such that two friends could co-exist for a couple days without getting on each other's nerves. Leaving Seattle on a Friday at noon, they rolled into the Kid Valley campground around three and it was already getting dark. Too late to string rods and fish, so they prepared a couple scotches after noting that the bottle had tipped over and leaked out half its contents.

"The Ballentine bottle tipped over and someone forgot to screw the lid on tight," Gerry said with a tinge of criticism as he held up the rectangular shaped vessel to measure the remaining volume. "It's a good thing it tipped on its edge otherwise we'd lost it all. This is supposed to last us for the weekend and it's already half gone"

"What soaked up the spill?" Dicky asked. "Maybe we can wring it out and strain it back into the bottle."

"Wouldn't work," Gerry replied as he craned his head to look into the cabinet. "It's pretty much absorbed into the shelf. Besides, all the good stuff has already evaporated."

Somewhat dejected, the fishermen sat across the table drinking their scotches and contemplated their evening. Eating would be first on their agenda. They came with plenty of food: the usual fishing trip fare of meat, cheese, bread, chips, a couple bottles of Gerry's homemade wine and a quart jar of pickles for which his dad, Sparky, was famous.

"We might as well eat," Gerry said as he reached into the refrigerator and pulled out a large package labeled 'jug meat'.

Also a Sparky delicacy, jug meat was an assortment of trimmings from other meat cuts, usually venison, layers of which are packed tightly into a gallon jar or crock, interspersed with handfuls of garlic, unspecified quantities of salt and other spices. After aging a few months in a cool place, the top, and usually moldy layer was discarded, leaving the remainder ready for consumption. On the camper stove, Gerry heated a liberal amount of bacon grease in a large frying pan and dropped in several pieces of the jug meat.

"Just smell that aroma," he said as he ducked away from the spattering oil and reached into a cabinet for a lid to place over the pan. "Here's a side dish you can open," he added, sliding a large can of pork and beans across the table, then, reaching back into the refrigerator, withdrew a plastic bag of pre-sliced cheese, a loaf of French bread and the quart of pickles. To round out the menu, he lifted from his fishing 'luggage' a bottle of red wine, on whose beer-style cap were two marker-pen letters: 'RA'.

For his wine, Gerry had long gotten away from the elaborate labels, foils and corks favored by most amateur wine makers and went straight to the chase. "RA' meant raspberry, 'E': elderberry, 'B': blackberry, and so forth. Vintage years didn't much matter and, in fact, it was a standing joke that 'Tuesday' was just as good as 'Friday' when it came to comparing his vintages.

"How do you keep these bottles from exploding?" Dicky asked, as he hinged off the cap with a beer opener and, not wishing to further waste any of their diminishing supplies of booze, quickly captured the first cup of fizz into his glass of scotch.

"I've never tried scotch and RA," Gerry said with a smirk as he produced a couple of wine glasses from the cupboard.

"S'not bad," Dicky responded, reaching for another pickle.

Dinner over, they washed and dried the dishes. Still too early to retire, they tied up leaders and several dozen yarn flies they might need the next day. Next they availed themselves to the only reading material in the camper: two old and damp *Outdoor Life* magazines found under the front seat. Then, after trying unsuccessfully to get a Sonics game on Gerry's transistor radio, decided to turn in for the night.

"Time really flies," Dicky said looking at his watch. "Already it's seven o'clock"

"Yeah, it seems like just yesterday we had supper," Gerry replied, quickly looking at his own watch to make sure Dicky wasn't kidding.   "For some reason I'm not hungry, though. Did you think to bring along any Tums?"

At five o'clock the next morning they arose after a fitful night, each having made an urgent trip to an outhouse fortuitously provided by the Cowlitz County Parks Department. Sometime after three AM, stomachs calmed down and they managed to sleep until about four-thirty, at which time they had all the prone time they could stand. They sat up in the warmth of their beds and talked for a half hour about the winter solstice and the follies of insufficient entertainment. It was still pitch black outside, so they prepared and ate a large breakfast of coffee, toast, scrambled eggs and bacon, after which they washed and dried the dishes, strung rods, donned waders and waited for it to get light. Eight thirty came and the stately firs of the Kid Valley finally allowed the first rays of light to reach the valley floor and the river. The Toutle beckoned to them, green, and slightly opaque, it hinted of good fishing for the day, what there was left of it.

Trips such as these gave Dicky much pleasure and the urge to return again and again. The anticipation of the first glimpse of water as he crossed the Kid Valley Bridge, the first cast of the day, the bright leaves of the vine maple, all these images kept him coming back. From work assignments as far away as Louisiana, Arkansas and Oklahoma, it drew him back. Prompted by memories: his biggest fish, fishless days, his first summer run, the longest night, it drew him back.

With the passage of time, Dicky slowly came to prefer the Toutle to My River. Time was not kind to either, however. Both were assaulted by relentless logging by the WTCo, but My River had to endure the runoff from not only the clear cuts, but from pastures and farmland. Each summer she had to share more of her water with the farmers until sometimes none flowed at all. Both contained good winter runs of salmon and steelhead, but on My River, half went to the Chehalis Tribe by virtue of the Treaty of Medicine Creek. An additional insult to My River was a pulp mill owned by the WTCo at the seaport town of Cosmopolis. It spewed effluent, which more than occasionally killed My Trout on their way to the sea. So the Toutle, by virtue of its lack of all things negative with My River, remained relatively pristine, and Dicky kept returning to her.

He planned to return one spring. Typically, the season opened on the second weekend in May, and he would journey from his home, now in Seattle, to the Kid Valley to fish for steelhead. Fresh from the sea, the early summer run were the most prized of all of the salmonoid species, and he always looked forward to the first strike of the season. Whether he landed one wasn't material—it was that first electrifying feel transmitted through the line to his rod and into his body that mattered most. It was addictive, and as he readied his gear after a long spring of no fishing, he could feel the excitement of opening day once again.

From Dicky's home overlooking Puget Sound and Mt Rainier to the south, a second mountain: St Helens could sometimes be seen when the air was clear, the sky cloudless. It showed up as a tiny cone of white just to the right of Mt Rainier. It functioned to remind him of the Toutle, and the many happy times he visited her.

But this day something was terribly wrong. Now, only a week from opening day, dominating the sky where Mt St Helens should have been, loomed a giant cloud of smoke and ash. Horrified, Dicky turned on the television to see images of the devastation caused by Mt St Helens. A helicopter-borne reporter was explaining how the blast and melting snow had overflowed Spirit Lake and how the boiling water was now rushing down the Toutle. As the TV camera panned away, Dicky could see the Kid Valley Bridge standing valiantly against the cauldron of logs and debris, then panning back in, it could be seen twisting away from its supports to be swept downriver. From another helicopter camera farther downstream, a steelhead was shown, alive and pitifully trying to swim ashore, away from the boiling water. As the reporter continued and the images became more horrific, Dicky stood transfixed, devastated at what he was seeing. A river that had given him such pleasure for so many years was now dying in just a few minutes. It was though he was witnessing the death of an old friend. Indeed, he sadly watched her burial beneath a million tons of Mt St Helens.

What struggled to the surface in a feeble attempt of resurrection would still be called the Toutle River, but never in Dicky's lifetime would she ever be the same.

15   A Taste of The Good Life

You learn that for many patients undergoing radical surgery, cancer returned after a few years, requiring further, and more invasive treatments.

All through high school, Dicky's life was pretty much that of a farm boy. Sure, he had been to Seattle a few times and felt at home cruising Chehalis Avenue in his '37 Chevy; but what he knew of life outside the farm was pretty limited. Not that this was bad. His city cousins would have benefited by his experiences on Lost Valley Ranch. Hard work in the fields, cleaning the barns, pitching hay to the livestock, chopping wood; it would be at least thirty years before city kids would be able to exercise like this in specialized exercise clubs with their Nautilus equipment.

Nonetheless, Dicky became aware and envious of certain elements of affluence beyond the Spartan existence on the Ellingson farm. Uncle Ralph's den and his collection of fly rods reminded him of this, as did the lifestyle of Aunt Louella and Uncle Claire. Their children, Carol and Gary, about Dicky's age, seemed to have all the material things teenagers wanted.

Uncle Claire, Elmer's brother-in-law, was the Safeway regional manager for Southeastern Washington and built a luxurious home in Walla Walla shortly before Dicky visited them in the summer of '52. A special treat for him, this visit coincided with a fly-in fishing trip to a lake in British Columbia Uncle Claire arranged as a birthday gift for Gary.

"Don't bring any fishing equipment." Gary said over the phone. "The guide service doesn't want to haul any extra stuff on the plane. They said all the tackle we'll need is already at the lodge. They have canoes and rowboats we'll use. All we have to do is show up at the airport."

Dicky only read about such a trip in *Outdoor Life* or *Field & Stream,* and the anticipation of such a fishing experience filled him with excitement. He again felt the same euphoria and sleeplessness as he did on the eve of his very first fishing trip with Uncle Ralph. Dicky wondered: *would great fishing trips like this always keep me awake the night before?*

Early the next morning they left in the family Oldsmobile for the drive to Spokane. There they planned to rendezvous with a guide service that would fly them into Canada. On the way, Uncle Claire had to complete some unexpected Safeway business that delayed their departure until the next morning.

Oh great, Dicky thought, *one more night of anticipation.* But he was so tired from the previous sleepless night, he went out like a light.

After a hearty breakfast at the motel, they drove to the Felts Aerodrome on the Spokane River. When they arrived at the huge de Havilland seaplane, Dicky and Gary could hardly contain their excitement. Four other fishermen were already there, having also scheduled this trip with the guide service, and it appeared that they too were excited.

They gave their baggage to the pilot for storage and scrambled aboard. The plane was equally huge inside; affording each a window seat they eagerly accepted. Fumbling to fasten his seatbelt under the direction of one of the other passengers, Dicky again became apprehensive. Except for a day trip in a Piper Cub that Mr. Smiley, his science teacher had rented from the Chehalis Airport, this would be his first flight in a larger plane, and although the

Otter still had only one engine, there was no comparison to the Piper.

As the pilot started the plane for takeoff, its huge engine belched fire, smoke and noise so loud Dicky became fearful that something was wrong. He glanced anxiously to the adult passengers who seemed relatively calm, so he tried to appear calm also, not wanting to seem like a greenhorn.

Then the plane really got noisy as the pilot shoved the throttle forward and the engine roared like a thousand Piper Cubs. The massive pontoons moved slowly through the Spokane River at first, and then rose to skim over the waves that had been created by the rapid taxi to the end of the takeoff area. Faster and faster the river flashed under, until finally it leaped into the morning sky, dipped its wing as if to bid farewell to Spokane and turned toward Canada.

Gary and Dicky both had their noses pressed to their respective windows and didn't notice the amused expressions exchanged by their fellow fishermen. It was just as well because they were the only kids—and greenhorns aboard.

The plane landed at Oysoyoos, BC on the Okanogan River for customs check, and then took off again for the BC interior to the northwest, flying under the high overcast and over the thousands of lakes below. Nothing Dicky had read in his outdoor magazines had prepared him for this. Surely any of these lakes could meet their fishing and camping needs, but the plane droned onward until no roads were visible—only lakes, and trees.

As Dicky was about to nod off from the drone of the engine, one of the fishing partners, an older gentleman, came forward and sat beside him. He introduced himself as Walt, and said he had been to this lake several times and had never been disappointed by the fishing. Walt had a grey beard blending into brown hair and a moustache that couldn't figure out which color to be.

"These trout are special," said Walt, puffing on a well-seasoned brier pipe. "They're called Kamloops Trout, and can get up to 20 pounds, but on this lake they're so many, they rarely get to be 7 or 8 pounds. They'll give you a tussle, though."

"Why don't they get bigger," Dicky asked.

"They would, except the food supply in this lake is limited for their numbers, and once they get to a certain size, they can't get enough to grow any bigger. Pretty soon, they'll all get to be the same size, and if we or the loons don't catch more to reduce their numbers, they'll get skinny and die from lack of food."

Thus, Dicky learned from Walt the law of diminishing returns as it applies to fish biology, although the real impact of how this might affect his fishing wouldn't sink in until years later.

Walt also elaborated on the trout's food supply. Dicky was surprised to learn that worms and salmon eggs weren't included. Not even close. Bugs, specifically water bugs named sedge, dragonfly and damselfly were what these trout ate. Dicky had of course seen dragonflies, and had only heard of the damselfly, but he couldn't imagine a trout, any fish, being fast enough to catch a dragonfly.

"These bugs aren't the flying type," Walt pointed out. "Before they fly, they swim underwater where the trout are. This is where they live most of their life. They only fly when it's time to mate and reproduce. Just before they get to the surface on their way to become flyers is when the trout really start feeding on them in earnest. This is the time when it's best to use a fly. A wet fly"

To emphasize his point, Walt extracted three long flies from an old sheepskin wallet from his coat pocket and gave them to Dicky. They were brown in color, tied on a long, rather large hook, and appeared to be made of pheasant feathers. "These are called Colonel Careys," he said with authority. "You fish these on the end of a floating line, just under the lake's surface"

Dicky nodded as though he knew all about floating lines and strange looking flies, but in reality, the only fly-fishing he had experienced up to this point had been with the flies copied from patterns in a Herter's catalog. These were mostly eastern patterns such as the McGinty, Grey Hackle Red, and the Paramachenie Belle.

Not really bug imitations, Dicky thought, *until garnished with a night crawler or periwinkle.*

Walt continued about fly-fishing and the special feelings he had about this particular lake. At the time, the excitement at just being able to catch a trout the size he had described, no matter the technique, kept Dicky from understanding just how special this trip must have been to him. At the time he failed to observe a tear that appeared on his well-trimmed beard. Walt's pipe had gone out and he busied himself at re-lighting it.

Finally they came upon their lake. From the air it seemed small until the pilot dipped the nose of the plane and descended to just above the treetops. Then it became difficult to see the end of the lake for all the inlets and bays. The pilot banked the plane in a steep turn and took a low pass over one of the larger bays. "To make sure there's no moose swimming where we want to land," he shouted to the passengers.

As if on cue, the passengers all peered out their respective windows to help the pilot look for moose. All they saw were a few loons and a lone boat at the end of the bay, its single occupant apparently ignoring the intruding plane. Swinging around on final approach, the lodge complex at the other end of the bay came into sight. A small cluster of people stood at the end of one of the docks—fishermen who had spent their allocated time at the lake and were now packed up and ready to embark on their return trip south.

The pontoons touched the lake's chop, then dug in and decelerated the de Havilland faster than the passengers expected. Seat belts not tightly fastened bit into laps and equipment loosely stored bounced along the floor. The pilot glanced at some of the offending gear that settled at his feet and glared back at the passengers. Without so much as saying so, a better job of storing gear on the return flight would be expected.

From his extensive reading of *Outdoor Life* and *Field and Stream,* the Lodge was everything Dicky expected. It had all the accoutrements of Uncle Ralph's den, and more. Massive log rafters supported a steep shake roof over walls of peeled logs. At one end of the giant main room was a stone fireplace with a grand log mantle stretching from wall to wall. Over the mantle hung a moose head, its waddle hanging at an angle as though frozen in death's position. Pictures of trout, loons and ducks adorned the walls and a mounted trout at least three feet long graced the archway to the dining room.

"This was one of our larger catches," explained the host.

In the dining room were pictures of large strings of trout held by grinning fishermen. Above a well stocked bar there were still more mounted trout. A framed grouping of flies, at least a hundred in all, hung over a framed photograph of a pipe smoking gentleman holding another string of large trout. To Dicky's surprise, this gentleman was Walt. He turned to see where he went and sighted him on the dock loading his equipment into a flat-bottomed boat.

He wasn't wasting any time getting out on the water, Dicky thought.

Seeing the party's recognition of Walt in the photograph, the camp host explained:

"Walt's been coming up here ever since we opened the lodge. This is his seventeenth year. A few times he's been up here twice in one year. He's kind of a fixture and knows this lake probably better than anyone. He'll catch fish when no one else can, but he's not secretive about his technique. We've learned a lot about fly-fishing this lake from Walt, and we're really going to miss him"

"Miss him?" asked Uncle Claire. "Is he going somewhere?"

"I'm afraid so," responded the host. "Walt says he has a deteriorating medical condition. He won't say what it is, but he thinks this is the last year he'll be physically able to come up here."

As they entered the dining room Dicky looked again out on the dock for Walt. He wished their conversation in the plane had been longer and wanted to tell him how much he appreciated his knowledge. Walt had already left the dock and was apparently on his way to his favorite fishing spot. Dicky's attention turned to getting out on the lake himself.

After a lunch that Dicky thought too lengthy and fancier than any he had before in such a primitive setting, Uncle Claire, Gary and another gentleman named Owen gathered their gear into one of the flat bottom boats powered by a Johnson outboard motor. Their host had supplied each boat with heavy rods, each strung with large strings of spinners— pop gear they were called. Trailing behind this pop gear were assortments of lures each festooned with treble hooks. In his excitement to get fishing, Dicky forgot about the flies Walt had given him. They were finally out on the water and he wanted to catch that seven-pound trout.

Trolling around the lake, many fish were caught, most less than the seven pounds expected, some in fact, of the size Walt predicted: skinny, less than sixteen inches and whose stomachs were devoid of insects. "These fish are stunted," our guide explained. "They don't have enough to eat and there are too many to be supported by the food in this lake. In the winter, many die off because of the lack of oxygen in the lake because it's too shallow." Their guide continued on with his appraisal of the growing problems with his lake: the means of his support that he so loved. The clients weren't totally sympathetic, however, being more interested in catching that trophy trout they flew up there for.

Later, back at the lodge and after a dinner more sumptuous than Dicky had ever experienced, the fishermen retired to the great room before the huge fireplace that had now been built to a roaring inferno. Walt had not been to dinner, but now settled into a great leather chair next to the fire and lifted a large snifter of brandy in a toast:

"To the Noble Kamloops Trout," he slurred, being somewhat influenced by snifters proceeding. "May they continue to flourish in ways we may not now perceive."

"Hear, hear!" the gathering of guests voiced in unison.

By now, many of the guests knew of Walt's plight. Embarrassed or unwilling to discuss it openly, they must have all secretly hoped their fishing days might be more certain, at least to the point they could perhaps be wheeled out on the dock to make their last cast at a ripe old age of ninety. Walt had seemed so young to be cashing it in so soon. Attempts were made to give best wishes and to express regrets, but no one knew what to say. Platitudes replaced true feelings and guilt became drowned by more brandies—all around—except for Dicky and Gary who were treated to Coca Colas.

As the de Havilland lifted off the Lake and turned south to return to Spokane, Dicky strained to see where Walt was fishing. Like Walt, he yearned to be able to go back again. Someday, somehow, he knew that he would.

16   PlayQuato

You learn that follow-on treatments such as radiation, has its own set of bad side effects such as a scared and shriveled colon, or increased incontinence.

There was a place just a few miles west of Chehalis, and just down the hill where, back in 1847, Great-Grandfather Stearns helped to establish one of the first pioneer settlements in Southwest Washington. This place was a dance hall. Built just after Prohibition, it provided a Saturday night release for loggers and farmers to kick up their heels and forget about the weeklong tedium of making a living. From outside, it resembled a giant Quonset hut, at least fifty by two hundred feet, with a smaller hut attached at the middle to form an entry vestibule. A large stage, elevated over an enormous dance floor, filled the main hut. The smaller hut contained a concession area where a bottle of Coca Cola or Seven-Up could be purchased, a few swigs taken, and then filled up again with the contents from whatever flask might be slipped from a pocket. The original owners named it PlayQuato, a contraction of its location: Claquato, and a place to come play. And folks from all over did indeed come to this place to play. Its biggest attraction: the music, was good, most often local Western, and sometimes a big band touring the area could be enticed to stop for a gig.

Sometimes PlayQuato could get rowdy, and on occasion a fight broke out, usually in the parking lot where large quantities of Olympia or Rainier beer were consumed. Fights flamed by the passions of youth, and usually over contested dance partners, were generally of the fist, resulting in a few bruises and bloody noses. Sometimes older men, loggers mainly, got into it with knives, and although never witnessing a knife fight, Dicky listened in fascination to stories, exaggerated with the passage of time, of knives of Bowie proportions, flashing in the moonlight.

So for him, PlayQuato was a place he came to when he wanted a diversion from the usually mundane grange dances.   The BawFaw Grange hall was located conveniently next to Boistfort High School and held dances every other Saturday night. Usually a trio or quartet of local musicians provided 20's and 30's music in four-four time, sometimes a fox trot, rarely anything fast, and the dancers shuffled counter-clockwise around the small hardwood floor to the beat. Around the floor on a narrow dais, curved-back benches were permanently installed to seat without discrimination, the hopeful, and the tired.

Dicky came back to PlayQuato for one last dance just before he was to report to the Armed Forces Induction Center in Seattle. It was November 1954 and he had just signed up to a four-year enlistment in the Air Force, subject to passing his physical. It had been dark for hours when he eased his '48 Plymouth coupe into the parking lot. He wanted to find a spot, lighted and in the open, remembering a previous time his hubcaps had been stolen. It was eleven thirty and someone had just left, vacating a spot near the entrance, which he quickly took.

Earlier, he had returned his date to her home after a movie in town and was now in the mood to dance. Pat, his sometime steady before they both graduated in May, wasn't much for dancing, but Dicky took her out on this last date, knowing it might be a long time before they saw each other again. As they parked in front of Pat's house that last night, they made promises to write often and to date when Dicky came home on leave. A chance meeting later that evening altered those plans however, and when he entered PlayQuato, the party atmosphere was already into its crescendo phase. After a particularly wild version of *The Yellow Rose of Texas* had subsided and Dicky returned his partner to her escort, he turned to find his next partner and came face to face with Cheryl.

She wore a flared skirt, a leather vest over a frilly blouse and boots that in any other venue might be called a cowgirl outfit. Here, she fit right in and could have been a member of the band. She smiled and accepted Dicky's offer to dance. It was a slow one, and she responded to his lead as though they had danced before. They dance again, and again, and when intermission came she led him to a corner table and introduced her aunt and uncle who were seated with another couple. By then, Dicky knew her full name was Cheryl Rogers. From California, she had been visiting for a week with her aunt and uncle who owned a cattle ranch just south of Chehalis. Pretty and aggressive, she kept Dicky's hand in hers even when they weren't dancing. As the evening wore down, he asked if he could take her home, and maybe to a movie the next day. She in turn asked her uncle who again eyed Dicky, now in a new light, and said it was OK, providing they follow them back to town—closely.

As they slowly drove to town, Cheryl seemed impressed with Dicky's car and remarked that it had been one of only a few she saw in the area that might compare with those from LA. Of course flattered, Dicky had modified it to the trend of styles he saw in *Hot Rod* and other magazines out of California, so the subject of cars occupied most of their conversation and he didn't learn anything more about Cheryl until their date the next day.

They saw an afternoon movie because Dicky had to catch an early train to Seattle the next morning, and Cheryl similarly needed to board a connection on West Coast Airlines to LA. West Coast Airlines flew DC3's out of the Twin Cities Airport to Seattle and Portland, and although

Dicky never gave much thought about flying; he didn't want to let on that he was impressed with her flight connections.

As they sat in his car in front of her aunt and uncle's ranch house, Eddie Fisher belted out *Any Time* on the radio. They made small talk they knew had to end too soon. Dicky talked about his pending train trip, how he was looking forward to the Air Force, his basic training in California, how he had been selected for Atomic Energy training; but finally, his curiosity could take it no longer and he asked about her parents. From her side of the conversation: her school experiences, life in LA, her knowledge of cars and horses; he had suspicions, but was almost afraid of the answer.

At first she avoided his question as though she hadn't heard. The first child of two very famous movie stars had long grown weary of the sudden change of attitude of new friends when they found out her true identity. With Dicky, she hoped to delay the inevitable, perhaps hoping he'd be different. Finally she looked directly at him for his reaction:

"They work in the movie industry," she said. "Daddy is Roy, my stepmother is Dale."

Even though suspecting and prepared, Dicky was astounded. But his expression must have been acceptable to Miss Cheryl Rogers, because she leaned over and kissed him on the cheek. Awkwardly, he attempted to return the favor, but she pushed him away, slid out her side of the car and beckoned him to follow. Holding hands, they slowly walked up the long sidewalk to the back door of the brick rambler. She let herself in and returned immediately with a slip of paper that she slipped in his shirt pocket.

"When you get to California, call me, she said, patting his pocket. "At least write and tell me how basic training is going. I'll write too…"

Her voice trailed off as she looked away as if to re-enter the house, then turned quickly and kissed him, this time on the lips. Eagerly he pulled her close, but she again pushed away, stepped inside, gently closed the door, and was gone.

17   The WTCo

You learn that hormone therapy is the next option after radiation, giving one feminine features such as enlarged breasts, then chemical castration, which takes away any remaining sexual drive. You also learn if none of these procedures worked, various treatments for pain were given to the final exit.

Dance halls like PlayQuato were popular back in the 40's and 50's because everyone danced. Well, almost everyone. I don't recall ever seeing Elmer take Mom to a dance after he lost his left arm in that accident at Camp McDonald. It made dancing awkward for him. Besides, in his mind there were better things to do on Saturday nights, and the accident made him a little bitter about doing things that needed a left arm. Dancing was one of those things.

The accident was one of those flukes that should never have happened.

It was on a Friday afternoon when most everyone's thoughts were on the Labor Day weekend and a well-deserved respite from the rigors of working for the Weyerhaeuser Timber Company. It had been after the fire season and overtime had been levied on almost everyone to make up for time lost when the woods were shut down. Elmer was working on a rail car, one of hundreds used to haul logs. It was pulled off the main line and placed over a pit in the maintenance shed so he could weld one of the wheels that developed a small crack. An overhead crane was used to hoist the wheel off the tracks and over a maintenance pit where Elmer could stand. It was a simple job, one he had accomplished many times; a job that could be done differently by having the wheel removed and brought into the shop, but the crack was small and someone decided it was faster to do it this way.

Meanwhile, a switching crew was in the process of moving other rail cars around the marshalling yard. The practice of sorting cars with a single switching engine was simple; a car to be sorted was given a shove toward the designated siding and the acting switchman flipped the rail switch at just the right time, sending the car off to join others in a string that eventually became the next train.

That day something went wrong. A car to be sorted wound up on a wrong track and came hurtling into the maintenance shop, crashing into the car Elmer was working on. The force of the collision knocked him across the pit just as a wheel, the track and his left bicep met in a bloody collision. Mercifully, the inside flange of the wheel pushed his arm down and away from the track, thereby sparing him an immediate amputation, but so much bone and muscle damage occurred, the result inevitably was the same.

Attempts to develop prosthesis to replace his left arm failed miserably, and the contraption supposed to enable Elmer to regain some utility and range of motion, wound up in the bottom drawer of a dresser, never to be used again. Dicky went with him to Seattle to see if he should sue the WTCo for negligence. The lawyer was convincing, but Elmer felt that a job was more important than a large settlement. A lawsuit would poison the environment, he concluded, so in the end, he went back to his old job, learned to cope, and continued working until he retired in 1970.

When Elmer first started working at Camp McDonald, he was excited about having a job that paid well, was close to home, and made good use of the welding skills he acquired while working at the Pearl Harbor Shipyard during the war. He was assigned to the maintenance shop where his initial job was to modify the dozen or so steam locomotives from wood to oil burning. This modification was long overdue as the sparks that flew from the old wood burners were a constant source of forest fires for which the train crews had constantly to be on the alert. Extra observers were placed aboard during particularly dry periods, an expense that Weyerhaeuser was loath to incur since all train crews, by contract were members of the National Union of Railroaders with salaries deemed exorbitant by Charlie.

Charlie Pearson was in charge of operations at Camp McDonald and could put up with the unions, to a degree. The International Woodworkers of America had recently unionized all of Weyerhaeuser and, except for the Railroaders, had received modest salaries and benefits after a long, contentious strike that ended just before the war. After the war there was a glut of labor so there were no thoughts to agitate for better wages. Moreover, there were no shop stewards to intervene when contract rules were bent. The workers went along with what Charlie wanted. After all, more hours meant more take home pay.

Modification of the steam locomotives, or 'lokies' was relatively straightforward. The wood tenders directly back of the engineer's cockpit were replaced with oil tanks. Because oil burned much hotter than wood, the riveted seams on most of the boilers in the older units had to be welded to preclude their blowing up. It was Elmer's job to rebuild these boilers. It was dirty work, and with the years of accumulation of wood soot on the outside of the boilers, Elmer often came home looking, in Grandma's vernacular, "like a darkie."

Later, as more of the lokies were modified, additional help was needed, and an apprentice was hired who happened to be an old friend of Elmer's by the name of George Gill. Gill worked with Elmer during WWII at Pearl Harbor where they were both shipyard welders. Prior to the war Gill worked as a cowboy in Wyoming. Small in stature, he must have ridden large horses as he had remarkable bowlegs that after years aground still hindered his walking. Those that didn't know his prior occupation assumed that it was probably a war injury and just as well didn't comment, as Gill's temperament was what all expected of a cowboy—not to be messed with.

Gill was unmarried, in his early 40's, and seemed the confirmed bachelor type. He was content to live in one of the several Camp McDonald bunkhouses that were home to other loggers who were either single or commuted to families on weekends. Typical of most of the single loggers, he was known to take a drink or two and went to town on Saturday nights in search of female companionship.

"Gill needs to settle down and get married," Mom remarked to no one in particular as she set another place at the table for him.

Mom didn't like his drinking, but put up with the few times he came to Sunday dinner somewhat bleary eyed from the previous night. She was particularly offended when Elmer broke out a few beers and they started reminiscing about the Girls of Pearl City—going so far as to opening old photo albums showing topless *Wahines* sitting on their laps, obviously in a photo studio setting. These were still early days of Mom and Elmer's marriage, however, and there were of course a few bumps to iron out. With familiarity, Gill became more civilized in Mom's eyes, as he was always extremely polite in her presence and brought her gifts on occasion. It was not surprising then, that her first born to Elmer bore his namesake. Gill was named the godfather to Dicky's half-brother who she named Gill Elmer.

At Camp McDonald one Saturday, when the shop foreman wasn't around, and only Elmer and Gill were working, Elmer asked if he wanted to come see what boiler making was all about. Dicky was fascinated by the workings of the Locomotive, of course, having made the trip of his life aboard old Number 104 some years earlier.

The biggest part of modifying the boilers, Dicky found, was to physically remove the entire thing from the bowels of the locomotive, cut through the old rivets with an acetylene torch, then weld it back together. This involved a lot of hot, laborious work, the whole process consuming large quantities of oxygen and acetylene. To Dicky's surprise and delight, Gill invited him to put on a heavy leather apron, goggles and hat and try his hand at using the cutting torch. He was shown how to adjust the oxygen and acetylene mixture such that the torch didn't retort with a loud pop when ignited. The first time, of course, was 'on Dicky' as he jumped a foot, much to their amusement. Once he got the hang of adjusting the mixture, Gill showed him how to get the half inch thick walls of the boiler white hot, first with just the initial mixture, then how to blast through the wall by applying an extra shot of oxygen with the squeeze trigger. It was simple, but it took a steady hand, and Dicky's first attempt looked like something seen in abstract metal sculptures.

Working with equipment like this was fun, but Dicky knew it wasn't something he'd want as an occupation. It was hot, dirty, confining work that he couldn't see himself doing all his life, but it did give him an appreciation of Elmer's job, and by that he felt Elmer had done both of them a favor. The shop was better than the woods when it came to working conditions, but Dicky's heart was more in the outdoors, and if Elmer had been a forest ranger or a game warden, he might have been more interested.

After all the boilers had been modified and there was no need for dedicated boilermakers, Elmer and Gill were moved to the welding shop where there was always work to do. A lot of this work went to sites remote from the shop at Camp McDonald, since things were always breaking around the logging operations. Huge, rail-borne donkeys, similar to the one Dicky remembered on Richter Hill were the main source of welding jobs requiring Elmer or Gill's expertise. Usually jobs such as these could be done on weekends when equipment was idle, but If something broke that interrupted logging operations, they were called to drop whatever they were working on in the shop and head for the woods, usually with a mobile Lincoln welder in tow. Speeders were initially the mode of transportation to the woods, but later, as more and more logging roads replaced rails, pickups and crew busses moved workers and equipment.

On one Saturday when again there were no bosses around, Elmer invited Dicky to accompany him on one of his jobs. This time it was high above the Valley to Camp Six where a rail car needed welding.

"Camp Six!" Dicky exclaimed, "Do you think it would be OK if I brought my fishing gear?"

Hearing rumors of large trout inhabiting the water reservoir above the now abandoned camp, Dicky envisioned a day in pursuit of his favorite quarry instead of providing Elmer with company while he worked.

Immediately Dicky realized his lapse in etiquette when Elmer said with apparent reluctance:

"I guess so, just as long as you don't forget to check with me from time to time so I don't have to come look for you after I'm through working"

If work were always like this, Dicky thought, *maybe it wouldn't be so bad having to drive miles into a private, gated and otherwise inaccessible area where there's fish to be caught.*

As Elmer guided the maintenance truck up the steep grade toward Camp Six, Dicky thought of all the streams and beaver ponds that he could get to if he had this job. They left the locked gate miles behind and crossed several streams that looked truly wonderful for fishing.

Gerry and I should come up here again sometime and check these out, he thought.

18   **Lessons Learned**

You learn there are different surgical procedures that might make a difference as to whether you would be sterile or not. One procedure developed by Dr. Patrick Welsh, Director of Urology at Johns Hopkins University, was intended to spare the nerves that control erection. You schedule another visit to Dr Rand to see if he had experience in this procedure.

In retrospect, I think high school graduation came too soon for Dicky. There had been little planning for college or what was to come next. Older sister Viv, Dicky's confidant on such matters had entered nursing school and was unavailable for consultation. The subject had been discussed with Mom and Elmer, but with minimal earnest because there was neither will nor sufficient funds within the family to pay for tuition, let alone room and board. Education past grade school had not been available to Elmer, and he felt that a high school diploma was the best he could provide Viv and Dicky at the time. First things first, he stressed: get work, save money, and then, maybe in a year, there'd be enough to pay for the first two years at one of the state's four year schools.

Since Elmer's employer, Weyerhaeuser was the only action in the community, Dicky's job application was submitted for any opening available, and was, to no one's surprise, accepted.

In the summer of '54, he was to become a general laborer, a carpenter's helper, or general flunky at $2.65 per hour—a salary twice anything Dicky had ever experienced. College became a distant goal. With this income, he could soon be totally independent.

Unfortunately, dreams of a long-time employment with Weyerhaeuser were almost immediately dashed. The International Brotherhood of Woodworkers voted to go out on strike. This had been Dicky's first and only experience with the foibles of union contracts. No contract, no work, and since he had only started a few weeks earlier, had no reserve or backup pay. It was back to square one, with no prospects for local work.

A few agriculture-related jobs in Eastern Washington, and a really bad experience working for a tree surgeon convinced Dicky that he needed to find something more permanent.

The tree surgeon, a muscular and rather handsome fellow named Larry had a contract with the Benton County Public Utility District to remove obstructing branches and trees from under and around their power lines. To minimize his expenses, he hired inexperienced kids, Dicky included, to don climbing spikes and do the work.

This practice wouldn't be tolerated later, because of the inherent danger of accidentally touching the power lines, some of which carried 64,000 volts. The inexperienced workers were provided no insulated equipment and the aluminum logger's hats they wore only better served to conduct the electricity to their naive bodies. But the pay wasn't bad, relative to sorting potatoes or boxing cucumbers in the local fields. Besides, Larry bought beer and provided free lunches on many occasions. He seemed to attract the local girls and demonstrated some of the finer points of seduction.

So the novices climbed and cut and hauled innumerable trees and branches by day, and at night partied with Larry and his many girlfriends. Dicky became enchanted with one such girl whose name was Cynthia. Older and wiser, she seemed to be attracted to Dicky—in the absence of Gary, at least. And on weekends when Gary was away to his home in Spokane, Cynthia and he dated. In his Plymouth coupe, they explored the backcountry roads of the Horse Haven Hills above Prosser and made out. Dicky had converted the front seat of his Plymouth so it reclined into a bed. At first, when fishing and the outdoors were his main interests, it was his camper, but he soon came to appreciate its superior use. Cynthia may not have appreciated its utility as much, because when Gary returned from Spokane, she opted for his apartment, and beer, and other things, that for Dicky, still undiscovered, he couldn't provide. Saturday night dances at the Benton City VFW proved to be the source of many less fickle girls, however, and Cynthia, although never forgotten, was forgiven her fickle and wayward ways.

These were fun times, and by the end of the summer it appeared that Dicky might have accumulated enough in back pay to at least buy tuition and a semester's room and board at Eastern Washington State College at Cheney.

Cheney seemed like the perfect place. Near Spokane, he could visit cousin Gary whose dad had been promoted by Safeway and had moved the family into an even bigger home. But when Larry's contract with the PUD had been fulfilled and it was time for pay to be divided, he conveniently disappeared. Calls to Spokane, the PUD and the sheriff produced no satisfaction. Without a written contract, the novice linemen had no claims that could be enforced. Two month's pay was lost and Dicky was devastated.

Lesson #1: no free lunch. Lesson #2: don't trust a playboy with your money—or woman.

Alone and disenchanted, Dicky decided then to join the military. There had been a war, or euphemistically, a police action going on between the French and the Viet Minh. Since it had indications of involving the United States, and since there was a military draft, it seemed to be prudent to avoid it by enlisting first. Moreover, Dicky's chances of going to college that year, and of getting a student deferment were destroyed by Larry's dishonesty.

19   Air Force

Your next visit to your urologist is pivotal in deciding how your sex life might be after surgery. "There's a tradeoff", Dr. Rand said. "The nerves that control erectile function are attached to the prostate, and if I spend too much effort cutting around the nerves according to Dr Walsh's procedure, there's a chance I won't get all the cancerous tissue."

The Air Force Recruiter for the Twin Cities of Chehalis and Centralia worked in an office out of the Chehalis train station. Dicky had long before decided that if he were to go into the military, he'd choose the Air Force. Neil Thompson and Scott Carpenter, both fellow BHS graduates, and both Air Corps pilots during the war, had distinguished themselves in combat and were heroes. But as Dicky talked to the recruiter, he had neither visions of flying the latest jet planes, or becoming anything other than a lowly airman third class, the equivalent of an army PFC. Larry's duplicity had totally deflated his sense of worth. He took the battery of tests administered to all recruits, however, and to his surprise, scored quite high in the technical areas, meaning he could have his choice of several impressive-sounding career fields. The field of atomic energy had a good ring to it, so after agreeing to be sworn in, Dicky was given a train ticket to Seattle where he would be processed through the Northwest Military Induction Center, a large complex where recruits received their physicals, were sworn into their respective services and given plane or train tickets to boot camp.

Before leaving for Seattle, however, Dicky had to return to Lost Valley Ranch for the last time to see Mom, and to get her blessing for this, his new adventure. She didn't object too strenuously because she knew he'd be better off in the Air Force than for working for Weyerhaeuser. Nevertheless, she made one more plea to attend college as soon as he got the chance. After packing his belongings, Mom drove Dicky to the train station for the trip to Seattle. Seeing her weeping as the train pulled away affected him deeply. He never experienced this outpouring of emotion for him like this, and reflecting on that moment, realized this set his resolve to go on to college, in whatever way that he could.

Ultimately, the Air Force provided the means.

After receiving his physical and another battery of aptitude tests at the Seattle Induction Center, he was sworn in with about 50 other recruits. After taking the oath, he began to have doubts about his decision. Seattle must have been truly a Navy town, because except for Dicky, every other recruit was going to San Diego for Navy boot camp. He was the only Air Force enlistee. Had he made a mistake? Gerald Erickson, one of his closest high school buddies had joined the Navy a few months earlier. Feeling very much alone, he was placed on a United Airlines Boeing Statacruiser bound for San Francisco. This was Dicky's first commercial plane flight and he was thoroughly impressed with its luxury and spaciousness. A Navy ship couldn't possibly compare to this, he reasoned. It had a second deck behind the pilot's cabin that he was allowed to visit, and because he was going into the Air Force, the crew invited him into the cockpit. All doubts about his decision evaporated then and there.

Parks Air Force Base was located across the bay from San Francisco and over the Contra Costa foothills, behind the city of Hayward. It had no airplanes, no airport, and looked more like the army camp Dicky remembered from an earlier train trip through Fort Lewis during WWII. It was located near the town of Pleasanton, and besides being used for the training of Air Force recruits, it was the processing center for military personnel being returned from Korea and other Far East assignments. Because most were being discharged from the service after spending their enlistments in conditions less than desirable, this part of the base had an unusually festive atmosphere.

The base exchanges and enlisted clubs were filled with happy GIs with pockets full of mustering-out pay, and the un-military attitudes of most were not exactly what the training cadre wanted new recruits to see. They were shunted off to their corner of the base as soon as possible, and given orders not to go to these places of iniquity unless they had passes.

20   Airman Second Class Rooski

You develop a gallows humor in your discussions with Dr Rand:

"So if we just go in and whack that puppy out, my chances of having to go through radiation, hormone therapy or castration are greatly reduced—is that what you're saying Doc?"

Everyone who went through boot camp, from the days of Valley Forge, to Paris Island, probably had a drill sergeant who was the worst, if not the most memorable of authority figures.

In Dicky's case, it was Airman Second Class Bronkowich, a diminutive refugee from the coalmines of West Virginia with an ax to grind. The recruits immediately referred to him as Bandy Rooski, or Rooski, for short. He in turn, was able to take them down to his level in whatever way he pleased. Four Eyes, was his favorite epithet for anyone who wore glasses, and anyone he felt was in the minority, or even appeared to be of ethnic origin was his favorite target.

In 1954 there was no such thing in the military as racial prejudice. A spade was called a spade, and no one in a subordinate position could argue the point. Unfortunately, one member of Dicky's training squadron was a black man from San Francisco, well-educated and more worldly than most of the recruits, but black nonetheless, and the brunt of Rooski's venom. This was Dicky's first experience with anyone whose skin color was a lot darker than his own.

Conflicted with his own identity, he might have otherwise been understanding and sympathetic. But he wasn't. Instead, he joined with the rest of the squadron in avoiding, if not castigating him as 'not one of us'. Most of the recruits were too preoccupied with their own insecurities to give the black man from San Francisco much trouble, however, so they didn't notice that he left the squadron about midway through the first month and they never heard from him again.

The issuing of uniforms and immunization shots were a few of the only memorable instances of boot camp. Neither fit very well. The shots, all eight or ten, were administered by a gauntlet of fiendish medics, all on the same day, equal number in each arm, not by hypodermic needles, but with multiple-jet air guns filled with gallons of serum: tetanus for wounds, typhus, malaria and yellow fever for the tropics, small-pox, typhoid and diphtheria for diseases not avoided as children, and for everyone else: the flu. Without exception, everyone came down with the flu, and not rarely, a combination of symptoms of the other inoculations as well. The infirmary was usually filled with sick airmen the day after the shots, and although it seemed that therein was a message for those in authority, this scenario continued as long as there were new recruits. Perhaps this was their way of identifying and eliminating the weak.

As for the uniforms, the recruits couldn't have cared less. Well, maybe not completely. The stiff cotton boxer shorts they immediately labeled 'Indian shorts...they kept creeping up on you. The blues, or class 'A's were of the type worn by the RAF and came in sufficient sizes to fit most of common stature. On the other hand, the fatigues, or one-piece coveralls worn by aircraft mechanics, came from the factory in one size, extra large. To compensate for the variety of sizes needed, the middle section was removed and then sewn back together. Four inches was removed for large, six for medium and eight for small; everything else, including the arms and legs remained extra large, and recruits were expected to tailor these to their own lengths. They quickly learned the rudiments of needle threading and loop stitching, but the lengths of sleeves and cuffs varied ridiculously, and the sight of their formation must have prompted the training officers to send everyone to the base tailor shop for corrective surgery. At fifty cents per garment, they finally looked 'uniform', but airmen of smaller stature still looked ridiculous. They took delight in executing rapid 'about faces, whilst their oversized fatigues stayed put. So much air circulated within, that long johns were one of the first things ordered from home, along with the customary Christmas cookies and fruitcakes.

Much of basic training was spent in classes of military order and discipline, Air Force history— of which, mercifully, there was little—and close order drill on the tarmac outside the barracks. Inside, the recruits were suffused with the traditional military set of priorities: ultra clean floors, highly polished shoes, well ordered footlockers, and tightly made beds.

Rooski had a novel way of making the floors uniquely clean. He had each recruit take a large portion of their laundry bleach with a mixture of GI soap and hot water and apply it directly, on hands and knees, to the wooden floors. If the flu shots hadn't made them sick, this concoction surely did, because the soft wood floors prolonged the pungent smell of Purex and lye for the remainder of their stay. The warmer the barracks were heated, the worse the smell. In the near-freezing cold of the Contra Costa foothills in midwinter, and in the absence of any bedding other than two very thin GI blankets, heat was very necessary. Moreover, the soft grain of the wood and the effects of the bleach liberated scores of splinters into bare feet. After several recruits reported to sick call with wood sliver infestation, much of their free time was spent undoing

Rooksie's brainchild, by sanding the floor—also on hands and knees.

21   More Lessons

Dr Rand says: "Every patient is different. You're relatively young, so I can spend more time cutting around these nerves. Some older patients don't care as much about erectile dysfunction and don't want to risk further complications..."

Before he can elaborate, you cut him off: "I care about erectile dysfunction. Let's go with Dr. Walsh's procedure."

One lesson learned by Dicky in boot camp was to keep his mouth shut.

He intensely remembered one specific instance during a disagreement with a mess sergeant while he was on KP. Kitchen Patrol duty was one of the recruit's less desirable extra curricular activities, wherein they were assigned specific tasks related to getting daily meals out to the thousand or so other recruits and training staff. Depending on the whims of the mess sergeant, these tasks ranged from food preparation, such as peeling potatoes, to washing dishes, or to serving food.

In serving food, certain inter-personal skills were necessary since portions often became a matter of dispute. The mess sergeants tested these skills at every opportunity, by yelling at the servers, to keep the servings small, and at the same time the 'servees yelled for more food. In spite of these trying conditions, the serving line was the more desirable of KP. The servers ate first, and sometimes last if there was food left over. Servers also were the first to finish with their particular tasks, and were usually free to return to the barracks after the last meal and the serving line was cleaned up for breakfast the next day. It was during this final clean up activity that Dicky ran afoul of the mess sergeant.

Activities around the serving line were hectic and workers were always bumping into each other, so it wasn't unusual that the mess sergeant and Dicky collided while Dicky was carrying a stack of serving pans to the washing crew. Nothing was spilled, and no harm done, except when the sergeant, who had a slight myopic misalignment handicap—that is to say, he was cross-eyed—said: "Why don't you look where you're going?" To which Dicky immediately replied: "Why don't you go where you're looking?" This untimely retort gained him the privilege of doing pots and pans—the lowliest and most undesirable of KP—for the next two weeks.

Another lesson learned while in boot camp was in the arena of making choices when it pertained to one's career. It's easy to see, decades later, how decisions then, had profound affects later, but at the time Dicky was essentially clueless as to how these choices would alter his future.

Military historians have by now written that the Eisenhower Administration too hastily de-commissioned the flying arms of the military after the Korean War. Consequently, pilots who left in droves to take lucrative jobs with airlines left a large gap in the officer corps that suddenly needed filling in the face of the Cold War. It was in light of this shortage of fliers that an order was given to all the training divisions to identify candidates for Aviation Cadet training. Aptitude tests taken during his induction examinations in Seattle somehow identified Dicky as such a candidate, so he was somewhat taken aback when the squadron adjutant summoned him to his office for an interview. Not knowing the reason, Dicky was apprehensive, thinking it might have been something to do with his run-in with the mess sergeant, so he was on his best military demeanor, sharply saluting and reporting:

"Airman Basic Stearns, Richard K, reporting as ordered, SIR!"

The adjutant, a second lieutenant, obviously a recent graduate from officer training, braced the young recruit as if he were one of his underclassmen, and might otherwise have broken his demeanor had it not been for Rooski's daily badgering on the drill field. Compared to Rooski, this second lieutenant was a pussycat, so Dicky was able to respond with the necessary and properly emphasized, 'Yes SIR! No SIR!' After what seemed like an hour of grilling, the adjutant must have been impressed enough to send him to the next screening, an interview with the Group Commander.

Lieutenant Colonel Sundstrom had been one of three Group Commanders at Parks AFB. He was there, ostensibly as a necessary link in the chain of command between Squadron Commanders and Wing Commanders, but in reality, his and many similar officer billets, normally filled by officers in the grade of captain or major, were created to enable WWII officers to complete their last assignment before retirement at 20 years military service. And at nineteen and three-quarter years, Lt/Col Sundstrom was, what is commonly referred to in military jargon as FIGMO.

Not aware of Lt/Col Sundstrom's status when he reported in his sharpest of uniforms and sharpest of salutes, Dicky was immediately disarmed with the Lt/Col's relaxed attitude. Feet on desk, in shirtsleeves, loose tie, and puffing on a cigar butt; he looked more like a detective in a Mickey Spillane novel. Dicky felt cheated. He expected to be grilled on a plane higher than the squadron adjutant, only to be asked, not ordered, to have a seat and a cigarette.

This meeting turned out to be the deciding point whether Dicky was to enter the Aviation Cadet Program.

Through their casual conversation, Lt/Col Sundstrom was able to extract the lack of Dicky's commitment to what amounted to be an additional 14 months of basic training.

In no mood for another Rooski in his life, at least not then, Dicky declined the offer to become a flier, an officer and a gentleman.

22   Other Choices

The radical prostatectomy was a success, according to Dr. Rand:

"There were no cancerous tissue in the nymph glands near the prostate which indicates that the cancer hadn't progressed outside the prostate area. That's not to say we're out of the woods yet..."

Christmas at boot camp gave recruits just enough free time to get into trouble. Those who had the means were allowed to go home for the period between Christmas and New Year, as the base was pretty much closed down. Many recruits who lived in California did just that. Parents, girlfriends or just friends flocked to the main gate to pick them up, a disheartening sight for those who were left with nowhere to go, nobody to see.

Dicky, on the other hand, had other opportunities, again, choices.

Early in December he received a letter from Cheryl Rogers. Along with the usual pleasantries was an invitation any red blooded recruit couldn't refuse. She wrote that her family was going to their Mohave Desert ranch for the holidays and asked him to come along as her guest. Moreover, she offered to pay for airfare to LA and back, and pick him up in her new car. She didn't say what her new car was, but Dicky could envision something convertible, with whitewall tires, and flashy.

Dicky's other choice was a weekend in San Francisco with the guys. They figured they could pool their money and hire a cab for two days to take in all the sights: Alcatraz, Seal Rocks, Fisherman's Warf, Knob Hill, the cable cars—all those, and more—if their money lasted. Where they stayed wasn't important—anyplace would be superior to the barracks. Besides, a couple of the guys were of drinking age and could get them enough booze to forget about the stifling environment of boot camp.

So what choice did Dicky make?

His weekend in San Francisco wasn't exactly like the shore leave you see in those movies with Frank Sinatra and his pals picking up chicks and getting into bar room brawls. Theirs was more like driving around all day, the six of them jammed in a cab seeing Alcatraz, Seal Rocks, Fisherman's Warf and the cable cars. Somewhere they missed Knob Hill, but probably wouldn't have recognized it anyway. As for getting drunk, none had much experience with booze and they crashed in their cheap motel rooms after about the second drink of sloe gin, the only booze name that someone remembered from a recent Humphrey Bogart movie.

This choice continued to haunt Dicky for many years. Somewhere he must have had his reasons, but could never reconcile them. To be sure, there were other choices later on, but where this one could have taken him, one could only imagine. In any stretch, Cheryl meant excitement and the opportunity to rub elbows with the Hollywood crowd. On their only date, they had fun and both wanted more, except then, there just wasn't time for their relationship to flourish. In retrospect, Dicky should have taken that plane trip, and if their relationship terminated after that week in Mohave, he'd at least have the memory. Now his recollection of that weekend in San Francisco was only a blur.

Basic training was supposed to end the middle of January, but there was an urgent need to get personnel into some of the secondary training courses, so not much occurred after the Christmas holidays by way of drill and classes. Instead, Dicky and others who were to go on to Lowry AFB in Colorado for electronics school, were given ten days travel to Denver, by whatever route they wished, as long as they reported not later than January 15th. Dicky chose to go home en route to visit Mom and to perhaps date Pat again. She after all said she would wait.

Shortly after Dicky arrived at the Greyhound terminal in Chehalis, somebody saw him get into Glenn Barr's pickup. Glenn happened to be returning to the Valley from town and stopped for Dicky who was in his class 'A' uniform. Whoever saw him must have notified Pat who immediately called Dicky's home through the Curtis party line switchboard, therefore innocently notifying everyone listening in that he was home. Mom took the call, and was affronted by Pat's anxious demeanor, not knowing that Dicky was even home. Shortly after hanging up, Glenn delivered Dicky to Lost Valley Ranch, and hearing Dicky giving Glenn thanks for the lift, she ran to the door just as he leaped the last step of the porch and delivered a huge bear hug. Tears welled in two sets of eyes before either could speak.

"Girls don't call boys and ask them to call back," Mom said later after delivering Pat's message. Dicky was flattered at the sudden attention, particularly when Carmen Wilson called not more than a half hour afterwards with an invitation to come over to her place. Mom just threw up her hands in resignation and laughed.

"Now what are you going to do?" she said. 'Who are you going to see first?"

Mom had met Pat and although she didn't necessarily approve of Dicky going steady with anyone, felt that Pat would be OK. Her mother had died of heat stroke the summer before, and Mom felt sorry for Pat.

Carmen, on the other hand was an unknown quantity, having moved to the Valley in the middle of her senior year. The only child of John and Carmen Wilson, they moved from Seattle and bought the Crossfield Ranch. The Wilsons took in foster kids shortly after settling in, giving the impression, rightfully or not, that they needed the extra income and hands to make a go at dairy farming.

Dicky worked for the Crossfields off and on during high school and knew some of the idiosyncrasies of the ranch. Crossfield, a retired chemist from Union Oil, designed innovations into his dairy operation, such as flushing gutters and chilled milk tanks that were years ahead of other local dairies. Dicky, out of curiosity perhaps, wanted to see how the Wilsons used these innovations, and seeing Carmen would be an excuse, or maybe it was the other way around. In the few days before he had to catch a train to Denver via Portland, they dated twice and promised to write. Mom again felt uneasy about this commitment on his part and said so.

"You have an opportunity to go to college and do a lot of things that will not happen if you get yourself tied down with someone right now" she said. "Your father and I married way too early and had to scrape by because he didn't have an education."

Then she said something that caught Dicky totally by surprise:

"Your father was a very charming and handsome man and I loved him very much." Again, tears welled, and she continued, "He had a roving eye though, and when you were born he had a venereal disease."

A huge lump formed in Dicky's throat as he tried to form a question he wasn't sure he wanted answered. In basic training, one of the courses dealt with VD and it's effects. And although these predictions could be partly to scare the recruits into using prophylactics readily sold at the BX, he had to know:

"Did...did I have it?" he stammered, embarrassed to be discussing something so personal with Mom. Subjects related to birds and bees were Viv's domain, but now she was off to nursing school.

Mom wiped tears from her eyes and said, "Fortunately for all of us, sulfa drugs were just introduced and we had to take treatments for several months. We watched you closely for a year after you were born and there weren't any symptoms".

Then she reached out to Dicky, pulled him to her and sobbed uncontrollably. He knew this had to be extremely difficult for her to admit and wished he could find words to console her. Now all he could do was hold her tightly and to try to keep his own emotions in check.

Later, after he boarded the passenger train to Denver at Portland's Union Station, Dicky tried to reflect on what Mom had to go through raising him and Viv under those trying times. Even in 1955 the subject of VD was taboo except in medical journals and in barracks humor. He wondered if, even now, he was really free of the disease.

23   **Biking with Doug and Shiela**

Dr Rand continues: "According to the pathologist who examined the prostate, there was cancerous tissue in the margin of the surgery, meaning there could be some cancerous cells left behind. What we do in all cases is monitor your PSA levels. If they remain at zero, we got it all. If not—we'll examine your other options."

It was snowing when Dicky arrived in Denver on the *City of Portland.* He had slept fitfully both nights en route, and the stopover in Salt Lake City hadn't refreshed him very much either. The snow was building rapidly on the streets and, by the time his taxi arrived at the main gate of Lowry, not much traffic was moving except on the main streets. Fortunately, the cabbie knew where the reporting squadron dayroom was, so after the guard at the main gate checked Dicky's ID and orders, he was delivered to the entrance of a barracks almost identical to the one he had been happy to leave ten days before. Except now he had to climb over a bank of freshly plowed snow.

He had to wait for his first class to start and was assigned to a barracks full of recruits like himself fresh out of boot camp. Each barracks contained eighty bunks, forty on each floor, twenty stacked on top of each other in two rows of ten. Apparently, the base commander felt it was easier to heat a barracks so occupied, because many adjacent buildings were vacant. Heating was a consideration as the Denver temperatures plummeted to below zero on some nights, and it was all the furnace tenders could do to keep the coal burners stoked. Furnace duty was full time and one of the most important of shifts that was rotated through some complicated lottery drawing

Dicky didn't understand. Because his turn never came up, he didn't bother to find out.

Wherever Dicky and his fellow students went in numbers greater than six, they marched. They marched to the mess halls and, when they had KP at the mess halls, they marched. When classes started, they marched. When President Eisenhower visited the base, they marched, this time on an airfield in a huge formation with a brass band.

This isn't any better than boot camp, Dicky thought.

The only difference was there wasn't a Rooski. For that, he was grateful, but the cold and dreary of Lowry in the winter began to wear on him. Classrooms were stuffy and overheated; causing many students to have recurrences of flu symptoms experienced after their basic training flu shots. Barracks crowding spread the flu, diminishing class attendance, thus delaying graduation until everyone could catch up.

It was late spring when Dicky and Doug found themselves waiting for the rest of the Basic Electronics 101 class to catch up. Fortunately they had avoided the flu and progressed to BE 102, but since there were not enough students to have a class, they were sent back to the barracks to wait until the next class started—in about ten days. Whoever was in charge must have forgotten about them because they were left to their own devices.

Doug was a husky towhead from Minneapolis who wore a crew cut—the kind where they used a ruler to make sure it was flat on top. He had a Harley motorcycle, so they took to exploring the roads and mountains around Denver. Doug had a distant cousin in the area named Sheila, and the three of them could be found riding tandem on the seat of the hog, her sandwiched between Dicky and Doug as they sped down the highway. They were invincible and, had tattooing been in vogue among impressionable airmen as it was for sailors, their mothers would undoubtedly have had conniptions.

An excursion to Colorado Springs found the trio motoring up Pike's Peak early one Sunday before the road was open for the season to the general public. It was easy for Doug to drive around the closed gate and over the barrier berm, and the two passengers hopped back on as Doug gunned the hog. They gleefully sped on to yet another adventure. They had Pike's Peak all to themselves.

Or so they thought. As they rounded a corner halfway up the mountain, they came face-to-face with a black and white highway patrol sedan. Its occupant, startled at seeing the gaggle of trespassers on a single motorcycle, first pulled over out of instinct, then stopped and attempted to hail the trio. Doug waved and they sped by. Dicky looked back and saw the ranger scramble back into his car and speed off to find a place to turn around. Now their visit to the summit had to be direct. The ranger would soon follow but they had the advantage of speed. As they rounded one of the many hairpin corners on their way to the summit, the ranger could now be seen several miles back, losing distance.

The trio reached the summit and was surprised to see another patrol car parked next to the only building on the barren peak. No one was in the car and, from the padlock clearly visible on the building's only door; it also appeared to be vacant. Doug killed the Harley's engine and started walking around the building, obviously looking for something.

"What are you doing?" Dicky shouted, as he tried to shake some circulation back into his legs. During the climb up the peak the combined weight of Doug and Sheila sliding backward toward him had put both legs asleep.

"We've got to get out of here before that ranger gets here."

Doug didn't answer, but disappeared around the building, re-appearing in a few minutes with an empty gallon can in his hand, apparently recovered from the pile of construction trash they saw next to the building. He went to the patrol car and, lying on his back, pushed himself under the rear wheels, can in hand. Dicky repeated, this time more forcefully:

"What the hell are you doing?"

This time Doug answered, his voice muffled from something he was trying to do.

"We're out of gas."

"What?" Dicky exclaimed as he nervously looked down the road, expecting the ranger to come around the last corner.

Without answering, Doug finally pushed himself back from beneath the patrol car. Standing with the can now sloshing half full of gas, he grinned. "This was the closest gas station I could find."

He casually strolled over to the Harley, unscrewed the cap of its gas tank and emptied the contents of the can. "Hop on," he said after the second stand on the starter and the Harley came back to life with a roar.

He didn't have to ask twice. Dicky and Sheila jumped almost in unison behind Doug, and the Harley leaped down the road just as the patrol car spun into the parking lot. There was plenty of room to maneuver and Doug skillfully turned his steed past the angry ranger who could only watch in frustration as the trio raced down Pike's Peak to the valley below.

Summer came, and Denver went from cold to hot. Dicky eagerly continued his studies in Electronics 102 but welcomed a break from the sweltering heat of the classroom afforded by a long Independence Day weekend. He earlier ditched Doug as a companion and means of transportation, figuring this motorcycle bandit was destined to get into trouble and was later befriended by Ted, who owned a brand new, red '54 Olds convertible.

"I'm going home for the holidays," Ted said. "Would you like to come along?"

Ted was a tall hayseed-type, and although likeable, was shunned by most of his classmates, apparently because of his appearance. From behind, he could have been any well-built, athlete who lettered in football, a lady's man; but in front, it was painfully obvious he was born with a clef pallet. His parents might have sprung for corrective surgery, except they were Christian Scientists and didn't believe in medical remedies. Instead, they bought him a new convertible when he graduated from high school, hoping it would compensate for his outward appearance. Inwardly, as Dicky soon discovered—he was a prince.

Ted lived in Carroll, a small town in west-central Iowa named after one of the signers of the Declaration of Independence. They figured they could drive there in a day, spend two days visiting his family, and drive back all night taking turns at the wheel so they could be back in time for roll call.

With the top down, they set off to the northeast on SR 6, which took them to the Nebraska border. There, US 30 would take them directly to Carroll, some five hundred miles farther. The warm sun mixed with the wind blowing through their GI haircuts, and the road sped under them. They savored the attention of occupants of less flashy cars they passed, particularly those cars whose occupants were females. It was then it occurred to Dicky why Ted wanted his company: He would be Ted's girl magnet. He had the handsome facial features that Ted, by an accident of birth, was denied. Ted, on the other hand, had the flashy car Dicky only dreamed of owning.

Carroll was a typical mid-western town. The county courthouse, centered within a flowered town square, was the tallest building. A banner draped over its wide façade advertised the county Fourth of July festivities at the fair grounds. Elm trees lined the wide streets, bordered by wide sidewalks and manicured lawns, populated by neat mid-nineteenth century homes, many with colonial-style columns. Ted's family lived in one such home just a few blocks south of the courthouse. His father owned the only furniture store in town and was president of the Chamber of Commerce. His mother managed and maintained their large home and, by her suntanned complexion, it was obvious that she worked the large rose garden out back. Rounding out the family was Ted's younger sister, Wanda. She would start her last year of high school that fall and, like Ted, had the tall and athletic bone structure clearly inherited from her parents.

Wanda would be Dicky's date, Ted declared, as he stowed his overnight bag in the guest bedroom. Ted had set up a double date for them before they left Lowry, correctly knowing Dicky wouldn't object. Wanda was the type who would be homecoming queen and, even in her junior year, she was. She had even been the county dairy princess— twice.

For their date, they would go to the county fairgrounds the next day and then take in the fireworks display over Swan Lake. Dicky visited with Wanda in the rose garden the next morning and learned of her ambitions. She would go on to Iowa State University and study agriculture. Her grades had already attracted several scholarships and she wanted to come back after she received her degree and teach the subject in her high school. She loved her community and never wanted to leave.

So much for any long-term relationship with this girl, Dicky thought.

Later that morning, Ted drove them over to his girlfriend's house. They rode in the back seat of the convertible, fully enjoying the privilege of being chauffeured. Ted's girlfriend, Sally, was strikingly pretty and, like Wanda, was tall and athletic. She and Wanda were good friends and could have passed for sisters.

The fairgrounds were located in a little town to the south, called Coon Rapids. It had a small midway with the customary Ferris wheel, carousel, and assorted twirley rides surrounded by game-booths and sideshows. It had a large assortment of dairy and produce displays and at least one barn for every type animal in the county. This day, Wanda was the center of attention, however, as her reign as dairy queen made her known to just about everyone. Dicky was flattered once again to be in the company of someone famous, remembering his short relationship with Miss Cheryl Rogers.

They went on all the rides, tossed baseballs at milk bottles, won stuffed pandas, ate cotton candy, hot dogs, and popcorn, drank lime phosphates, and saw all the animals, all the time acknowledging the recognition of Wanda, wherever they went.

Later in the afternoon, they went to Swan Lake. A large park with walking paths that surrounded the lake and at one end, an 'oompah band performed on a raised gazebo. On a dock, a crew was setting up the evening's fireworks. Children splashed gleefully in a large roped-off area, and adults dove from boards and platforms. Around the lake, almost every picnic table was occupied in anticipation of the evening's show. As the evening waned into night, swing music replaced Souza, and people started dancing on a small deck surrounding the gazebo. Japanese lanterns were lit, adding to the magic of the evening. Dicky and Wanda danced, experiencing the magic by swaying to tunes like *Night Train,* which segued into *The Very Thought of You,* then into *Midnight Serenade.* Ted and Sally sat out the dances and later suggested they go park so they could see the fireworks from the comfort of the convertible.

Finding a parking spot at the end of the lake, Ted gathered up a blanket from the trunk and led Sally off to a place they could watch the fireworks by themselves.

Dicky yelled back at Ted, "This place is too public, I think we'll move the car to another place. We'll be back to pick you two up after the fireworks."

Ted answered with a reply Dicky thought was: *OK...don't hurry.*

The fireworks were less than spectacular, and the magic of Dicky and Wanda's attraction wore off because it was clear that nothing more than a few kisses and hugs would be the fare for the evening. Wanda was probably still a virgin, given her family background, and Dicky was still recoiling from his conversation with Mom.

So as they sat in the front seat of the convertible, they spoke of the stars, of how Dicky's sister Viv described the galaxies from the back seat of the old model 'T' on Richter Hill, how Wanda learned of astronomy from a recent visit to ISU. Their conversation droned on, and they were soon fast asleep.

The *chillurp... chillurp... chillurp* of robins was the first familiar sound Dicky heard the next morning. A light fog was drifting off the lake and it took a few more seconds to realize where he was. Wanda, still asleep on his shoulder, had numbed his right arm so he could barely move it. When he did, she awoke with a start.

"Omigosh, we must have slept all night," she said.

With those words, Dicky realized the gravity of their situation. They had failed to pick up Ted and Sally, and Dicky could now visualize them walking back to town, blanket under arm, hoping they wouldn't be seen by anyone they knew. Dicky drove the convertible back to the place where they had left them, hoping maybe they had slept there all night, too. Nothing.

And there was nothing left to do but drive back to Wanda's place and face the music. Wanda knew her parents would be angry, but reasonable, given a good explanation.

"What are you going to tell them?" she asked.

24   **Fellow Travelers**

Now this acronym: PSA, would become part of your vocabulary, your preoccupation and your fears. Prostate Specific Antigen, measured in nanograms per milliliter, derived from a blood sample, then compared to previous samples to determine its progression—as in watching the rate of one's own mortality.

Graduation from electronics school finally came. Dicky and his classmates were assigned to "casual" status in their barracks, awaiting the long anticipated transfer to advanced training at Sandia Labs in Albuquerque.

Earlier, they completed the necessary paperwork for their security clearances and indeed, heard from friends back home that the FBI was asking unusual questions. Mr. Tovera, Dicky's baseball coach, almost had a seizure, thinking the Feds must have nailed him for filing one too many late tax returns. Rumors went through the school like wildfire when a special agent visited Superintendent Jarrell, asking whether Dicky's attendance was exemplary and if he had been associating with any known Communists. Fortunately, Dicky hadn't included Mr. Smyth, his physics teacher as a reference, as he was an admitted socialist, close enough in 1955 to being subversive, and to the FBI, a definite "red flag."

One other name on his security application was Gerry who just happened at the time to be engaged in moonshine running for his dad, Sparky. By coincidence, his last run was just a few nights before the FBI agent was at the school asking questions. Needless to say, Gerry was less than casual during the FBI interview and if polygraph tests had been used in 1955, he likely would have been a candidate for further interrogations.

But Gerry, Mr. Tovera, and Mr. Jarrell must have responded satisfactorily regarding Dicky's character, because interim top-secret clearances were granted and shortly thereafter, along with five classmates, he was ordered to report to Sandia Labs.

They were offered options of travel: privately owned vehicle, bus, train, or commercial airline. They were granted sufficient funds to defer the cost of any option, including a small per diem for lodging and meals while en route. It was determined by some bureaucrat that it should take two and a half days to travel from Denver to Albuquerque, so they determined to milk the system by traveling the cheapest way possible, getting the most return for doing so, and garner a few extra dollars and days of vacation.

One of the travelers, Airman Callo, owned a car, having brought it from home on a short leave while awaiting his clearance. A vintage Nash two-door sedan, one of those body styles immediately drawing derisive remarks like, "sowbug" or "overturned bathtub," it was roomy enough for all six travelers, so they could draw their maximum individual travel allowances, each one chipping in for gas.

What a deal, they thought.

Late in the afternoon they arrived in Trinidad, a small mining community located just north of the Colorado-New Mexico border. A good place to stop for the night, they reasoned, as the increasing altitude was effecting the performance of the Nash as they climbed toward Raton Pass some thousand feet higher, and they didn't want to get stuck somewhere in the dark. A single motel with a glowing neon vacancy sign beckoned. They checked into the two remaining units, each with two double beds and a rollaway.

Again the frugal travelers were presented the opportunity to save a few dollars by doubling up. They split the total cost for the rooms, partook of a steak dinner at an adjacent restaurant and summarized their expenses. They already saved more of their travel allowance than anticipated for the entire trip. A bar at the entrance to town seemed to be a good place to celebrate.

It was early in the evening, but already the bar was starting to fill with the Saturday night assemblage of local patrons. Dicky and his fellow travelers filed into a wooden booth at the edge of a well-used dance floor and, pleased that no one seemed to notice their GI haircuts; each ordered their own brand of poison. Recalling what sloe gin had done to him back in San Francisco, Dicky conservatively ordered a Coors. Waiting for his order from the busy waitress, he strolled over to the Wurlitzer, inserted a dime, selected two Eddy Fisher ballads and looked around to see if he were noticed. If any available girls were in the bar, they would be looking—from experience, he knew this. He watched from the corner of one eye as his first selection was plucked from Wurlitzer's circular magazine, twisted 90 degrees and plopped onto the turntable. A click of needle on vinyl, then the familiar strains of *Tell Me Why* floated across the dance floor. The girls at the bar seemed to be unimpressed and apparently were occupied with dates. No action here, the GIs jointly concluded; so after one more round of drinks, they decided to drive to the other side of town where another bar was located just off the main drag.

They piled into the Sowbug and it soon became obvious that Callo was having difficulty with his two scotches and the 6,500-foot Colorado altitude. This condition was not unnoticed by a local deputy who red lighted them to a stop after skillfully dodging Callo's attempt of running him off the road.

"Kind of erratic tonight, aren't we?" the deputy caustically understated, as he examined Callo's drivers license. "You fellows must be from Fort Carson."

The deputy concluded correctly that he had pulled over a car full of GIs, but assumed incorrectly they were Army grunts from the post at Colorado Springs. Callo responded with a nod, but then became agitated when the deputy continued:

"Let's look at your registration."

After rummaging around in the glove compartment for a few minutes, Callo said unconvincingly: "It must be over at the Motel"

"Where's that?" the deputy replied.

"The Trinidad Motel," Callo slurred.

"Fine, let's just go there and get it," the deputy responded.

Callo retreated: "No, I must have packed it with my uniforms. They're being shipped to Albuquerque"

Now the deputy had lost all sympathy for this carload of GIs whom he would have probably let go with a warning, except Callo was obviously too evasive.

"You guys will have to follow me to the station where we can get this all straightened out," he said, taking back Callo's divers license as hostage.

Callo continued to be uneasy as he steered the sowbug behind the deputy's car and slowly caravanned to the sheriff's office looming ominously across the lone traffic-lighted intersection. Next door to the sheriff's office was a square adobe building, obviously old, and built for one purpose.   Above the door an equally old carved sign proclaimed: Las Animas County Jail.

This did not look good.

As they nervously waited behind the deputy for the light to change, Callo suddenly put the sowbug in reverse and, gunning the Nash's meager engine, let out the clutch. Fortunately there was no one behind, and they lurched backwards toward a mid-street alleyway. By the time the deputy could respond, they had shot down the alley, careened into the next street and, save for Callo's lack of driving skills, were on their way to becoming unwilling fugitives.

Fortunately, Callo's driving expertise was not up to the two scotches, or they might have all been wrapped around some light pole. Instead of bombing out of town, he skidded the Sowbug into a snow bank at the end of the street and proceeded to get it stuck in the deep snow.

Unimpressed at their attempted flight, the deputy ordered all out of the sowbug and marched them single file to the sheriff's office. He had obviously been in the military, probably just recently, because not only did he know the correct commands, he gave execution orders on the correct foot.

Everyone expected they'd be thrown into the jail next door, but the deputy had dealt with GIs before. He knew that Callo was the only one who had broken any laws; and after calling the MPs at Fort Carson, he escorted him to a back room holding cell and drove the remaining GIs back to their motel.

"I suggest you see about catching a bus for the rest of your trip to Albuquerque," he said after they explained their situation.

"Your friend Callo is going to have to answer to the MPs tomorrow; and the CO at Fort Carson doesn't have much sympathy for this sort of thing. We'll impound his car until we get his registration sorted out anyway."

He continued after handing back their ID cards: "Meanwhile, you guys stay out of trouble and get on that bus first thing tomorrow morning."

Next morning, waiting for the southbound Trailways bus, they couldn't help but notice the army sedan parked down the street in front of the sheriff's office. In about ten minutes Callo emerged, flanked by two MPs who unceremoniously deposited him in the back seat, turned the sedan around, and, as if to remind the now sober GIs of their transgressions, drove by slowly so they could observe the potential consequences.

They never saw Callo again, although they were told he was denied his top-secret clearance and was assigned to an aviation and electronics maintenance squadron in Wichita Falls, Texas. Dicky thought to thank the deputy for being lenient, because this unforgettable evening could have been critical to his Air Force career. He soon forgot the deputy's name, however.

25   Sandia Base

The first few months after your surgery, all symptoms of cancer seemed to disappear. Your monthly PSA tests stayed at zero point zero nanograms per milliliter—exactly as they should for someone without a prostate. So far the news was good.

Arriving at Albuquerque after a long and scenic Trailways bus ride through Northern New Mexico, with a comfort stop at Santa Fe, they transferred to a city bus which dropped them off at Sandia Base's main gate. Checking in at the adjacent security office, they were instructed to report to the adjutant of the 1092nd Support Squadron.   The 1092nd was a tri-service organization whose mission was to house, feed and more or less tolerate the assorted military members who would be trained to maintain the various new weapons of the U.S. nuclear arsenal.

Tolerate was the operative word, because for a military organization, there was not much by way of discipline. In the student body, there were army privates with PhDs who just wanted to serve out their two-year draft obligation and get back to working on their tenure. Conversely, Air Force and Navy enlisted were considered to be 'lifers' and had up to that time, been taking military discipline seriously.   The officers were somewhat intimidated by the free wheeling attitude of the instructors, who for the most part, turned out to be those same PhD privates.

Some students, Dicky included, still hadn't been granted their final clearances, so they had to wait for the next class to start. They were selected to do support work: KP, squadron maintenance details, motor pool drivers—all the undesirable things Dicky remembered at Lowry, except this duty was demeaning to the PhDs who made life miserable for the non-commissioned and junior officers in charge of these functions. Consequently, an edict was proclaimed by the base commander that students would not perform any details set forth in a list drawn up by—the PhDs.

So rather than single out the PhDs, all students were granted 'light duty'. The first week the Lowry graduates took their cues from the PhDs who just sat around the barracks and worked on dissertations, read books, or discussed amongst themselves subjects which were totally alien or of no interest to those 'lifers'. But their ivory tower attitude rubbed off on some of the more impressionable young airmen and sailors who developed their own bizarre behaviors.

One group of sailors started building and flying kites off the top of the barracks. At sea, flying kites from ships and aircraft carriers apparently was one of their favorite pastimes. Like the high seas trade winds, the New Mexico spring gales provided a great laboratory to fly different kite configurations, but when the PhDs became involved, things really got out of hand.

A huge box kite was conceived and designed. It was constructed of heavy butcher paper 'procured' from the mess hall. A sturdy frame was needed, so one of the engineers took up the challenge and constructed one from aluminum tubing, also 'procured'. To get it to the barracks roof, an ingenious hinging system designed into the frame enabled it to be folded and stored inconspicuously until the day of the test flight. Unfolded, It was so big it was agreed that it had to be flown at night so as not to be kyboshed by the base authorities. To be seen by the launch crew, a

Coleman lantern would be hung from the tail, it's weight calculated as part of the kite's flight dynamics.

Word soon got around about the box kite project, and more and more of the engineers and scientists lent their expertise toward assuring its success. A meteorologist suggested that winds in excess of 30 knots would be detrimental to lofting the kite to a desirable angle. From somewhere he provided an anemometer, which they mounted on the barracks-top, launch platform. A cable spool was converted to a large reel, which could be anchored to the barracks roof floor. Someone produced a thousand feet of 100 lb test nylon cord. An aeronautical engineer recalculated the tail design for best stability. Materials scientists suggested that the butcher paper be reinforced with a varnish coating, but when tried, it defeated the ability of the kite to be folded. This set off a squabble between engineers who favored the 'folding' concept and those who wanted to do a final assembly on the roof. The meteorologist prevailed when he pointed out that the average wind speed on any given day would be too severe for the kite to survive, irrespective of how it was stored on the roof. He added that since the launch window was highly dependent on wind speed, the kite shouldn't be exposed to the elements until launch day.

All of this fuss and scientific deliberation was wearing on the sailors who just wanted to fly their box kite. But they were clearly losing control of their project, and decided one night after having a few extra beers, to surreptitiously move the kite to the roof when the winds were a steady 20 knots from the west. The Coleman lantern was lighted, the kite unfolded, and an uneventful launch was executed. From ships, these sailors did this before. No problem.

But this was 1955; the height of the Cold War, and Sandia Base was considered one of the prime targets of the Soviet Block. Kirkland Air Force Base, adjacent to Sandia, had several missions: the primary one being the protection of the top-secret nuclear research and storage facilities. Two main threats from the Soviets were perceived: sabotage through ground based infiltration, and airborne assault. To counter the first threat, a large presence of tri-service Military Police were kept in a constant state of combat training. Kept on constant alert, the second threat would be met by the 1092nd Fighter Group. This group had the very latest in interceptor aircraft and prided themselves in having the fastest scramble rate in the entire Air Force.

Normally a kite wouldn't show up on radar. Typically its skin and frame being made of carbon materials such as wood and paper, wouldn't reflect radar—a fact that wouldn't go un-noticed years later when stealth aircraft were introduced. But this kite was different. An aluminum frame and Coleman lantern produced a blip not unlike that of a MIG 15.

Immediately the base was put on alert and interceptors scrambled. Ground controllers vectored the fighters to the box kite, but when it didn't move like a bogey, confusion ensued. A helicopter was launched and soon identified the source of the light, but it took some time to determine whether the kite was subversive or not, and by the time the MPs surrounded the barracks, communications between perpetrators and defenders finally established calm and order.

After the box kite incident, more rigorous work details were established to defray the boredom of waiting for classes to start. The sailors who launched their kites were given particularly challenging details, and all stairway doors to barracks roofs were padlocked.

But it was still difficult for the authorities to keep the PhDs happy.

Two such students decided they should take up butterfly collecting. It seems the desert and mountains east of Albuquerque contained one of the largest populations of butterflies in North America. In several field trips to Sandia Crest, the tallest peak and landmark overlooking Albuquerque, they had collected many species they chloroformed and tacked to the walls of their rooms. But many species were elusive, so an alternate means of capture was devised.

An old delivery van purchased from a local used car lot was taken to the base hobby shop and retrofitted by cutting a large hole in the top, sufficient for two people to stand with long handled nets, while a third drove the van in pursuit of the elusive butterfly.

Imagine, if you will, this old van, with two eccentric looking, pipe-smoking academics, standing in the cutout opening of their van with butterfly nets, wearing pith helmets and Bermuda shorts, tooling out the main gate of a top secret military base. It had to make the authorities really wonder what people were being allowed into our national nuclear weapons program.

It was of little coincidence that eccentricity was the hallmark of some of the participants of this program. Once the students were introduced to the awesome power of the devices with which they were to be associated, some of them went off the deep end.

Take Corporal Gary Mason, for example: Graduating cum laude in physics from a small Midwestern college, he procrastinated just long enough about going on to graduate school that the draft caught up with him. After his induction into the army for a two-year stint, it was determined he was a natural candidate for the nuclear weapons school, but for one small detail: he was a pacifist.

His strong religious background, combined with a sense of moral outrage toward the growing military industrial complex and its huge expenditures in weapons production, made him at first very outspoken about his unjust assignment. When this outrage got him nowhere, he became sullen and introspective, so much so his roommates began to express their concerns to the squadron adjutant, CWO Kelley.

"We don't like the way Gary is acting. Since that training film showing the after effects of Hiroshima, he's been sort of weird," his roommate, Staff Sergeant Adrien, said. "He hasn't gone to the mess hall for the whole weekend and missed several classes since the first of the week. I tried to pull rank on him and order him to go to class, but he told me just to screw off. For a religious guy, this is wholly out of character."

"I agree," said his other roommate, Corporal McIntire, "He seems ready to do something drastic."

And as if on cue, Corporal Mason suddenly barged up two flights of the barracks, ran to the end of the hall, opened a window and jumped out. Fortunately, the window he chose was directly over a newly spaded landscaped area, which essentially broke his fall.

Undeterred, he picked himself up, ran back into the barracks, this time up three flights of stairs, to the end of the hall and again jumped out the window, resulting in the same results, only this time he made a larger impression in the flower garden.

As he again picked himself up to make an apparent third attempt, his roommates wrestled him to the ground and held him until the MPs came to haul him away to the hospital. His second attempt at suicide had indeed broken a hip and he was placed in traction. This gave the school commandant time to find a more suitable assignment for Corporal Mason, and last heard he was transferred to an Army arctic weather research site in Greenland.

Sensing the student's unbound restlessness, the adjutant, CWO Kelly, a crusty old warrant officer who was serving out his twentieth year of service before retirement, asked those scheduled to start class in a few weeks whether they wanted to work at the officer's club. It wouldn't be KP or sweeping floors, they were assured, and so they agreed and reported to the club the next morning.

Much to Dicky's delight, he was assigned to the Officer's Club swimming pool—as a lifeguard. Dependents, specifically girls from high school and college, he fantasized, would all be hanging out under his perch like a harem. Dicky's classes weren't scheduled to start for two weeks, and he was told he could work weekends if he wanted. What an opportunity!

Maybe my clearance could get misplaced and I'd have to spend all summer at the pool, he thought.

But things didn't quite work out that way, and Dicky was disappointed that the expected bevy of girls didn't show up. Most of the time a bunch of screaming juveniles came who violated pool rules and ignored his whistles and admonishments until he finally exerted his newfound authority and ejected a few. Fortunately, these belligerent officer's dependents were never told that the lifeguards were lowly enlisted men, so his admonishments were usually taken seriously.

Dicky made friends with a few of the regular teenage bathers, but was told by CWO Kelly to steer clear of the flirting girls who were not to be trusted. Wives of officers off on temporary duty were another story. One wife must have thought Dicky was particularly to her liking, coming on to him in a big way as he returned from the locker room one afternoon. And she wasn't too subtle:

"Hi big guy, I'll bet you'd be good in bed."

Dicky was totally dumbfounded. He had never had any female come on to him this way and he stammered clumsily, not wanting to seem the novice he obviously was:

"I...I suppose I am," he stammered. Not knowing what more to say, he looked around desperately for someone to come over and be an excuse to change the subject. But there was nobody around, nobody to bail him out of this embarrassing situation. She continued her seduction:

"I've been watching you for the last few days and know you get off at five. How would you like to come over to my place and get off on me?"

Now Dicky was more in control of his faculties and said:

"I'd... I'd like to, but...but I said I'd go downtown tonight with the guys to the Albuquerque Folk Festival." Now his mind was racing.   "There's supposed to be some great food and music..." Then, realizing the stupidity of his response added:

"Would you like to come along?"

Dianne, as he later learned her name, responded:

"Sure, if you think it will be OK with the guys. I always like good food and music, and..."Her words trailed off as she leaned into him seductively: "...a good roll in the hay."

Dicky was hemmed into a corner not of his choosing. Dianne, not short of good looks, clearly was of the type CWO Kelly warned about: an officer's wife, bored, and on the troll for young studs in the student body of the Nuclear Weapons School. What better place to troll, than at the Officer's Club pool.

As Dicky expected, when he finished his shift at the pool she was waiting for him again, this time parked at the pool service entrance in a black MG Roadster. She had changed from her bathing suit into an outfit clearly intended for seduction: low cut to show off as much cleavage as was legal, and a flimsy chiffon skirt that crept up her legs. She twirled in a graceful pirouette as she removed herself from the roadster and invited Dicky to drive. She held open the driver's door with a flourish and gave him a quick pinch on his behind as he squeezed into the bucket seat.

This will be a night to remember, Dicky thought. As he attempted to appear suave about his situation, he fumbled with the gearshift and promptly killed the engine— twice.

Dicky's roommates either didn't show up at the Festival or the time or place of their planned meeting didn't materialize. By then, he was grateful they didn't rendezvous, as he was becoming comfortable with this older woman on his arm and, emboldened with his newfound 'studliness', sneaked a few tweaks of his own on Dianne's supple fanny. They had a great time at the Festival, eating many of the ethnic Mexican foods, watching the dancers perform and trying some of the dance steps on their own. Dicky, being a good dancer, managed to impress, at least she said so, and they swayed under the romantic spell of la musica Latina.

Later, they ended up at Lt. Commander and Dianne Cameron's on-base quarters on Sandia Base. At the Festival she had plied him with just enough cervesa to remove his inhibitions, what few of them remained, and prepared him with expertise for her coup 'd grace.

Their affair was brief, as Commander Cameron was to return from his temporary assignment somewhere in the South Pacific, and Dicky's classes started the next week, requiring his full attention. They had one more overnight fling in a motel room paid for by Dianne, and it was over. Dicky, more than Dianne, was sad of it's ending, but months later their paths crossed when she volunteered as hostess at the base Army, Navy and Air Force (ANAF) Club. There they danced, perhaps indiscreetly close for the last time, but agreed any further liaison would be unwise: for Dianne, as she very much enjoyed her role as an officer's wife, and for Dicky, who didn't want to lose his security clearance.

Another critical path and lesson in Dicky's life was established: stay clear of older women, particularly those already married.

26   Atomic Testing

*"You should work on your keigel exercises", Dr.
Rand recommended. "They're supposed to correct
any mild incontinence you might be experiencing".*

Their camper van pulled into the North Las Vegas
headquarters of the Nevada Test Site at 6:55 AM, minutes
before the tour bus was to take them some 60 miles back to
the north. A visit to the historic site of over 200 atomic tests
was part of the vacation itinerary DeVonne and Dicky
planned as an adjunct to a trip to Reno, Las Vegas and
points farther south in the spring of 1998. Now, after a
month of planning and anticipation, they almost missed their
scheduled meeting.   Forty-three years earlier Dicky had
driven through Las Vegas on the way to Sandia Base in
Albuquerque. There he had been assigned to the Armed
Forces Special Weapons Project (AFSWP), a super-secret
agency responsible for the development and maintenance
of atomic weapons. Then, Las Vegas seemed as merely a
truck stop with a few casinos and marriage chapels, so it
came as a big surprise that the distance from the hotel
where they stayed was well over 20 miles away, and the
morning traffic through the suburbs seemed more like LA
than the sleepy desert town Dicky remembered.

Hastily, they signed in at the NTS lobby and joined
35 others who also applied for one of the monthly tours
sponsored by the Department of Energy. On the bus PA
system, Ernie their tour guide, announced his credentials.
He had also been assigned to AFSWP in the early 50's and
had participated in many of the atomic tests, both at the
NTS and in the South Pacific. A 35-year civil service
employee, his entire career had been centered about the

nuclear testing program, and now, after retirement, he was called back to show off his former workplace.

They had something in common, Ernie and Dicky, so they conversed between his obligatory announcements to the tour group. As they spoke, Dicky tried to remember his previous association with the NTS:

It was in the fall of 1955. At the Atomic Energy Commission's facilities in Albuquerque, Dicky had completed a course of specialized training in special weapons fusing systems—military jargon for the electronics in atomic bombs used for detonating the beasts. He, along with several other students were waiting for orders to their next assignments when those with specialized training were directed to perform radiological sampling after one of the atomic tests at the NTS. The particular test was called Apple II, one of thirteen in a series code-worded TEAPOT. The primary purpose of Apple II was to study the effects of atomic blasts on civilian structures. A typical city of the 50's was constructed within a mile of ground zero. Streets were laid out complete with lampposts, furnished homes, stores, cars, and mannequins representing people in various stages of occupancy. Shielded cameras were hard-mounted everywhere to record blast and thermal radiation effects. These recordings, declassified almost immediately after the test, would become those infamous images shown in schools, and at civil defense seminars everywhere. The scene, in slow motion, would be forever remembered: sides of homes spontaneously burning from the thermal radiation of the 30 kiloton device, followed by the blast leveling all the wooden structures and many of the brick and concrete buildings, and finally the immediate reversal of the blast created by the rapid rise of the mushroom cloud, a hideous, unseen force sucking everything back toward ground zero.

Outside the view of these cameras, were other items under test that would neither be recognizable nor revealed to the general public—items of interest to Dicky's team. These were mockups of atomic weapons, or rather training devices complete with the electronics and fusing components, but without the high explosive trigger that might be secondarily detonated by Apple II. Their task was to take radiation samples of electronic devices with which they had familiarity by virtue of their recent training. The experiment for which these samples were to be taken was never explained, and their efforts were not entirely successful as the difficulty of disassembling and accessing their respective devices while wearing heavy protective clothing—gloves, coveralls, masks and boots—was made doubly difficult by the oppressive heat of Yucca flats.

So just as they were surreptitiously flown into the site of Apple II's mayhem, they were flown back out without ever knowing much about what they accomplished. With great difficulty, they took and recorded a few radiological samples—or so they were told. Ironically, with their top-secret clearances, they also weren't allowed to view first hand, what the general public would be shown repeatedly on film over the ensuing years: the devastating effects of Apple II on that typical city of the 1950s.

When Dicky and his monitoring team returned to Sandia, they were ordered to turn in their film badges. Nothing was ever reported back to any of them as to what levels of exposure they experienced on Yucca Flats, but in those days no news was good news, so none the wiser, they were sent on their way to new assignments. Dicky was assigned to Barksdale Air Force Base, Louisiana.

Somewhere, somehow, before reporting to his next assignment, however, he got married. It must have had something to do with those letters to and from Carmen, because before he knew it, he had proposed and she accepted.

CWO Kelly stated his opinion succinctly:

"You must be out of your cotton-picking mind."

Regulations stated that anyone below the rank of E4 had to have counseling from their squadron commander to get married. This task was delegated to CWO Kelly who had just the right temperament to discourage even the most headstrong.   In Dicky's case, however, CWO Kelly somehow knew of his fling with Lt Commander Cameron's wife, and figured the best way to quell any resurgence of this messy situation was for him to get married and direct his hormones elsewhere. The squadron CO concurred.

Dicky had fifteen days to get married and report to Barksdale AFB. He checked in with flight operations at Kirkland and found he could get a hop part of the way home: to Hill AFB just outside of Salt Lake City. But it was leaving almost immediately, and Dicky hadn't packed anything. He rushed back to his barracks and upon returning with his duffle hastily packed, watched first in disappointment as the giant Globemaster C124 rushed down the runway, then in horror as it failed to gain the necessary speed for liftoff and skidded into the perimeter fence at the end of the runway. It's landing gear collapsed and it fell grotesquely onto its right wing. Miraculously, it didn't catch fire and, Dicky learned later only one person was killed: a young airman going home on leave.

A day later, and still very sober at the thought of what could have happened had he been on that C124, Dicky boarded a C37 'Goony Bird' for Hill AFB. No subsequent flights would take him farther toward home, however, so he took a Greyhound bus to Chehalis and hitchhiked to the Boistfort Valley. He never told Mom of what might have been regarding his near-mishap, nor did Mom object too strenuously to his intent to marry Carmen. Perhaps she felt, as did CWO Kelly, that Dicky needed a permanent woman in his life.

The honeymooners left for Albuquerque in Dicky's '48 Plymouth coupe that had been in storage at Lost Valley Ranch. Laden with luggage and gifts to start a new home, they chose a route down the Oregon coast, through Yosemite, Death Valley and Las Vegas. A stop back at Sandia was necessary to pick up the remainder of his belongings, and to introduce Carmen to CWO Kelly.

Carmen possessed the striking beauty of most Italian women of her age. Jet-black hair and dark eyes, her lineage was Sicilian. While still in high school, her mother met and fell in love with Antonio Vallerio, a charming and seductive orchard worker from Wenatchee. Carmen and her mother were never apologetic of her heritage.

CWO Kelly was very impressed on the other hand.

"You 'sumbitch," he said after handing Dicky his transfer orders. "You must be one of the luckiest studs around. If you mess up and make her unhappy in any way, I'll personally hunt you down and kick your ass."

Dicky's first operational assignment was to a Strategic Air Command (SAC) base: Barksdale AFB in Louisiana. It was his job to maintain and test the electrical components of the nuclear weapons for which he was trained at Sandia. It was also Dicky's job during SAC alerts to monitor the loading of weapons of his particular specialty onto B-47 bombers, to determine their readiness to detonate, but most important: to assure all the necessary electrical and physical safeguards were in place to prevent premature detonation.

Within the military reservation of Barksdale AFB, lay Flag Lake. Because it was restricted to military personnel, the fishing was pretty good, but only for bass, crappie and other warm-water species. To Dicky, fish were fish because he had been away from My Trout for over a year, and seriously needed to exercise his casting arm. A series of connecting bayous to Flag Lake contained the best fishing, but they also contained snakes: cottonmouth moccasins and others much more poisonous, if one counted the coral snake. It was said, however, the coral snake, because of its small mouth, could only bite places with loose skin, like ear lobes and between fingers. This was small consolation to any one bitten, because any bite was fatal. This fact alone prompted many locals who fished the bayous to carry a snake gun: either a small gage shotgun or 22-caliber pistol with birdshot.

Dicky rented a sixteen-foot flat bottom jon boat at the small marina run by base special services and loaded his equipment. Narrow and long jon boats were popular fishing platforms in the Louisiana bayous because they could be easily maneuvered in shallow water and between cypress trees. Carmen had given him a spinning outfit for his birthday, and after a few practice sessions, he was prepared to cast lures under the shoreline vegetation where he was told large bass could be caught. It took a few hours for him to get the hang of it, but eventually he had two nice largemouth bass on his stringer. Now he wanted to try for some white crappie, and being told their habitat was in the bayous, proceeded to row to the mouth of the closest one. A small, almost unperceived current flowed out of the lake and Dicky, preoccupied with catching crappie, soon found himself farther into Fifi Bayou than he anticipated. So occupied was he with fishing, he didn't sense his situation until the jon boat bumped into one of many large cypress trees populating the bayou. Immediately the boat swung around in the current and bumped into another cypress, this time with enough force to knock something loose from its low hanging branches.

It was a snake. Fortunately, it fell onto the front seat of the boat, some six feet from where Dicky was seated. Otherwise he surely would have jumped overboard to perhaps some worse fate. It immediately coiled, and Dicky could see its head was that of some species of viper: flat with eyes protruding forward, piercingly, menacingly at him. His immediate reaction was to grab an oar to knock it into the water, but realizing the oars were fast to the boat, gabbed the next longest thing in the boat: his prized birthday-present spinning rod. Unfortunately, he had reeled to the rods tip, a lure festooned with triple hooks, and as he swiped at the snake he snagged it deftly, making it strike ferociously at the rod, and dangerously close to Dicky who was now torn between throwing snake and rod overboard, or trying to separate it from the lure. First things first: flip snake and lure overboard and out of harm's way. Now break off snake—no, leader's too strong. Reel in snake and lure to tip and try to break it off that way—no, might break tip. Finally out of desperation, he grasped the rod in both hands, baseball style, released about two feet of line so the snake was dangling free of the tip, and with as much force as he could muster from his seated position, slammed the snake into the cypress trunk. It tore loose and splashed into the bayou, skipping once before it swam frantically away.

Shaken, Dicky grabbed the oars and quickly rowed back to Flag Lake, swearing never to again enter *any* bayou without a snake gun.

27   Screaming Eagles and Sputnik

"What about this impotence?" you ask.

"Give it a few more months", Dr. Rand said.   "I was careful not to cut through any more nerves than possible, but it typically takes three or four months for healing and for you to be able to have normal sex.

"Such confidence", you think. You reverently hope he's right.

The escalating Cold War of the 50's prompted a buildup of Strategic Air Command (SAC) bases throughout the United States. A new base, Little Rock AFB in Arkansas, was under construction and needed a cadre of specialists to maintain the nuclear weapons to be stored there. Dicky was identified along with other technicians to set up on-the-job training programs for specialists being transferred from other bases. Because there were new weapons to be maintained, he was sent back to Sandia Base for a month to learn their fusing and testing characteristics. While there, he wondered if Dianne still trolled at the Officer's Club pool, but remembering CWO Kelly's admonitions and his wedding vows, decided not to find out.

Dicky and Carmen rented a small apartment in North Little Rock, some 15 miles from Little Rock AFB. The road from the base was a two lane county highway, winding through farmland, and was ill constructed to handle the sudden impact of commuting contractors and airmen. Just off the main gate, apartments and homes became available for rent or sale in the small town of Jacksonville, but the locals, seeing the opportunity for sudden income, raised their rates well beyond what a lowly airman could afford. So the young couple settled on an apartment next to the railroad tracks and just adjacent to the 'colored' district in North Little Rock.   While in Louisiana, they had become exposed for the first time to segregation and blatant racism; but now living close to their black neighbors, they didn't feel threatened like many of the white locals who expressed opinions with which neither of them could agree, much less understand.

"These uppity niggers just want to integrate our schools so they can date and marry our kids," said Mr. Trent, their landlord.

Mrs. Trent sat back in her rocking chair, nodding in agreement. In retirement, the Trents were almost as poor as the blacks living across the tracks, but seeing an opportunity to supplement their income, partitioned their modest two-bedroom house into a duplex.   The single bathroom was shared, as was a large porch that circled halfway around the house. The stifling heat of the Arkansas summer forced both couples into conversations air conditioning might have spared, but Dicky and Carmen learned to keep their liberal opinions to themselves, lest they be evicted as 'niggra-lovers'.

But school integration was more than just a casual topic for porch conversations. The Supreme Court recently ruled on Brown vs. Board of Education, and now it was up to President Eisenhower to enforce the integration of Little Rock's Central High School. In defiance, Governor Faubus stood in the way by commanding the Arkansas National Guard to prevent the 'Arkansas 9' from entering. Having no other option, Ike nationalized the Guard and called in the 101st Airborne.

Dicky was just getting off work and had been driving past the flight line where several C123s had just completed unloading the 2nd Battalion of the Screaming Eagles. They formed a convoy of trucks and jeeps, blocking his exit from the base. Now he had no choice but to wait for the last vehicle, and follow it on the only route to North Little Rock. But outside the gate there was bedlam. Scores of media vehicles and photographers swarmed about, hoping to film or otherwise document history. Before they could fall in behind the last vehicle of the convoy, an Air Policeman who had been directing traffic, allowed Dicky and several other commuters to proceed first. Now the maneuverings began. Frantically, to gain an advantage, reporters from ABC, NBC, CBS and several other news services attempted to pass commuters to photograph the convoy as it proceeded to its destiny with history. Several times Dicky was almost run off the road when they attempted to pass on curves, on bridges or against oncoming traffic. Finally, he pulled over and let them all go on their way, figuring he could more safely watch this idiocy on the evening news.

The launch of Sputnik came as a shock to America. Not so much for its scientific achievement—after all, it was only a tiny ball containing a radio transmitter—but because as a nation, we were complacent in our own scientific capabilities. Critics said we no longer valued scientific education the same as the Soviets. Moreover, our estimates of the capabilities of the USSR regarding missile capability were put into question. Compared to our capabilities, theirs suddenly seemed greater. This comparison became known as the 'Missile Gap'.

Dicky had been assigned to Little Rock Air Force Base when Sputnik was launched. He didn't think much of it at the time, being more concerned about his work as an Atomic Weapons Electronics Technician. Graduation from leadership school, promotion to Staff Sergeant, upgrading his technical skill level—all were important milestones. With less than three years service, it seemed his Air Force Career was on a fast track.

Meanwhile, wheels in the Pentagon were turning to close the 'Missile Gap'. Defense contractors throughout the nation were gearing up to design, develop and integrate missile systems. Concurrently, training of personnel to operate and maintain these systems would be necessary. Time being of the essence, calls went out to identify personnel to receive this training, so it wasn't surprising that orders sending Dicky to one of these defense contractors would be forthcoming. The nature of the orders was a little unusual, though:

"SSGT RICHARD K. STEARNS. AF19509551 will proceed from this station to Philadelphia, Pa, on or about 18 April 1958 for approximately 71 days for the purpose of attending Reentry Vehicle Systems Analyst training at the General Electric Company. During this period, airman can be contacted at the Penn Sherwood Hotel, 39th and Chestnut Streets, Philadelphia, Pa. Security clearance for this training is Top Secret."

Dicky's contemporaries at work could hardly believe it. Live in a hotel, eat in restaurants, and train in a civilian facility—all luxuries previously unheard of. Up to this point all his training had been confined to military classrooms, lodging in crowded barracks, and eating in chow halls.

This was like nothing he had experienced before. When he checked into the Penn Sherwood Hotel, he discovered there would be about a dozen other students taking the same training, so rather than spend most of their daily allowance on individual rooms, they decided to rent several suites for the duration. Each slept four comfortably, six with rollaway beds, so they found their individual quarters allowance useful for other things. On weekends they visited historic places, museums, and theaters. They saw major league baseball.   They went to lavish parties thrown by GE. These were days when the Military Industrial Complex, as forewarned by President Eisenhower, was just starting to reach out with its tentacles.   There were no guidelines for the military in those days, no rulings on conflicts of interest, so Dicky and his fellow students took full advantage of GE's hospitality. They referred to GE as 'Generous Electric', and filled up on their free dinners, drank their free booze and used their free tickets to local events. It was a dream come true for Dicky who had seen little of this world, and graduation came much too soon.

For their graduation exercise, a special event was scheduled in which they were to demonstrate the operation of the reentry vehicle around which their training was centered. Addressing their graduating class and observing their demonstration would be no other than Vice President Nixon.   To provide sufficient space for the expected entourage of congressmen, generals, company presidents and other hangers-on, an auditorium on the ground floor of the *Philadelphia Enquirer* was rented.   For those that so carefully observed the top security surrounding their training, this was bazaar.   The only thing shielding the general public from their work were long drapes hung over floor to ceiling windows facing the Thirtieth Street Train Station—possibly the busiest west of Grand Central.

For a week, Dicky's team practiced their demonstration, part of which was intended to simulate the operation of the reentry vehicle as it re-entered the atmosphere. To accomplish this, the birdbath shaped RV was placed on a large test fixture that moved in six degrees of freedom to actuate spin, roll and yaw sensors. In turn, these sensor sent signals to gas jets intended to stabilize the reentry vehicle during its fiery path to the target. Within the reentry vehicle would be a dummy thermonuclear warhead to receive the appropriate signal to simulate detonation. Contemplating this signal reminded Dicky of the way in which the detonation of a Mark Six gravity nuke had been simulated to a cadre of Air Force Cadets back at Barksdale AFB. Captain Bragg, their team leader, didn't think the VP would appreciate the bursting of a blown-up paper bag, however, so the team instead devised a red light mounted on top of the dummy warhead that would illuminate at the appropriate time.

The day of the demonstration arrived and the team was notified that Nixon wouldn't be present after all. It seems an unruly crowd in Lima Peru assaulted him and Pat in their limousine several days previous, and neither were now in a mood to visit the City of Brotherly Love. This was just as well, as the demonstration didn't go as expected.

Part of the demonstration was to show how the reentry vehicle was mated to the top of an Atlas missile. As it was rotated in its cradle, several hold down clamps came lose and allowed the fifteen hundred pound reentry vehicle to drop with a resounding crash some five inches onto the missile mockup. The team had practiced so much, the hold down clamp bolts became stripped of their threads and decided to let go at the most inopportune time. In the audience were several high-ranking designers of the Atlas missile, one of whom came up following the demo and asked in an accent emblematic of the original Von Braun team:

"Vot vill happen to my missile if this vould happen on der launch pad?"

The answer was clear: because the Atlas frame was designed like a balloon to minimize its weight, any unexpected shock would likely cause its collapse. That day, design changes were made to the hold down clamps.

28   Vandenberg

Two years after your prostatectomy, a troublesome increase in the levels of prostate antigen begins to show in your semi-annual blood tests.

What this means", said Dr. Rand, "Is one of two things: Your body chemistry is settling out and is now reflecting the residual prostate tissue left after the surgery, or there is still some cancer present..."

Simultaneous with Dicky's training at GE, cadres of Air Force technicians and officers were being trained at other contractor facilities around the country for eventual assignment to a large military reservation on the remote coast of Central California. Mothballed since the end of WWII, Camp Cooke eventually became Cooke AFB, then Vandenberg AFB, named after the late Air Force Chief of Staff, Hoyt S. Vandenberg. This isolated base became the ideal operational testing site of most of the Air Force's missile programs: Thor, Atlas, Titan and Minuteman and for launches of many research satellites requiring a polar orbit.

Arriving with hundreds of other Air Force and Contractor personnel in the autumn of 1958, Dicky was confronted by an Army post whose infrastructure was overrun by sand dunes and scrub brush. Fog rolled in from the Pacific Ocean year-round, making everything damp. In keeping with a crash program to get the first missiles operational, the original buildings of tarpaper and wood were renovated rather than replaced. Dicky's quarters were similar to those of basic training except open bays were converted to rooms: singles for officers and non-coms, doubles for other enlisted personnel. The early days at Vandenberg weren't exactly typical of the glamorous California assignment he anticipated, but there were unexpected benefits:

The extensive coastline within the military reservation had essentially been unexploited since Camp Cooke was deactivated in 1946. Among its shoreline rocks and within its surf lay a treasure of sea life. Huge abalone could be pried off the rocks at low tide and large surfperch could be caught at high tide. Steelhead still migrated up the Santa Yenes River that bordered the base; and off the coast, Bonita and Yellowtail were plentiful. Wild javelina and deer were everywhere; the javalina introduced to control rattlesnakes that were said to have populated the sand dunes. Dicky never saw rattlesnakes, so he assumed they did their job; but it was necessary to control the deer, as they were a hazard to planes taking off and landing on the new airstrip built to bring in everything from missile components to building materials. Deer shoots were conducted by the Air Police and the resulting carcasses were made available for the mess hall cooks. Some found their way to barracks barbeques, as would an occasional javalina. Some of the surfperch that survived, un-fished for years, could have been of record proportions, but Dicky and his fishing friends never gave it much thought as they happily delivered their catches to the mess halls. But as the population of Vandenberg steadily and relentlessly increased, so did this bounty decrease. Finally, and perhaps too late, strict regulations were implemented and enforced, but fishing would never be the same.

In the next few years, missile launch pads, gantries and silos appeared in increasing numbers all along the coastline of Vandenberg. Early on, five Thor launch pads were constructed for the 672nd Strategic Missile Squadron, which conducted training for England's Royal Air Force launch crews. The RAF would operate the missile sites in England, but in keeping with the United States' policy of maintaining strict control of our nuclear warheads, the USAF would train its own personnel in their maintenance and installation. For training launches, the US would supply to the RAF, reentry vehicles with the appropriate telemetry to score successes, partial successes, or failures. Early on, most were failures, in fact for each type of missile; the first launch or two were spectacular failures. I recall one in particular:

It was a test launch of a Thor, in which the RAF crew would demonstrate their capability to deploy back to England after a long and arduous year of training. The countdown proceeded through a series of holds, some normal, most to clear up glitches. Dicky was in the blockhouse with the launch crew and a score of onlookers who wanted to watch the action up close. Dicky's job was to monitor the functioning of the reentry vehicle and dummy warhead through launch and during liftoff, after which a crew high on a hill overlooking the base would take over. Included in this crew was the ever present and necessary Range Safety Officer (RSO). The blockhouse was central to several launch pads and was designed to withstand an explosion of a fully fueled missile, should one fall back during the preliminary stages of liftoff, which often they did. Remote TVs, although available, weren't too reliable and couldn't be panned very well, so once the missile was launched, it was anyone's guess within the blockhouse where it might be going. After liftoff, one function of the RSO was to give the all clear, at which time the huge concrete doors to the blockhouse could be flung open and the launch crew could dash outside and watch first hand as Thor arced gracefully over the Pacific on its way downrange.

This was the plan that day, but just as the range safety officer gave the all clear, Thor did a one-eighty and gave every appearance of returning to its pad. Observing this, the RSO pushed the destruct button, but now the wide open blockhouse doors were jammed with RAF personnel and contractors, some outside frantically trying to get back in, others unaware of the danger, still wanting to get out. Required to remain at his console, Dicky didn't get caught up in the crush, but instead watched TV images of the flaming remnants of Thor raining down on the parking lot some five hundred feet away.   Fortunately, no one was hurt—either by the falling debris or the doorway panic—but several cars were demolished.   After that episode, range safety rules were revised and the blockhouse doors remained closed until Thor showed little inclination toward homesickness and was well down range.

Launch failures such as these made work at Vandenberg more than interesting.   On another occasion Dicky was in the blockhouse, again at his console for a test launch of an Atlas ICBM, when similarly, Atlas did a loop-de-loop several thousand feet after liftoff and the RSO punched his destruct button. The film footage of this failure made it into every newsreel and even a couple Disney movies, but what wasn't followed was the reentry vehicle being flung on a high arc towards the tracks of the Southern Pacific Railway several miles away.   Missing the tracks by just a few feet, it pummeled into the side of the grade and instantly crystallized the sand under its impact footprint. This reentry vehicle was of the same type demonstrated at Dicky's graduation in Philadelphia. On reentry, it employed the principal of heat retention in which a ten-inch thick copper heat shield shaped like a huge birdbath protected the warhead from burning up in the atmosphere. True to its function, it spun into the railroad grade, and managed to keep all its top-secret warhead components from scattering to the four winds and making the job of recovery much easier. The components, of course were totally destroyed, clustered in a jumble inside the copper shield, ready to be secured.

Nobody at that time knew this, and for all the recovery team knew, they were scattered out in the open for all to pick up as souvenirs. So it became imperative for the team who stood by for such emergencies to get over there post haste, particularly because a maintenance crew of the Southern Pacific had left their speeder and was strolling casually toward the impact area. Last thing needed was for them to start picking up and taking home top-secret components. First it was necessary to get the Air Police to secure the area, and being a member of the recovery crew who was closest to the scene, Dicky was airlifted along with the Air Police via helicopter to the closest level area, some hundred yards, from impact. As they landed, the Southern Pacific crew now stood above the RV, curiously looking down at its jumble of components. Dicky shouted at the APs to get over there and chase them away. A young airman took off madly across the sand dunes, waving his sidearm in the air, blowing his whistle and falling down in the loose sand several times before the Southern Pacific crew, watching his antics with amusement, casually returned to their speeder and left.

One of the security anomalies of Vandenberg was this Southern Pacific Railway that wound its way along the coast and through the base. Its busy schedule meant launches had to be accomplished within certain windows of time. Moreover, any passenger on the train could easily observe the activities on the launch pads and the building of new facilities. It was particularly ironic that Khrushchev traveled through the base as such a passenger, just after he had been denied for reasons of security a visit to Disneyland. Perhaps, for him, our Atlas ICBMs standing in their gantries, on alert, like sentinels overlooking the railroad, were a suitable visual substitute to Disneyland.

But for whatever visual deterrence the Atlas might have presented, the reality of their ability to launch in a moment's notice was widely understood by most who worked on them. There were two obstacles to launch readiness. One and most important, was the immaturity of the technology: from unreliable circuit boards, to untried materials, to incompatible sequences, all suffered from too much haste and too little testing. In time this was fixed, but the other obstacle took longer: it was the ever-present salt air and fog that enshrouded Atlas and all its support equipment. If not hosed down periodically, everything developed a thin crust of salt-induced corrosion. Most understood if Atlas wasn't either launched within two months of its being placed on alert or recycled back to the hanger, it would become corroded to its launch pad.

Over time, technology improved and even the salt air was subdued, not because of the development of corrosive-proof materials, of which there were some, but out of more pressing necessities: everything went indoors. Site hardening became the latest buzzword coming out of the Pentagon, so not only did Atlas go inside, her home became hermetically sealed and concrete encased. First, coffin-like structures were built wherein its concrete lid slid open and Atlas rose like Dracula during countdown as she became fueled and readied for launch. As reaction times became critical, she was then stood in silos, unexposed to the elements until just minutes before launch where she rose vertically on her pedestal. This last launch configuration wasn't without problems, however, as one particularly horrendous failure demonstrated: As Atlas was being fueled, something went wrong and while still inside her silo, she exploded. It didn't take much imagination to envision the ensuing damage: a tunnel connecting the underground blockhouse to the silo acted as a conduit for the blast wave, sending two concrete doors intended to contain such an event, crashing into the final door to the blockhouse. Moreover the silo lids, constructed of two thirty-five ton interlaced concrete clamshells, were blown skyward like autumn leaves, landing some two hundred yards away. It went without saying: in the blockhouse that day, a few eardrums were popped.

The stimulus of Vandenberg, its launches, and its technology became the impetus for the furtherance of Dicky's education. While at Little Rock AFB, he had taken night courses at Little Rock University, managing to complete several before Sputnik. Now the opportunity came again in the form of on-base courses offered through a small junior college in Santa Maria, some twenty miles away. Several instructors were engineers from on-base contractors who offered a new dimension to his education. From his classroom training, his thought processes touched on the theoretical, but never delved much deeper. Now, from one engineer, he learned the physics of space flight in ways in which he couldn't in a regular university; another presented practical solutions of calculus and analytical geometry problems that tied directly into his work. Dicky was fired up to become an engineer, and when once again a call went out for people to fill the technical vacuum perceived by the USSR's first manned space flight, he was ready.

The program was called the Airmen's Education and Commissioning Program, and to qualify, Dicky had to be able to complete an engineering degree in three years—fewer would increase his competitive standing. First, Dicky needed the recommendation of his Squadron Commander, and, almost as an afterthought, a bunch of bureaucrats thought it would be a great idea if he took a series of aptitude tests. Whether or not these had any bearing on his acceptance to the program, their results were nonetheless interesting and predictable. On the low end of the scale, his aptitude for being a mortician was slightly above that of being a life insurance salesman, and, as expected, his highest aptitude was that of aviator, next a science teacher, then an engineer. Slightly under these, and also not surprising—at least not to Dicky—was 'forest service man'.

In the end, he was accepted into the program that would make him an electrical engineer, not so much for what he wanted—under different circumstances he would have preferred to be a forest service man—but because that's what the country needed.

29   OSU

Dr Rand Continues: "If there are still cancer cells, we'll continue to see an increase in the PSA readings, in which case we can take appropriate action. Watching and waiting is the appropriate action, but if you're nervous about inaction, external beam radiation can be done now, but you need to be aware of the side effects."

Several schools of engineering participated in the Airmen's Education and Commissioning Program. Dicky had a choice of any having vacancies, providing he could complete his degree in the required three years. This would prove to be difficult unless allowed to challenge several of the core courses, like freshman chemistry. Including his meager thirty-three semester hours already obtained through night school, he would need an additional one hundred and ten semester hours to graduate.

"Holy Smokes!" Dicky's engineering advisor exclaimed as he sat sweating in Professor Akin's office. It was late June 1961 and the morning temperature on the Oklahoma State University campus was already hovering in the 80's—still a little under the humidity, but gaining fast. Dicky wondered if this program was going to be such a great idea, as Professor Akin continued on his appraisal:

"Unless you're able to complete eighteen hours a semester, and I'm talking about engineering courses with additional lab hours, it's just not possible for you to finish in three years." For effect, his voice elevated half an octave on *possible*.

"Can I challenge any more courses?" Dicky asked. Shortly after arriving, he successfully tested off chemistry and engineering drawing, having studied for two months during his leave en route to Stillwater. Now he was asking the impossible.

"You aren't going to have enough time to study for any more course challenges," he replied. "It's going to be difficult enough to find time to study for the course work ahead."

He was right, of course. Together they agreed on a Herculean schedule of ten hours for the first summer session, twice the normal, then nineteen hours of math, physics and engineering courses the fall semester. If Dicky survived that, then another eighteen hours awaited in the spring. For a breather, two hours of music appreciation was included, the only course that first year for which he received a grade of A.

Carmen and Dicky rented a small two-bedroom house just north of the campus on Knoblock Street. Daughter Candy, a little under five years old, could play in the fenced back yard as could a newly acquired white Spitz puppy they named Trixie.   In one corner of the kitchen, Dicky set up his study area next to a phone from which he anticipated collaborating with classmates. For the duration, that's where his hours at home would be spent: hunched over his desk, back—literally—to family.   He spent Christmas and Spring breaks catching up, and precious few hours were made available for socializing. They managed an occasional dinner out, and a movie; twice he explored Lake Blackwell, the only fishable body of water within fifty miles. Except for a few bass, an occasional crappie, the fishing was mediocre which just as well, as fishing was a diversion his grade point average didn't need.

Another diversion *nobody* needed was the weather. Stillwater was directly on a line between Wichita Falls, Texas and Topeka, Kansas—Tornado Alley. Hardly any of the cheaper homes in Stillwater had storm cellars, so in the case of an imminent tornado, they were told to huddle in a closet on the southwest side of the house and open all the windows on the northeast side. What good this would do, Dicky's family hadn't a clue, but it gave them something to do while awaiting their demise, I suppose. Only one tornado touched down on the campus during the time Dicky had been at OSU. It was on the night before his graduation and it raised hell, injuring many and killing one coed. Other, lesser storms accompanied by thunder and lightning, were common, and in the summer they were welcome as it meant a ten or twenty degree drop in temperature. Lightning strikes, on the other hand, were not welcome as they were often too close; thanks to a fiendish ham radio operator across the alley whose name was Bert. To support his hobby, he erected a tall metal radio antenna topped with a lightning arrestor, so whenever lightning thought of striking within a mile radius, Bert instantly was on the minds of all the neighbors who secretly wished he were sitting at his key when the lightning arrestor failed to do its job.

For his first lightning strike, Dicky was a few hours into REM sleep after a long study session to prepare for midterms. It was typically hot and muggy, and he had put the swamp cooler on full reverse, to draw outside air through a partially opened window and across bodies as they lay, sans covers, stuck to sweaty sheets. On the advice of a neighbor, Dicky installed a used swamp cooler in the kitchen window. Swamp coolers consisted of a large fan and water wheel arrangement designed to blow moisture-laden air into the house, ostensibly to increase the humidity, and hence, lower the temperature. It works well if the humidity is low already, but Stillwater in the summer isn't exactly Arizona; so rather than blow moist air in all night with marginal results, Dicky reversed the fan before coming to bed. So here they lay, finally asleep when the storm approaches. In his subconscious, Dicky can hear thunder in the distance, approaching. Ever approaching. Closer. Then the explosion of a million volts screaming down Bert's lightning rod brought everyone immediately to a sitting position. Simultaneously, the brilliance and charge of the lightning, and the smell of ozone filled the air—instantly overloading all Dicky's senses. He couldn't remember being so terrified. For the remainder of their stay in Bert's neighborhood, Dicky never slept during an approaching storm.

According to OSU promotional brochures, the School of Engineering has a long tradition of excellence. In 1961, little of this excellence had anything to do with student body diversity. Dicky's ability to qualify for graduation in three years with so few qualifications, had less to do with his sterling credentials, and more to do with the fact he was a white male under a full government scholarship. For the Good Old Boy Network, Affirmative Action was alive and well—long before it was invented by LBJ. This was the case with all engineering students except one.

Carol was perhaps *the* token white female, and so far as anyone within the Good Old Boy Network knew, was the only minority within the entire school of engineering. Being moderately pretty in a masculine sort of way, she fit right in with the rest of the guys. Normally her masculinity would give them pause as to her sexual orientation, except she slept with them—or at least, it seemed, a lot of them. She selected only the eligible, unmarried engineers with good grades. Her grades weren't bad as she demonstrated a natural affinity for things mechanical, electrical and technical; but all agreed they could be better except for her study habits. For any given study session, her attention soon went from solving an engineering problem to how to crawl in bed with her study partner. Everyone also agreed that her study habits were akin to a slave trader: she was looking for the best sex partner, ultimately with an eye to getting that 'Mrs.' degree. Collectively, this attitude represented the mind set of the Good Old Boy Network in the 60's, but Carol rose above it all and got engaged to one of the Air Force graduate students, Norman, thereby obtaining a certain modicum of vindication.

Being a pilot further helped elevate Carol's status among the Air Force students. One favorite story about her flying exploits dealt with her renting a small two-seater to tour the English countryside. It seems she ran out of petrol and found it necessary to land in one of Queen Elizabeth's cow pastures, stampeding some of her prize Herefords and setting off an international incident. This notoriety, coupled with her disdain for anything domestic didn't put her in good graces with wives. As Norman's fiancé, she was naturally invited to social functions, but instead of joining wifely conversations about babies, diapers and the like, she gathered with the men, foot elevated on a chair as though it was the first rail on a corral fence, and offered her own off-color jokes. Secretly, most of the men probably wished their wives had a little of Carol's pluck, and although she probably wasn't a major factor, by the time the class of '63 graduated, almost half of the Air Force students had divorced or separated.

During WWII, when OSU was still Oklahoma A&M, AFROTC students trained for their pilots wings at a dirt field west of Boomer Lake. Because it was more important to field pilots, most left to fly for the Army Air Corps before they could graduate. After the war, many came back and finished their education on the way to distinguished careers. Several became generals, and were influential in deciding the direction the Air Force would take in educating its officer corps. Consequently and on average, more Air Force personnel were assigned to the OSU schools of engineering and aeronautics than other universities. This had a tendency to overload some of the engineering classes with motivated people, thereby skewing the grading curve, much to the chagrin of the local students. In the 60's it was difficult to distinguish Air Force students from locals because the Age of Aquarius hadn't reached OSU; and given their conservative bent, locals wouldn't dare flaunt long hair for the next ten years. So everyone pretty much looked like your typical engineering student: hair crew cut, long right arm from carrying too many books, short and permanently bent left arm from chain smoking cigarettes. And always the omnipresent slide rule hanging from a belt loop. So even though the Air Force students were somewhat older than the average local, the distinction faded when they became seniors and graduate students. On one occasion, however, no one mistook who was who.

A short distance west of campus, near the town of Enid, was Vance Air Force Base. In addition to being the administrative headquarters for the Air Force students— they went there for medical needs, commissary goods—it was also a facility for advanced flight training. Consequently, many OSU graduates who wound up going there for advanced flight training couldn't resist the temptation to buzz the campus during at least one of their training sorties—a reminder to all toiling in their hot classrooms that the wild blue yonder still beckoned. On one particular occasion, a new jet was introduced to the campus: an F-4, later to be used extensively in Vietnam and nicknamed 'the Phantom'. It was, by itself an imposing craft. Flying low over the rice paddies of the Mekong Valley, it flushed many Viet Cong from cover. With afterburner, it probably contributed to their loss of hearing also.

None could tell if this alumna actually took his Phantom through the sound barrier as he buzzed the campus—it didn't really matter. The effects of the afterburner were devastating: cracked windows, lab gear crashing to the floor, students diving for cover, irate calls to the base.

And to a man, every Air Force student in every class that moment could be uniquely identified—by their red face and sheepish grin.

30   Officer Training

"What side effects?" you ask, already knowing of most clinical *studies from your extensive research on the Internet. A website support group is your connection to thousands of other men who had undergone the same procedure and were now facing the same decision.*

Dicky's classes ended at OSU at the end of the 1963 summer session. The day had been somewhat ominous because the night before a tornado tore through the campus and left a shamble of fallen trees. A student was killed by one of several downed electrical wires. Electricity had barely been restored for the commencement ceremonies and less than half the graduating class showed up to receive their diplomas. Dicky proudly accepted his Bachelor of Science in Electrical Engineering from the Dean of Engineering, however, and acknowledged the congratulations of Carmen and daughter, Candy. No other family member was there, but he sorely wished Mom could have been. Her fondest hopes for her oldest son were realized that day, and by her absence, he felt less than fulfilled.

For Dicky, Class 63D of Officer Training School, was like basic training only with less hassle. Some of his contemporaries were also from enlisted ranks, but most came directly from college and had no prior knowledge of military protocol. Nowhere was the difference more noticeable than on the drill field. Given the temporary rank of Flight Lieutenant, Dicky's first task was to shape up his flight of plebes and teach them how to march. This was his first taste of authority, and although he might have relished regressing to the persona of his basic training nemesis: *Rooski*, he didn't. Instead he spent extra time with the less coordinated and earned the respect of his flight after they were honored to lead the squadron during their first Saturday parade. *Flight Tiger-Twelve*, they named themselves, and when called to formation each morning, each would emit the loud growl of their mascot as they exited the barracks on their way to formation.

"What's the motto of Tiger-Twelve?" Dicky would yell after taking roll call and bringing his flight to attention.

"Every man a Tiger, SIR!" was their throaty response.

With that, Dicky would execute a smart about face, salute his squadron commander and report:

"Every Tiger...uh...man, present and accounted for, SIR!"

This bending of protocol went on for the first week of drill, but finally, one of the training officers squelched it, saying it didn't reflect well on the squadron, particularly when the "Every man a Tiger, SIR!" retort could be heard across the parade ground and all the way to the Base Commander's reviewing stand.

After the rigors of engineering classes at OSU, drill competition had been a welcome diversion for Dicky. He enjoyed taking his flight of plebes to new heights of marching perfection and when he learned that President Kennedy might be stopping at San Antonio during his visit to Texas, he was excited his flight might compete for the coveted role of Honor Flight when JFK emerged from Air Force One.

Events in Dallas that week erased all excitement, however, and instead, Dicky led his flight, along with the entire base military cadre, to a hastily organized memorial service. His voice broke with emotion as he echoed the command to present arms.

On that cold November afternoon, taps were played for Dicky's President.

31   Piloting Spy Satellites

Some made the right decision about opting for follow-up radiation therapy. Others waited too long and now were truly faced with their mortality. Painful and expensive hormone injections might gain a few years, but the inevitable would come, and everyone in your support group knew it.

Shortly before graduation at Officer Training School, first assignments were posted on the squadron dayroom bulletin board. Those who had prior military service already had some hint of where they were going because they were given a set of choices before finishing their undergraduate programs. In Dicky's case, he was eager to get back to the Pacific Northwest, and knowing of a new program at Boeing called DynaSoar, stated this as his first choice. Second, he chose 'Satellite Control Facility', not fully understanding what they did there, but it was located at Sunnyvale California, the next place closest to Seattle. He chose third the Nuclear Weapons Lab at Albuquerque, a town he liked from his days at Sandia. Dicky's thought process of selecting location instead of potential for challenge or advancement was simple: If he liked where he lived, the job would come easy, if not, no matter how challenging the job, he would probably not be as happy.

Scanning the assignment list, he was disappointed his first choice didn't materialize. Somewhere he heard the DynaSoar Program wasn't going to be funded, so he wasn't totally surprised to see his second choice listed instead. After the commissioning ceremony, his training officer, Captain Segal, delivered Dicky's orders and remarked:

"These are the strangest assignment orders I've ever seen."

Dicky looked at the single typewritten sheet containing one sentence. He was to report not later than 26 January 1964 to the Lockheed Corporation, Building 104, Sunnyvale, California in civilian clothes.   No further instructions were given.

So on January 20th, he entered the lobby of the Lockheed Missile and Space Company and identified himself to the receptionist. She immediately called someone, who sent an escort to deliver him to another building across the street, a large rambling, single story structure with multiple wings of modular offices, sprouting large arrays of microwave and other non-descript antennae from its roof.   Inside, another lobby with Lockheed uniformed guards, blocked entry into the inter sanctum that would be Dicky's place of work for the next eight years.

The first thing impressive about this assignment was the absence of military uniforms. All the officers wore business suits or sports jackets and tie, the reason given they were an extension of Air Force Headquarters in the Pentagon, which had similar uniform rules.   Except for a few administrative NCOs, all personnel assigned to the Satellite Control Facility were officers.   A scan of the duty roster revealed a collection of over two hundred officers whose specialties were mainly in the science and engineering fields, ranging in rank from second lieutenant to colonel.   No one was addressed by his or her rank, even though the order of command was tacitly understood, and recognition of rank was often replaced by respect for one's performance in a technical specialty.

Dicky's first assignment was to go back to school. For six weeks he returned to the 104 building for classes in orbital mechanics taught by the University of California

Department of Astronomy.   Later, he was sent up the peninsula to Stanford University for a series of lectures on satellite-borne computer systems, which, although still in their infancy, would be the crux of his work for many years. While at school, paperwork was processed to clear him for an ultra-classified satellite surveillance project, by the top-secret codeword: 'Corona.'

The need for reliable intelligence during the apex of the Cold War had prompted the Corona Project, which would orbit reconnaissance satellites to image the USSR at altitudes above that nation's airspace. It was, by any stretch of one's imagination, an ambitious undertaking by a small band of engineers, scientists and intelligence officers to create and operate a new kind of revolutionary space surveillance platform.

After a series of security briefings and the signing of the first of many non-disclosure contracts with nameless agencies, Dicky was introduced to a team of officers and contractor engineers in a small, windowless room with rows of drafting tables and desks.   On the walls were floor to ceiling maps of the world with orbits overlaid at angles that suggested, from his recent classes in orbital mechanics, polar orbits from launches in a southerly direction from Vandenberg Air Force Base.

From an engineering point of view, these were heady years for Dicky. The challenge and opportunities presented by the Corona Project left him working long hours, some well into the night, as he worked on programs to secure photographs essential to the security of the free world. Working along scientists and engineers from Lockheed, TRW, GE, and Eastman Kodak, he helped develop some of the tools and techniques to make equipment in space work in ways never before tried.

As Dicky's knowledge of satellite intelligence gathering systems progressed, he was assigned to a team to evaluate the results of each mission. Known as the Payload Evaluation Team, experts in each specialty: optics, thermodynamics, orbital dynamics, cartography and payload computers; were sent to a covert location to pore over the thousands of photographs returned from orbit by reentry vehicles released from polar orbiting satellites. The crux of the PET team's evaluation was primarily to determine for the intelligence community, exactly what resolution each payload or camera delivered. One of the means of making this determination was to position progressively sized images made of white canvas in known locations and take pictures of them—from orbit. It was Dicky's task to take these pictures by programming the camera systems. Because there would be more film on board than could be used before the depletion of the satellite's other expendables such as battery power, stabilization gas, and orbital maintenance propellant; Dicky was permitted to program targets of opportunity.

On one particular satellite mission, there was just enough film to cover several long strips of the Continental United States on the final north to south passes; after which the film was recovered via reentry vehicle as it was de-orbited over Hawaii. C-119 'Flying Boxcars' were deployed from Hickam AFB to snatch the reentry vehicle mid-air as it hung beneath its recovery chute. Using an ephemeris program to predict the satellite's ground pass, and using weather predictions from Strategic Air Command to determine the probability of seeing the ground, Dicky contacted a covert contractor to position the resolution targets in a vacant field in Eastern Colorado, after which he programmed the payload camera to photograph them. This accomplished, Dicky determined he could also photograph a fifteen mile-wide swath from Seattle to the Columbia River on a subsequent north-south pass before the film ran out.

32   George Creek Revisited

"The side effects of radiation are varied", said Dr. Rand. "But the most common are rectal burning from radiation 'spillover' and urinary complications such as increased incontinence. Also there will be the added scar tissue that complicates any other surgery that might be necessary. In view of these considerations I would recommend waiting a little longer."

They nicknamed her Charlotte. A select team of engineers and technicians contracted by the National Reconnaissance Office built and named her. All her components were assembled to perform a precision orbital ballet for a single purpose: to photograph areas of the earth denied access to the United State by any other means. She was launched in the summer when the sun would be at an optimal angle to illuminate those areas. Weather forecasts for the duration of her mission were favorable, and the orbit selected to cover most of the areas desired by the intelligence community would be easy for her to attain. Once in orbit, all her functions performed exactly as expected. When Dicky's final set of commands were assembled and uploaded to her memory, she was ready to expend the last of her film on the targets he chose: the resolution patterns in eastern Colorado and an area of Western Washington from just north of Seattle to the Columbia River—an area to include George Creek.

After Charlotte's reentry vehicle was recovered and flown with its precious film contents for developing, copies were made for immediate distribution to intelligence consumers and to the Payload Evaluation Team who flew to a rendezvous location to review the developed photos. Separated into rolls corresponding to each day Charlotte was in orbit, the photos could be reviewed as they were drawn across large light tables specially made for photo interpretation. Dicky's task would be to review rolls of selected days to determine Charlotte's ability to convert computer commands to photos of pre-selected areas on the earth's surface. Armed with detailed topographical maps and printed ephemeris data of Charlotte's trace over the earth, he could be found over the next several days hunched over his light table, staring through an eye loupe at landmarks not before seen from space.

As the long strip of film moved beneath his loupe, Dicky imagined himself looking down on the earth from a virtual cockpit within Charlotte as she hurtled through her polar orbit. Although not a photo analyst, he examined every detail, thinking perhaps he could see heretofore, unexplored images important to the intelligence community. Sometimes he noted particular images, and consulted on these with Al, hunched over his own table.

Al was a CIA analyst and had lots of experience bending over light tables such as these. His associates claimed his shiny nose was from being pressed against photo images over his years in the business. His analysis was valuable to the PET team and he enjoyed the challenge of reviewing the imagery of each new satellite mission.

Dicky returned to his task and later came to the images of the last day of Charlotte's mission. First, the resolution targets he had deployed to Eastern Colorado came under his loupe, bright and clear. Again he exclaimed to Al about his find, and this time, Al agreed that this mission of Charlotte might indeed be special. Measurements were taken and Dicky's excitement grew at what he might see on that last strip of film over Washington State. In his mind's eye, he flew over the Snohomish River near Everett as the first seconds of imagery came into view, then south he flew, over Silver Lake, then Green Lake— easy landmarks to identify, even without topographical maps. He fished both of these lakes years before with Uncle Ralph.

Now his attention was riveted to the last few feet of Charlotte's payload. Again, he vicariously flew in his space capsule: over Vashon Island, Olympia and on south to landmarks he knew from childhood. *There's Bunker Creek*, he said to himself as he adjusted his eye loupe to get a better focus. Now the Boistfort Valley came into view and excitedly he followed the South Fork—My River—to Lost Valley Ranch.

"Somebody logged the upper twenty," he said to Al who was still hunched over his own table, obviously more concerned with imagery in the Soviet Union than mere logging operations in Washington State. Farther south, Dicky's loupe settled on the small two-bedroom home Mom and Elmer moved into shortly after Dicky joined the Air Force.

He consulted a detailed topographical map in preparation for the climax of Charlotte's mission—at least as far as Dicky was concerned. After many failed attempts of finding George Creek on that weeklong exploration with Gerald and Gerry, he wanted to see its location relative to BawFaw Peak and other landmarks. With precise measuring instruments available to Charlotte's photo interpreters, he could determine exactly the location of George Creek, and by what route would be best to get to her once again.

He expected to see roads down to her upper reaches—the WTCo had started them when the three teenage explorers made that memorable fishing trip. What he didn't expect to see was the devastation of what had been George Creek. All the stately and massive old growth cedar along her banks were gone, replaced by a grotesque slash of logging debris and erosion caused by the dragging of logs through her stream bed. Except for a thick stand of alders that struggled against the now all too frequent floods, all that remained was total and absolute devastation.

The elation of being perhaps the first human to study the Boistfort Valley from earth orbit was quickly replaced by a deep sorrow of seeing this demise of George Creek. Still hunched over his light table, Dicky pushed aside his loupe, buried his head in the crook of his arm, cursed the WTCo, and sobbed quietly to himself.

33   Stanford and Friday Golf

With Dr Rand's recommendations of watching and waiting fresh your mind, you go home and review several cases in your support group wherein some patient's PSA tests with little warning, increased geometrically.

You vow you won't wait too long.

The Vietnam conflict was heating up as Dicky was at the zenith of his challenging work at the Satellite Control Facility. Within the government and particularly the military, there existed a demand for more education among the scientist and engineer corps. A special call went out to those who could finish out their master's or PhD degree and return to their current assignment without having to make a permanent change of station—PCS in military jargon. By virtue of taking his astronomy and related courses at Cal and Stanford, Dicky was in a unique position to answer this call. Moreover, he had a sponsor in Colonel Gorrighan, a Stanford School of Engineering alumnus, and a Corona field test force director.

"You'll find this Masters of Engineering program at Stanford to be a real challenge," Corrigan said. He rocked back in his desk chair and puffed on a large cigar he had some difficulty lighting, finally giving up and resorting to chewing it instead. He continued:

"Your studies will be strictly anonymous insofar as your work here is concerned. In fact, you'll be expected to blend in with the student body—grow a beard and let your hair grow long, if you're comfortable with that."

Dicky thought back to his undergraduate days at OSU. There, most of the Air Force students maintained their military demeanor, even while wearing civvies. Now he knew why this had to change: Vietnam and the growing unrest on campuses made it difficult for military students not to get into discussions—or worse. Best to blend in, he concluded. His attention returned to his sponsor's admonitions:

"We want you back here to do bigger and better things after you get your degree, so be very careful not to form any close associations with classmates or faculty who are foreign nationals. You won't be debriefed from Corona, so you can drop in on occasion and keep abreast of what's going on..."

He fiddled with his cigar some more, finally abandoning any hope of getting it lit, then added almost as an afterthought:

"...Which is all the more reason to be careful."

Dicky started his classes with some trepidation. Keeping his identity anonymous wouldn't be difficult. Identifying foreign nationals more so, but his biggest worry was personal: was he prepared to tackle the ambitious program of study expected of him? He had just two years to complete his studies, his thesis could take longer, but uncertainty grew with the growing college unrest over Vietnam. His contemporaries at Stanford were for the most part also concerned about their studies but for a different reason: they didn't want to flunk out and face the draft.

Sooner than expected, his worries were substantiated. One of his classes involved the use of Stanford's new and only computer lab. Computer programs were submitted in batch, and on one occasion as Dicky was on his way to pick up the printout of one of his runs, he noticed smoke coming from an area housing the ROTC classrooms. Students were running toward the fire and as Dicky pushed closer, he could see other students dancing with glee as they chanted: "Burn baby, burn." They had apparently torched a Navy ROTC classroom, and now the media was there, taking pictures. The Tet Offensive in the highlands of Vietnam had set off protests on campuses everywhere. This particular protest had serious political undertones, involving members of the Weather Underground and other groups labeled subversive by the FBI.

In addition to the FBI, this protest also caught the attention of Dicky's security people because shortly thereafter, they summoned him back to their office in the Satellite Control Facility and gave him some very grim news: Apparently Dicky's autonomy had been compromised and they couldn't take a chance of him being targeted by anyone who had any possible connections to the 'other side'. Who this 'other side' might be, wasn't explained, but someone in higher authority decided the stakes would be just too high for him to continue at Stanford and still maintain his relationship with the SCF.

Dicky knew because of his sensitive work at the SCF, he could be a target if he were to travel outside the United States; hence his travel was severely limited. To travel to friendly countries, he had to get prior permission, to unfriendly places it was forbidden. This didn't bother him too much because it kept him out of Vietnam. But this was the first time he heard of having a travel—or study—restriction within his own country.

At first he was crushed. Here, he had a golden opportunity to get an advanced degree from one of the best schools in the country. But then he recalled his worries about the difficulty this program might bring, his fear of failure, of having to face Colonel Gorrighan and the rest of his associates back at the SCF, of telling Mom he couldn't hack it. Now he had an excuse, and his attention turned to several alternatives: He could start the next semester at either the Santa Clara or San Jose State Universities, both down the peninsula and both with good engineering schools.

Colonel Gorrighan shared Dicky's disappointment, but knew Security's decision wasn't made lightly. Dicky didn't let on that he was more relieved at getting into an easier program of study than being removed from a situation where he might be 'targeted'. He still didn't comprehend what that meant until he had a conversation with the SCF Chief of Security.

"You apparently were identified by someone the FBI was watching at Stanford," he said. "That someone possibly even talked to you when you took that computer course up there before you got your clearance. Once they tie you to the SCF, you're on their list. It's likely they even took your picture as you walked out of a contractor's facility on one of your PET trips."

"But how could someone like this be a danger to me?" Dicky asked.

"There's more than just physical danger," he replied. 'We've learned that their best means of getting information on our systems is through academia, or technical symposiums. Seemingly innocuous conversations are engaged with their 'targets', and they can tie together an amazing amount of detail that way. The FBI apparently knows that one person who targeted you, and now there are others. Their investigation into the torching of the ROTC building alerted us to that."

"So, better to remove me from their area of operations, is that right?" Dicky asked. "And what's to prevent them from following me to San Jose State, or Santa Clara?"

"The FBI hopes they do," the security chief replied. "That way their identities can be correlated and they can be kept under surveillance."

Dicky left Security's office not fully satisfied with their explanation. They left something out of the equation, but he didn't want to delve further into the workings of the FBI's 'spook' operations—even if he could.

Classes at San Jose State started in the summer session. Dicky's graduate advisor estimated that with coursework already taken at Stanford and Cal, he could finish his master's in electrical engineering in less than a year. Dicky chose San Jose State over Santa Clara because SJS had a larger selection of evening classes preferred by engineers at the sprawling IBM laboratories nearby. These engineers, Dicky surmised, could influence into the curricula, certain aspects of computer science theretofore untaught by the faculty. Then, the field of computer science would be still in its infancy in a place yet to be known as Silicon Valley.

Compared to OSU and Stanford, Dicky couldn't believe how easy the course work was. Because computer labs were in their infancy, he used his access privileges at the SCF to use one of the many large-scale, state-of-the-art systems to circumvent the batch turnarounds that hindered his contemporaries at Stanford and SJS. He found his SJS contemporaries, unlike the ones at Stanford, were older and not as concerned about the draft. Some had definite opinions about Vietnam and were surprised to learn that Dicky was an Air Force officer, although in most conversations he was content to pretend he was just another engineer from Lockheed or IBM taking night classes.

After the summer session, he increased his course load and still found time to play golf every Friday. He and a couple fellow students figured they could play a different course every week and never repeat any of them. They played as far south as Carmel and as far north as Petaluma. Freeways were fast and gas was cheap. These were fun times for Dicky and Vietnam seemed so very far away. One or two times on their way through San Francisco, they drove through Golden Gate Park or the Haight-Ashbury to view the hippies.

"They put so much stock in dropping out, turning on, and not conforming," said Dicky, as they gazed in amusement at the flower-painted Volkswagen vans lining the streets along Golden Gate Park.

"But to me, they all look alike."

As more Air Force students came to SJS, Dicky, by virtue of his seniority, was appointed liaison officer between the SJS registrar and the Air Force's Institute of Technology who administrated all Air Force graduate programs. This meant he would be responsible to insure his fellow Air Force students had the necessary coursework and resources to finish their respective degrees in the allotted time. With this responsibility came a third-floor office in the AFROTC building, and, with the relative political calm of the SJS campus, a quiet place to study.

A call came to his office late in his last semester of study that made another significant impact on the direction of his career: The call was from Don Seed. Lieutenant Colonel Seed had a rather unique authority within the SCF. In the national chain of command, his was only two layers from the Secretary of the Air Force, but his title wasn't in any way ostentatious: Field Director, Secretary of the Air Force, Special Projects (SAFSP). His small office within the inter sanctum of one of the Satellite Control Facility's complexes, contained four simple desks, each with a two drawer Deibold safe and a single phone. The only thing unique about Don Seed's desk was a red phone connected to a crypto machine locked in an adjacent closet. Three officers under Don's supervision occupied the other desks. Their titles were simply: Project Officer.

"Hi, this is Don Seed" came his greeting, as Dicky answered his phone with the informal identification: "AFIT office."

"Yes sir, what can I do for you?" Dicky replied. He knew Don by his status, nothing more, but he figured the fact he was calling had to be significant.

"I understand you're about to graduate and come back to the SCF," he responded, getting right to the point: "I will be having a vacancy in my office soon and would like you to consider filling it. I think you'll find the work challenging."

He added after a pause: "And the benefits are pretty good."

34   NRO

Five years after your surgery there's bad news: "Your last PSA test came back 1.0 ng/ml," Dr Rand said over the phone. "I think it's time we took some action to correct this progression before it gets any higher. I'll refer you to an oncologist over at the Swedish Tumor Institute."

To Colonel Gorrighan's chagrin, Dicky accepted Don's offer. Dicky heard through the grapevine that a flurry of higher echelon objections were made all the way up to the Secretary of the Air Force—after all, with his newly acquired degree paid for out of another account, Dicky *was* supposed to return to his original organization. But the SecAF prevailed, needlessly sighting their needs as superior.

After joining Don's group, he learned the SecAF Special Projects designation was cover for a covert organization called the National Reconnaissance Office. The NRO was organized in 1960 under executive orders signed by President Eisenhower, its mission to develop and operate satellite reconnaissance systems. The organization, and even the name of the NRO would remain secret for another thirty years.

Dicky's new job was simply defined: Implement national reconnaissance requirements into an enhanced version of Charlotte. Not so simple was the implementation, because Charlotte's new software had to be constantly modified to meet changing requirements. Armed with his knowledge of Charlotte's capabilities and limitations, he teamed with contractor engineers and scientists to develop this software. Because of the intelligence community's insatiable appetite for more and better pictures, he constantly had to strike a balance between this appetite, with Charlotte's hardware and operational capabilities. This balancing act was Dicky's biggest challenge. He argued with intelligence officials on the satellite's limitations, while at the same time cajoling hardware engineers into getting more performance. His task became known as 'squeezing blood from the Charlotte turnip'.

Normal earth orbiting satellites depend wholly on Newton's law of physics to keep them flying in predicted orbits. Charlotte was designed to be one of these normal satellites, but because it could be maneuvered through the use of extra thruster fuel, its altitude and predicted footprint over the earth could be altered. This fact didn't go unnoticed by the intelligence community, and soon they were agitating to move Charlotte's orbit closer to high priority 'targets' at times a normal orbit wouldn't allow.   Closer sometimes meant lower, however, and any orbit below a given altitude had to be closely monitored because of atmospheric friction. Friction tended to degrade orbits, so it became necessary to determine how much friction or atmospheric drag could be expected, hence, a 'drag team' was recruited from the scientific community. This team consisted of atmospheric scientists, climatologists, and experts in solar flare phenomena.

With this team in place, Dicky and his small group of software engineers could now 'fly' the satellite over time critical targets. They in fact, became known as the 'scarf and goggles' crew, similar to Snoopy swooping his Sopworth Camel over the enemy. This capability proved to be extremely important during the height of the Cold War, and although no recognition could be publicly given the team, several members of this pioneering effort were subsequently honored at a White House ceremony.

35   Kern Plateau Golden Trout

Dr Tovler seemed like a nice chap. One had to be pleasant to be an oncologist, you reason. So much death seemed to surround this profession. In medical school there had to be a course in dealing with grief, and if one failed this course, a different specialty was recommended.

Commuting between Dicky's job at the SCF located in Sunnyvale and his headquarters in Los Angeles was a frequent and sometimes boring part of being a NRO project officer. He carried in his wallet an impregnated, miniaturized copy of his travel authority from the SecAF that essentially allowed him to travel anywhere and anytime, expenses to be charged on a Diner's Club card paid out of some special fund he never worried about. Often he traveled with fellow NRO engineers who weren't above clowning around with stewardesses to relieve the boredom.

"Hi, Jack," one might shout to another engineer seated across the cabin as a stewardess entered into her 'fasten seat belts' routine.

This was before it was illegal to speak of hijacking, and often the pilot would join in and jokingly speak of diverting to Cuba en route to LAX.   One such Pacific Southwest Airlines pilot would go into his monolog, complete with Victor Borge accent, to keep the passengers entertained.

But the possibility of being hijacked to Cuba was a real possibility that wasn't ignored by NRO security. Later they implemented a plan to use military airplanes or charter private aircraft between Sunnyvale and LA. A cleared project engineer owned one such aircraft, a twin Cessna, so when he needed to commute, he and his Cessna were called into service to fly extra NRO-cleared passengers. On one of these commutes, Dicky asked him to divert his flight plan to fly over the Kern Plateau. Immediately south of King Canyon National Park, the Kern Plateau was a unique part of the Sierras, home to the prized golden trout, a species Dicky had yet to catch, and he wanted to see first-hand what terrain he might encounter on a hike to their habitat.

From the air, it appeared the Kern Plateau was just that: a plateau with meandering creeks connecting small lakes, before combining into a larger stream that cascaded into the Kern River some three thousand feet below. Entirely without roads, the Kern Plateau beckoned to Dicky, and he immediately made plans to go there.

His assault would be from the small community of Lone Pine on the eastern slope of the Sierras. A climb of some two thousand feet over ten miles, he would require the company of several more hikers with sufficient stamina to make the round trip. Bob LaCroix, another project officer and would-be fly fisher, enthusiastically volunteered. So did Gerry after Dicky sent an information packet to his home on Mercer Island, just east of Seattle.

"Greetings," was his usual phone salutation in response to Dicky's invitation. "After reviewing all the maps, brochures and other stimuli you sent, how could I *not* want to join you on this trek? Should I bring some elk jerky for trail food?"

Dicky recalled that Gerry finally bagged an elk on the old Keller homestead and had made enough jerky to last two years.

"Yeah, bring the jerky, and while you're at it, stop by REI and get some freeze dried stuff," Dicky said.

Recreational Equipment, Inc was a warehouse store in Seattle that carried a large selection of camping and hiking equipment. Founded in 1938, it was structured as a consumer cooperative to purchase high-quality climbing equipment from Europe because such gear could not be purchased locally. It was also one of the few outlets for freeze-dried food and lightweight back packs. Dicky and Gerry made REI a necessary stop whenever he visited Seattle.

"Oh, and be sure to get a couple ice axes," Dicky added.

The trailhead to the Kern Plateau was near the end of Horseshoe Meadow Road some twenty miles southwest of Lone Pine. Already the hikers found themselves at seven thousand feet and out of breath before they got a half-mile from their car.

"My legs feel like there's ice water running down them," Bob said.

Bob LaCroix was not quite in the shape he let on to be, and his sixty-pound pack was heaving from the huge breaths he was taking.

"I think we should stay awhile at this altitude and camp overnight," Dicky said.

He remembered reading somewhere of the dangers of driving from sea level and then striking out before acclimating to the altitude. Some hikers had come down with an illness called pulmonary edema, even died, he learned.

So they broke out their tents and made camp on a windswept rock overlook beneath Wanga Peak, elevation 10,371 on Gerry's topographical map. The bone-numbing cold crept into their down sleeping bags and they slept fitfully in their clothes. The next morning, they had to thaw snow to make coffee, their canteens being frozen.

"I'm still wondering if this is such a good idea," Bob said again.

His breathing was not as labored, however, and agreed the overnight delay was at least a good idea. Bobs parents were French-Canadians who came to Boston after WWII and sacrificed to send him to Northeastern University and then to MIT. His Boston accent, not usually pronounced, came through when he was agitated.

"Looking at the 'topo map, there's not much more of a climb," Gerry said, tossing coffee grounds from his cup and scooping it clean in the snow.

"I think once the sun warms things up a bit, the hiking will be a little easier."

At the time, neither Dicky or Bob associated the ease of a hike with the sun's warmth, but together with Gerry they broke camp and commenced the slow trudge up Little Cottonwood Creek.

At the end of the second day, they finally reached the lakes Dicky saw from the Twin Cessna. They had actually dropped in altitude and now scrub pine and sorghum meadows beside small streams greeted them. They could see trout scurrying under cut banks as they approached, and rings on lakes revealed larger trout feeding on flies yet to be identified. Quickly pack rods were assembled and in a few casts, eager golden trout of about six to eight inches were caught. Four more casts, brought to hand four more fish of the same size.

"It can't get much better than this," Dicky declared as he cut a willow branch for a makeshift stringer. "We might as well make camp over there by those trees."

They stayed at their Cottonwood Lake camp for a week, catching and releasing hundreds of golden trout, frying others for their meals in adequate supplies of butter and bacon grease, having learned from their fledgling experience on George Creek to bring plenty. In all that time they saw not one other human, save for a troupe of girl scouts who hiked by, single file, just as Dicky was taking a bath, au natural, in the crystal clear lake. Meekly he waved at the youthful leader who yelled at her flock to avert their eyes. They all did except for the last scout who used both index fingers in a universally recognized gesture of *shame, shame on you*.

After they broke camp and headed back down Cottonwood Creek to their car, a huge thunderstorm blocked their path. Lightning strikes marched up the ridge toward them, and seeing no visible place for protection, they took cover in a ditch along a forest service road that led to the trailhead.   Huddled under their raingear and fully expecting the next lightning strike to take them out, they were instead shocked when a forest service pickup drove by and drenched them with mud from the rutted road. In the downpour they must have either looked like rocks to the driver, or he was just as anxious to get out of harm's way. They never saw him again and returned to their car thoroughly soaked and muddied from the experience.

36   Trinity River Half-Pounders

After the first week of daily radiation treatments, things become routine: travel to the Tumor Institute by ferry, back home via a drive south through Tacoma and over the Narrows Bridge. Friends volunteer to drive, although for the most part, the effects of radiation aren't debilitating, only tiring to the point where it would sometimes be nice to nap on the way home.

Now Dicky's enthusiasm for fishing was restored. Being diverted from his first love by the intense stimulus of his job at the NRO, he remembered there was more to life than technology. He returned to work more missions of Charlotte, but there was something lacking. An opportunity to develop software for a new NRO satellite restored his interest, however, and he again took up the challenge. He worked with another project officer, Ned Gaylord, to implement algorithms developed by Ned into a complex command and control system. Ned, a brilliant scientist, received his PhD in electrical engineering from Purdue. He had a keen sense of humor, and used it to make his point to contractors who wouldn't listen or would disagree with his technical position.

"Let me ask this question differently," he would say, then restate the question exactly the same way. His technical expertise was unchallengeable, however, making him the ideal officer to oversee this highly technical contract.

Dicky, Ned and several other project officers spent the next year overseeing the development of this software during which time Dicky and Ned enjoyed their mutual technological challenges—and their means of recreation:

fly-fishing and sailing. They shared a sailboat, a Coronado 25 they kept at Marina Del Rey. Their slip was next to Doris Day's, but her boat was so much larger it was difficult to see what was happening on her deck from theirs. On several occasions they sighted other celebrities coming and going: Denver Pyle and Rock Hudson being the most noteworthy, but they could never be sure of the others, and in fact never did see Doris Day. Ned rented a cabin on Henderson Lake in the Sierra foothills where they vacationed with their respective families and hiked into some of the nearby lakes to fly fish for Eastern Brook Trout.

Dicky's continuing pursuit of trout took him to Northern California over one Christmas holiday. His prey, immature steelhead were known to be in the Trinity River that ran by an old historic hotel in the little town of Lewiston. After convincing his family such a vacation would be fun, he contacted the hotel manager and booked two connecting rooms. It was snowing when they arrived. After checking into their rooms, and placing their Christmas presents under a tree in the lobby, they gathered in front of the huge stone fireplace where other guests were singing carols. Someone produced a guitar and Dicky accompanied the group in a couple rounds of *Jingle Bells*, *Deck the Halls* and of course: *Silent Night.* Daughters Candy and CaraMia thought this was the best Christmas ever. Dicky and Carmen had to agree.

Later that evening it stopped snowing and a full moon illuminated the river. Dicky read somewhere that some of the best fly-fishing could be at night, particularly in the moonlight, so he excitedly donned his waders and assembled his fly rod.

The moon was at its zenith and the riffles of the river could be clearly seen as they flowed past the hotel into deeper drifts and glides. He imagined at first he could see trout feeding along the edges. Then he saw and heard a splash that couldn't be mistaken for anything else. A Black McGinty was already tied on his tippet, so he made one false cast and clumsily dropped it near the now disappearing ring of the rise. Immediately there was a large boil and a connection. Unexpectedly, a steelhead was on his line, heavy and angry. Then nothing.

Shaken by what he experienced, Dicky fumbled in his fly box for another McGinty. Finding none, he attempted to tie on a substitute: a Black Gnat, but he couldn't see, even in the bright moonlight. Without a flashlight, he retreated to the porch light of the hotel and secured a stronger tippet before tying on the Gnat, the last black dry fly in his box. Now he returned to the riffle and, more skillfully this time, presented the Gnat. Nothing. Once more, another cast. And another. Finally, a vicious strike produced a fine steelhead of about twenty inches. Called half-pounders by the locals, these immature, or precocious sea-going rainbow trout were the main attraction of flyfishers in Northern California. They populated the Trinity and Klamath Rivers in large numbers and came readily to a fly presented in the right manner.

At night, the right manner wasn't important, however, and Dicky caught and released several before he was totally satisfied. Before turning in, he killed one, a fine two-pounder, and presented it to the hotel desk clerk with instructions on how it should be prepared for breakfast.

37   Technology Versus Trout

During your radiation treatments, sleep didn't come easy at night and conversation with your drivers would sometimes be fragmented—in and out of consciousness, but always philosophical. It was a good time to have so many friends.

Now it was time for Dicky to decide on his future. By virtue of his high profile position at the NRO, he could go on to bigger and better assignments. Two such assignments were available: At the Los Angeles headquarters of the NRO field office, he could continue to work with Ned where improvements in optimization algorithms needed to be implemented. Ned however, would eventually be promoted into an assignment in Europe, so Dicky would essentially fill his position. The other assignment would be at the Pentagon, at NRO headquarters. This job was less defined, but would continue to put him in the limelight of superiors who could, and would promote him above his contemporaries. Rosie, his predecessor at the SCF was a good example. Under Don Seed, he progressed rapidly from the rank of captain, to lieutenant colonel, staying at major less than a year. Then, before his twelfth year out of Annapolis, he was promoted to full colonel. Another full colonel in Rosie's office in Los Angeles was even younger. At age thirty, Bob's youthful appearance and demeanor, sometimes got him into trouble.

Because NRO officers needed to keep a low profile in their travels around the country, they sported the bell-bottoms and leisure suits of their contemporary civilians, wore their hair long, and looked like anything but senior officers in the military. Nicknamed 'The Mod Squad' by some of their detractors in other directorates, they indeed looked the part of the TV personalities of the then popular series. On the way back from a visit to NRO headquarters, Bob stopped at Wright Patterson AFB, Ohio where he had no business, but having those travel anytime, anywhere orders, decided to look up an old girlfriend. While at the officer's club, he was confronted by the base commander who figured him to be an imposter and demanded to see his ID. Obviously he didn't look like a full colonel, much less an officer, so he was detained until his boss, the SecAF, could vouch for him.

So Dicky could either choose one of two assignments offered him, or look for another job. One particularly excited him: It was at the Air Force Plant Representative Office at the Boeing Company in Seattle. Again, he used his *go anywhere-anytime* orders to divert to Seattle on a return trip from the Pentagon, ostensibly to attend a contractor's briefing on a new program. Since the briefing was in the same building as the AF Plant Representative Office, he dropped in to visit the AFPRO commander and asked about possible jobs in Seattle.

Rosie dropped in to visit Dicky after being told of his decision to leave the NRO.

"Where is your patriotism?" he started in, hoping to appeal to Dicky's vanity. "You are a national asset. You have the talent to contribute to the security of this country, and you want to go to...Seattle?"

Somewhere Dicky heard this comment before, so he was prepared.

"There are things other than satellites," he replied. "The only promise I can see in the NRO are maybe a few below-the-zone promotions, a lot of interesting work, and places to live I'm not too keen on. These are the killers. Washington DC? LA? No thanks."

So, three years before his eligibility for retirement, he moved his family to Seattle and went to work at Boeing. Carmen was ecstatic and they purchased a home not far from her family and even closer to where she grew up. Dicky was equally happy as he was once again close to My Trout.

38   Boston and Reel Collecting

The end of radiation treatments came after thirty-five round trips to Seattle. The last trip was made in your sailboat Ruddy Duck. An overnight stay at the Des Moines Marina, dinner at Anthony's and a courtesy ride to the hospital with a friend marked your final day of treatment.

Dicky was assigned to the Seattle detachment of the Airborne Warning and Control System (AWACS) Program Office. Their headquarters was at Hanscom AFB near Boston, and he traveled there frequently to discuss technical matters with his associate in residence, Lt. Col Jim Tomson. Jim was a former pilot who flew fighter-bombers out of DaNang and took a lot of flack from the North Vietnamese gunners. By the grace of God, he was spared being shot down, and rotated back to the states somewhat the less for wear. Except Jim had an attitude. Whether it had been developed as a result of his war experience, or if it was just his New England heritage—it didn't matter. He tended to disagree outwardly with the wrong people, particularly superiors; so when it came time for him to retire, he did.

But he and Dicky developed a friendship, primarily centered about their common love for fly-fishing. AWACS, being a large government program encompassing many diverse contractors, provided jobs for just about anyone who had any connection whatsoever. In Jim's case, he had been influential in Boeing's decision in granting a generous sub-contract to Hughes Aeronautical Systems, so after his retirement, they returned the favor and offered him a management position at their Anaheim plant in California. For Jim, travel to Boeing from Anaheim was frequent enough to fish Northwest waters with regularity, so he bought an Alaskan camper on a pickup truck, a boat, and drove the distance to Seattle whenever he had the chance. He must have had a notion he would soon quit Hughes, however, because within a year he moved his family to Seattle and accepted a similar position with Boeing.

Dicky continued traveling to Boston and for something to do during weekends, took up collecting fly-fishing reels. The hobby had not yet caught on among serious flyfishers, making it possible to find many antique and classic reels in and around Boston. On any Saturday, he could be found traveling into Vermont and New Hampshire, haunting garage and yard sales in the quest of fly reels. His display case soon filled with assorted fly reels: Pfluegers, Vom Hoffes, and Hardys. Later, his collection included bamboo fly rods, particularly when there was an opportunity to use one as a barter item. And there were many opportunities.

A weekend ad in the *Boston Herald* drew Dicky's attention to a large, three story mansion in Lexington, not far from the hotel where he was staying. The ad was for a B.F.Nichols antique fly rod for twenty dollars, and although he didn't know much about B.F. Nichols, he figured somebody did, and twenty dollars seemed like a reasonable price for some trading stock. He knocked on the front door of the mansion and heard a voice from somewhere he couldn't at first determine:

"What da ya want?"

The source of the voice came from somewhere outside the house. Dicky stepped off the porch and responded:

"I came about the fly rod you advertised," he hollered to no one in particular.

Now the direction of the voice came from the roof of the mansion.   The owner was apparently cleaning the gutters, and peered from around one of the giant elms guarding the front porch.

"Look inside the front door," he said.   "It's on the portico table.   If you want it, leave twenty bucks and it's yours."

It was a fine specimen: Sixteen feet long in four pieces with extra tip, rattan wrapped handle and German silver reel seat.   All the guides were in place and it looked almost new.   Dicky placed a twenty dollar bill in its place and yelled back at the owner as he descended the front steps:

"You just made a sale. Thanks a lot."

In the ensuing years, Dicky traded this B.F. Nichols, clearly a collectible antique, for a quite useable classic Winston two-piece rod of 1950's vintage. He fished the Winston on several trips to special lakes and rivers, and later displayed it over the mantle of his fireplace. Much later it garnered a respectable $1,500 on eBay. His extensive reel collection languished in his den display case until they too found new collectors—via eBay.

For Dicky, collecting fly reels, as in fishing, had its rewards. But in fishing, rewards were more related to the pursuit, than in the possession.

39 Vietnam Avoided

"Now we go into another period of watching and waiting", explained Dr. Tovler. "We'll monitor your PSA every three months, and if we managed to radiate the cancer successfully, we should begin to see the levels decrease to zero."

Dicky avoided serving in Vietnam, a fact that sometimes weighed on his conscience. Several of his classmates from Officer Training School went, some didn't come back; but Dicky's security clearances, and their associated duty and travel restrictions gave him an excuse. Now he couldn't go if he wanted to. He even needed permission from Security to visit Canada. Still, he felt guilty.

Work at the AWACS field office at Boeing was interesting, although not nearly as much as when he worked at the NRO. But he was now at Seattle, near My River, and he could go fishing just about any weekend. Gerry also worked in Seattle, at the Army Corp of Engineers, so they resumed going to places they fished many times, many years before.

"Wheredoyawannago?" Gerry said after Dicky called his office on a Friday afternoon. The question, or more accurately the suggestion, was the usual:

"Greetings; let's go fishing."

"I thought you'd never get to the point," Gerry said.

"Let's head north. I'll pick you up at seven tomorrow. I'll furnish the wine and bread, you provide the meat and cheese." Dicky said.

As they met the next morning the first words from Gerry were:

"Pour the wine."

Typically, a bottle or two of homemade elderberry or raspberry wine was intended to supplement a streamside repast of meat, cheese and bread. Before getting underway, sometimes a sample was necessary to make sure it was good.

"Mighty good," Gerry exclaimed after sipping a dash of elderberry poured into a plastic wine glass.

"Yeah, my quality assurance is better than yours," Dicky replied. "That last time out, we had to go through a whole case of yours before we got a good bottle."

"I think my case was pretty consistent," Gerry said. "It's just as we sampled through to the last bottle, they got progressively better."

"Yeah, it's interesting how the quality can vary like that in just one case. Wish we could figure out how to get to the good bottle first."

Dicky steered his pickup across the Mercer Island East Channel Bridge, and they headed north to the Stillaguamish River. That day they would fish for searun cutthroat on the Lower 'Stilly', and maybe pick up a Pink Salmon or two. It was 1973, an odd year, meaning there would be a fall run of Pinks, or Humpies as they were named for the hump they grew after entering fresh water.

The Lower Stillaquamish River entered Puget Sound after it flowed a dozen miles through farmland and salt marshes north of the city of Everett. The Game Department provided several access points below the hamlet of Sylvana and they figured it ought to be easy to wade and hike along the river. At the first access, Dicky parked the pickup and they proceeded to string rods and put on waders. As they sat on the tailgate and focused on their first riffle, it became apparent the going might be difficult: The river was about a foot above normal, and the accompanying silt would make visibility difficult.

"No sense fishin here," Dicky said. "I thought for sure it looked OK when we crossed the bridge up river."

"Just wishful thinking." Gerry replied. "I suppose it'll be better upstream where it's probably clearing up already."

"Let's go up there, maybe above Deer Creek," Dicky said. "The Humpies won't be up there yet, but maybe we could turn over a steelhead in the Fortson hole."

The Stillaguamish River was subject to the foibles of logging operations on its upper reaches. One of its major tributaries, Deer Creek was once home to some of the finest steelhead runs ever, but it was mercilessly logged in the 50's and never recovered. A clay bank, severely eroded after a carelessly built logging road washed out, will likely for decades muddy the water whenever it rains.

As expected, Deer Creek was indeed the culprit. The river above was clear, so they continued on to the general store at WhiteHorse and turned left toward the parking lot serving the trail to the Fortson Hole. Fortson had been a sawmill back in the 30's and left a series of ponds adjacent to the river. The ponds drained into the river, and along with the outlet of a steelhead hatchery farther upstream, formed a sizeable eddy above a long drift where at most times, several steelhead could be seen holding in their respective positions.

As they ducked through scrub alder guarding the trail, it was apparent from footprints in the mud they wouldn't be alone. Indeed, when they broke out onto a long gravel bar, three fishermen were waist-deep, intent on covering an imaginary line of steelhead.   Farther down, a lone angler was casting to a spot under a hanging alder. No one was moving and no fish were apparent, so they decided to drive back to the millpond side and see what they could make out from the high bank directly across from the gravel bar.

The sunlight was just at the right angle, and their Polaroid's revealed no fewer than twenty steelhead lined up along the edge of the drift where the three anglers were casting. They were placing their flies ten or fifteen feet beyond fish that appeared to be almost at their feet.

Why should we tell them of their error? Dicky thought. Occasionally, a well-drifted fly swung close enough to a fish to make it move aside and let it go by. Fascinated, they watched for a long time, finally becoming convinced the steelhead in that drift to be immune to all flies presented.

Downstream, several alders hung over the lower drift, and remembering how he used to watch salmon below Lost Valley Ranch on My River, Dicky scaled one and looked down on four steelhead holding in a drift not more than three or four feet deep.

"I've got an idea," Dicky said after climbing out of the alder. "Why don't you climb up here, and when I go back on the other side, you can tell me where to cast, and how the fish react?

"I've got a better idea…" Gerry answered, but before he could finish, Dicky cut him off saying:

"It's my idea. Besides, you're not too keen on driving my pickup. And I have the keys"

After driving back to the parking lot, Dicky met two anglers returning to their cars, fishless and obviously discouraged. They exchanged the customary: "How'd it go?…Not so good…Too bad…Well, g'luck anyway"; and he continued eagerly to the lower drift where Gerry was now standing on a branch in the alder.

"They're still here," said Gerry, trying to keep his voice to a loud whisper.

Carefully, Dicky waded mid-river and payed out line as he side-armed one, two, then three false casts and dropped his fly under the overhanging brush, some twenty feet above Gerry's perch.

"I can't see your fly," Gerry said. "What did you tie on?"

"A skunk pattern," Dicky replied. "Maybe I should tie on something brighter?"

"That would be a good idea. Otherwise we'll be wasting our time. It's not as light as earlier. I can see the fish, but not your fly. Try something brighter. Like a cutthroat yellow."

Gerry's favorite pattern was the cutthroat yellow. It was a gaudy fly, tied with an abundance of red, yellow and white materials, not intended to imitate anything a trout might eat, but attractive, nonetheless; and for Gerry, quite effective. It was almost the only fly he fished, but with it, he out-fished Dicky, so it was hard to argue with success.

Now the cutthroat yellow drifted along the line of steelhead to where Gerry could clearly see it, and their reaction to it.

"They just move aside and let it drift by," Gerry said. "I don't think it has enough action."

Dicky moved upstream and allowed his line to straighten out so he could swing the fly back and forth in front of the steelhead. Pointing his rod straight downstream, he stripped line in, and then let it out again in hopes of stimulating a strike.

"One picked it up then let it go," Gerry said, his voice elevated. "Now they're darting all over the place."

As he was about to say "Where's my fly," a vicious strike ripped slack line out of Dicky's hand, and before he could react, a bright steelhead took off downstream in a flash of leaps. Line screamed off the Hardy St. John whose retort echoed upstream to the two flyfishers still covering their drifts. A series of runs up and down beneath Gerry's perch, punctuated by leaps of decreasing vigor soon yielded a gasping female of about ten pounds at Dicky's feet.

He reached down and twisted the fly from the corner of her mouth and kneeling to hold her upright, pushed her back into the faster water.

40   Casualty Affairs: A Price Paid

Good news: "Your last PSA test came back 0.2 ng/ml", Dr Tovler said with his usual display of pleasantness.

It's heading in the right direction, and if it continues this way, we should be able to declare you to be in remission."

Words of assurance, to be sure, but…

Working at the AF Field Office at Boeing wasn't all about fishing. There were more serious aspects to being an Air Force Officer during the Vietnam War, even if one didn't go there. With casualties approaching forty thousand, many were Air Force personnel from the Seattle area. Families had to be notified, and who else to do so, but those who, for whatever reason, were 'homebound'. For the folks at the Pentagon, somebody had to do it, and the local guys stationed at Boeing were likely candidates.

Each week, a duty roster was drawn up for casualty affairs, meaning two officers, captain to lieutenant colonel, were on call to don their dress blues and notify a family of the loss of a loved one. Their territory was from Everett to Seattle; meaning chances were good—or bad—that notifications would come up with regularity.

Dicky drew two notifications. The first was for a Staff Sergeant who was killed in a vehicle accident outside Hue. His next of kin was a brother who lived somewhere in Everett, but his address of record was out of date, so a good part of the day was spent in the Snohomish County courthouse tracking him down. He was finally found in a run-down apartment on one of Everett's seedier areas near the waterfront.   Dicky knocked on his door with apprehension. He rehearsed his message of condolence, but expected a grieving relative's reaction to be anything but predictable.

A bleary-eyed and unshaven man in his forties came to the door in his jockey shorts.

"Mister Johanson?" Dicky asked.

Mr. Johanson's first reaction to the two officers dressed in blue outside his door was probably natural for someone who likely had more than one run-in with the police. After a lengthy explanation of their identity, Dicky finally conveyed the bad news.   Unexpectedly, his reaction was not of sorrow for his brother, but of concern as to how soon he might receive survivor benefits.

The next notification some months later, was a real heart-grabber. Again, the casualty wasn't a direct result of combat, but also because of an accident. It seemed this young Airman fell from a hotel balcony in Saigon. Technically, she was a Vietnam casualty because she was waiting for an R&R flight to Honolulu from her assignment in DaNang where she served as a triage medic.

As they approached the ornate front door of the lakefront home, Dicky felt the POW/MIA bracelet on his left wrist as it rested against his wristwatch. A mini-skirted Pacific Southwest Airlines stewardess gave it to him when he was commuting between San Francisco and LA. She said the name carved on it represented one of thousands who were either POWs or MIAs. She didn't know the person whose name was engraved on the simple stainless band, but felt an obligation to distribute them to whoever might wear them in sympathy. Now the weight of the bracelet could be felt as if it were made of lead.

It was Dicky's turn to ring the doorbell, and as soon as the woman saw the two uniforms, she immediately knew the news was bad. Dicky had again rehearsed his delivery, but some of the words stuck in his throat:

"Mrs. Bettencourt, I regret to convey to you the sincere condolences of President Nixon. Your daughter Airman First Class Ann Bettencourt was killed in an accident in Vietnam, and…"

Dicky had steeled himself for the worst, but he barely caught Mrs. Bettencourt as she sank to her knees and screamed in agony.

"I'd rather be toting an M-16 in a rice paddy over in 'Nam, than have to do any more of these," Dicky finally said almost in a whisper as he steered the government sedan back across the Evergreen Point Bridge to Seattle.

Neither of the somber casualty affairs officers said anything else that evening, but when he finally got home, Dicky started with a double scotch and got fairly drunk.

41   Returning to My River

*"I think we're going to have to do something about
this damn incontinence," you complain to Dr Rand
over the phone.*

In his sixties, Uncle Ralph hadn't slowed down a bit
in his enthusiasm for fishing. During the winter steelhead
season, he still drove his Ford regularly and just as fast to
his favorite drifts on the Green, Cedar and Tolt Rivers. He
still deployed his cartop boat to Silver and Cavanaugh
Lakes, where he took limits of Kokanee with his usual
expertise. It was as though in his November years, he was
on a quest to fish as much as he could.

Sometimes Dicky would be his fishing partner, but
trips with him to Dicky's favorite rivers: the Toutle and My
River became infrequent—particularly after Grandma
Richter died. With her gone, Uncle Ralph and Aunt
Emmagene had less reason to visit the Boistfort Valley.
Dicky's attraction for My River diminished also. He brought
his fishing rods when he visited Mom, but most of the time it
was either out of shape due to flooding, or practically dry
from too much irrigation. Consequently, he went to other,
more predictable rivers.

The Green was such a river. Flowing out of the
foothills of Mt. Rainier, a dam isolated the upper river, which
by virtue of it being part of the Tacoma water supply, was
protected from logging. The lower river flowed from the
dam for twenty miles to the flat valley at Auburn where its
former oxbow meanderings were dredged and straightened
by the Army Corps of Engineers until it joined the Black
River at Tukwilla. Then together, they formed the Duwamish
River and flowed into Elliot Bay at Seattle's waterfront.

Above Auburn, the Green came very close to another river, the White, which normally flowed into the Puyallup. The Puyallup, like the Green, also drained into Puget Sound, only at Tacoma's waterfront. But depending on the vagaries of geology and hydrology, the White sometimes flowed not into the Puyallup, but into the Green. Floods from either river, combined with deep and porous gravel left by glaciers, contributed to its diversion, at most times unpredictably. Later, as farmers settled both the Green and Puyallup valleys, they saw the advantage of influencing this diversion, and used dynamite when they saw nature wasn't doing it their way. Of course, the farmers in the opposing valley took umbrage and for the next flooding season, used more dynamite.

So it became an annual event. At the peak of the runoff from Mt. Rainier, usually around the Fourth of July, farmers from both valleys would set off succeeding and larger charges, until finally the Corps of Engineers stepped in and built a dam at Mud Mountain, thereby controlling the White from further flooding. Later, they built a similar dam on the Green, making everybody happy.

There were many drifts along the Green for Dicky to fish after work. His office overlooked an old oxbow of the lower river, giving him a view of whatever species of salmon might be migrating. Whenever salmon were jumping, he found it hard to concentrate on work, so if something important needed to be done, he closed the blinds.

A call from Gerry reminded him of what he might be missing, however. Gerry's office at the Corps of Engineers overlooked the same water some five miles downriver, and he saw the same action.

"Have you looked at the river?" he said. "There are hundreds of silvers jumping. We should check this out."

There were several spots where access was easy. A favorite was upriver from Kent, adjacent to the Auburn Golf Course. Its long drift could be easily covered with roll casts—the high bank made most back-casts difficult—but nonetheless easy access for an hour of fishing after work. They met in the pro shop parking lot and quickly assembled their rods.

"I can't see how these guys can concentrate on golf when there are so many fish out there," Gerry said, pointing to the flurry of jumping salmon on the river.

"I know what you mean," Dicky responded. "Uncle Ralph and I were fishing here for steelhead last winter when it was freezing cold, and they're out here playing like it's the middle of July. Pretty weird, I'd say."

The salmon that evening were fickle. Time and again they followed flies cast and retrieved to within a few feet of the bank, only to turn back and resume jumping, cavorting or whatever ritual they performed preliminary to spawning farther upriver. It was a frustrating evening, but for Dicky and Gerry it was good to be out, away from their respective offices, and it was not considered a waste of time by any stretch.

42   WFFC

"This incontinence is much worse since the radiation treatments, and it's progressed to the point where I'm starting to avoid social situations for fear of embarrassment," you complain to Dr Rand. "Moreover, I'd like to pick up my golf game where I left off eight years ago, but it's impossible to concentrate on my golf swing and my sphincter at the same time."

A Boeing Engineer with whom Dicky worked on the AWACS program was also a fly fisherman. He was avid in this hobby, and he invited Dicky to a meeting of the Washington Fly Fishing Club so he could see what serious fly-fishing was all about. A recent past president of the WFFC, Pete knew nearly all of the hundred-plus members by their first name. By the time introductions were made, Dicky's head was swimming. So many names he had heard of before were members, many Boeing managers, even a vice president, but one name he remembered from his childhood: Roderick Haig-Brown.

To qualify for membership, Dicky had to meet certain criteria: Two members in good standing had to be sponsors, he needed to attend at least two regular meetings, and he had to participate in one club outing or work party. Needing the kindred fellowship of flyfishers in his life, he wanted very much to be part of such an august membership. For the next nine months Dicky went to each meeting, club outing and work party.

One work party was at Lenice Lake in Eastern Washington where a general cleanup of the shoreline was organized. Lenice was one of a series of lakes formed by water seeping through the porous basalt formations below Grand Coulee Dam. Trout introduced to these lakes grew unusually fast and large, giving the club impetus to help the Game Department in their management.

Dicky was told to rendezvous with Pat, his other sponsor, at the trailhead to Lenice on the morning of the work party. Pat was another Boeing manager who also took his fly-fishing seriously. Managing a fishing camp during the summer in British Columbia, and wintering in Mexico where he fished the Sea of Cortez, Dicky wondered how he was able to convince Boeing to give him so much time off to go fishing.

By the time he fought the Friday night rush hour out of Seattle and drove to the trailhead to Lenice, it was dark and he was tired. The pickup headlights illuminated a Game Department sign designating the parking lot, and seeing no other vehicles, he parked in an obscure area. Without exploring further, he entered his pickup camper shell, crawled into his sleeping bag and was soon asleep.

Sometime later, one of the last electrically driven trains of the Milwaukee Line sped through the night on its way from Spokane to Seattle. As it silently approached the crossing to the Lenice Lake trailhead, Dicky had just entered into a deep sleep and could only subconsciously sense its arrival. Now, only a few hundred feet from the crossing, it emitted a screaming wail, immediately bringing him upright, only to smash his head into one of the camper shell supports, and returning him to an even deeper slumber.

Early next morning he awoke from his interrupted sleep with a splitting headache. Now, the parking lot was filled with assorted RVs and cars owned by WFFC members. Someone had set up a camp kitchen and already made coffee. The smell of frying bacon reminded Dicky he hadn't eaten since lunch the day before.

"That's a hellova bump on your forehead," said Pat before he started making introductions.   "Are you sure you're going to want to be bending over to pick up garbage all day?"

"I'll be OK as soon as I have a cup of that coffee and some breakfast," Dicky said.

43   New Perspectives

"I'd like to think this is the last time you'll see me here on your operating table," you say to Dr Rand just before the anesthesia took over your consciousness.

You don't hear a response. How wonderful these new drugs, you think, as you quickly drift into la la land.

Dicky was sworn into the WFFC at its November 1974 general meeting. Only two members per month could be so inducted, so he felt privileged to be included in such an exclusive group who readily shared their knowledge of this challenging and historical sport. Founded in 1939, it was then the only fishing club in a state where fly-fishing was looked upon more with curiosity than respect. Although versed in fly-fishing from articles read in magazines, and from his long experience of fishing with fly-fishing tackle, he found there were infinitely more things to learn. He listened with rapt attention to presentations given by guest speakers, attended seminars on fly tying, entomology and casting, and became thoroughly engrossed in every aspect of fly-fishing.

The WFFC and fly-fishing became Dicky's new obsession. Thoughts of what he could have achieved, had he remained in the NRO, soon disappeared.

Still, he had one more opportunity to rejoin the NRO. Nine months before reaching his twenty years toward retirement, orders came down giving him a choice: transfer to NRO headquarters in Washington DC, accept a promotion and a commission in the regular component of the Air Force, or retire. Up to that point, he had turned down repeated offers of a regular commission, and now he was happy he did. As a 'regular' officer he would not have had this choice, but in his reserve status he could retire. He gave notice to do so upon his twenty years of service.

At age 38, retirement would give Dicky the means and freedom to pursue his love. At a November meeting of the WFFC, a guest speaker, Dave Whitlock, gave a presentation on fly tying that inspired the following letter:

"Dear Dave: I came away from your presentation last night envious at what you do for a living: tie flies, write articles and give presentations on fly-fishing. Can you give me any advice on what I could or should do to get started in this business? I know this is a rather limited sport, but here in the Pacific Northwest, I think it has potential and if I'm any indication, there's plenty interest..."

Dave wrote back:

"Dear Dick: Thanks for the compliment. I enjoyed presenting my program to the WFFC and I just love Seattle! Regarding your questions: you can scratch out a living tying flies, but to be successful, you need to concentrate on a unique aspect of fly tying and expound on that. Being from Arkansas, I started by tying variations of bass and crappie flies and wrote on their use in various fishing magazines. Once you become known through lectures and writing, you can branch out to other aspects depending on your audience and readers. All it takes is a lot of dedication and hard work."

Inspired, Dicky started tying in earnest. He sent samples of his best ties to Dave, who sent back comments and suggestions. Soon, he could whip out a dozen pretty good *Doc Spratley* patterns in an hour. Now he entered into an aspect of this new business where he had absolutely no experience: marketing.

On a fishing trip to British Columbia, he stopped at a fishing shop just north of the border to get his fishing license and like flyfishers are prone to do, perused the selection of flies for sale.

"I notice you're running out of Doc Spratleys," Dicky said.

Without looking up from his task of filling out the license application, the shop owner replied:

"That's the most popular pattern up here this time of the year. That, and the Carey Special patterns."

Trying not to appear eager, Dicky clumsily made his presentation:

"I can have a couple hundred of these for you in a couple days. What do you pay wholesale?"

Now the owner looked up quizzically at Dicky and chewed thoughtfully on his unlit pipe.

"You tie?" he asked.

Instead of fishing the next three days as intended, Dicky spread out his portable kit on a nearby campsite picnic table and started tying. He learned to pre-cut his materials and package them by size, greatly increasing production. On the second day, he had completed one hundred fifty, but the wind started cutting into his efficiency, and his eyes were starting to cross from fatigue. Finally he assembled his promised two hundred by going into his own fly box for the last twenty and returned to the shop. The owner looked at his offerings, rejected several, and said:

"I'll give you thirty-five cents each or you can have something of equal value in trade."

Dicky looked with renewed interest at a display case containing reels and other goodies. He fondled a couple Hardy reels, a brand not available in the States, finally settling on a Princess model. A fly line with backing evened out the trade. *Perhaps not much to account for two days work*, he postulated, but considering he got something of higher intrinsic value than thirty-five cents a fly, he came away satisfied.

But fly tying for a living just wasn't his forte. *Not enough return for the work involved* he decided, and besides, he didn't want to confuse work with his pleasure. He would need to find some other way to earn a living—and to fish.

44   A Bunch of Good Guys

The installation of the artificial sphincter took one hour longer than expected.

"Much of the scar tissue left by the original prostatectomy and the radiation treatments had to be dealt with", explained Dr. Rand some time later. "After you've healed in about two months, come back and we'll activate the device. You should be back playing golf again."

Members of the WFFC were an eclectic group. Common only in their interest and love of the sport, they represented a cross section of professions and crafts that came together once a month to talk not about work, but fly-fishing. There were carpenters, engineers, physicians, electricians, and lawyers, even a retired United States ambassador. There were a few who made their living in businesses relating to fly-fishing, but most didn't hawk their wares at club meetings, lest they incur a fine from the club Ghille whose role as Sergeant at Arms was to keep decorum and order. Most members donated their time freely when it came to the common benefit of the sport and everyone came away being a better practitioner.

This was not to say there weren't a few rotten apples. A few slipped through the member screening process and used the club for their own personal gain. Jack 'The Hat' was such an individual. The club had a dress code which required the wearing of coat and tie during its dinner meetings. Either Jack's sponsors didn't get the word to him before sending him on to the membership committee, or he snowed everyone through the entire interview process. Not only didn't he wear a tie, much less a jacket; he wore an old slouch hat to all meetings. Some who saw him fishing said he apparently never took it off.   For profit, Jack collected old fishing reels and advertised the fact whenever he had the opportunity. He would badger members known to have their own collection into bringing reels to meetings for his inspection, then try to lowball a purchase. The most egregious of his antics came when one of the club's most senior and respected members died and left a large collection of classic rods and reels to the club's foundation. Before designated club members could visit his widow to assess the collection, Jack called on her unannounced, and made a ridiculously low offer for the whole lot, saying he was there on behalf of the club.   She, of course, saw through his ruse, but to the club's board of directors, this was the last straw. He was unceremoniously uninvited to further meetings and asked to turn in his club decals and patches.

Some said Jack had been blackballed, but those who knew the history of the club wouldn't have used that term.

Early in the club's years, candidates for membership were voted on by the means of a wooden ballot box passed around. Each member in good standing was given two marbles, one white and one black. If, after all votes were cast, one black marble appeared in the box, the candidate was refused membership—"blackballed." That process was used until the mid sixties when the first candidate of African heritage was brought up for membership. Not only did the process change; but also that candidate, in just five years, became one of the club's most progressive presidents.

But to the WFFC membership, progress had its limitations. The club's charter stated unambiguously that members were restricted to males over the age of twenty-one. This was not to say, wives or girlfriends had to be excluded from all activities, only from dinner or party functions where their attendance might be deemed inappropriate. After all, off-color jokes were agreed to be the domain of males when the club's charter was drafted, and meetings, particularly those whose 'wet fly' events meant bellying up to the bar before dinner, needed to be left uninhibited. Several times, the subject of women associate membership was broached at board meetings, but only once was it passed on to the general membership for a vote. The board knew this might be a contentious issue, and it was. Passionate speeches were given, pro and con, but when the final vote was tallied, the club would remain male only. More than a few good members resigned in protest, however, and never again did the subject get past the board of directors.

45   Some Good Places to Fish

*Your six-month visits to Dr. Rand become routine.
He now has a machine from which the PSA
analysis can be done the same day. Your
anxieties are lessened as the readings continue to
be less than 0.1ng/ml.*

It had been many years since Dicky had been to
British Columbia to fish. That trip in the spring of 1950 with
Cousin Gary to an interior lake, its name long forgotten, was
his last recollection, but it had been a fond memory. Being
away from the Northwest for the last seventeen years didn't
allow opportunities to fish much in his familiar waters of
Western Washington, so he spent his first few years after
moving back to Seattle just catching up.

It was at a 1973 Christmas party meeting of the
Washington Fly Fishing Club that Dicky first heard of
HiHium Lake. His co-sponsor, Pat owned a fish camp and
ranch in British Columbia by the name of Circle W. To
promote his business, he donated three days of fishing and
lodging to the club. To Dicky's delight, the first thing he won
from his first WFFC Christmas raffle was Pat's donation.

In those days, real estate in Canada was relatively
cheap and could be owned by U.S. citizens. Pat, a
resourceful Boeing manager, purchased Circle W in 1954
from Bob Walters who had developed it from the original
land grant holdings. These holdings, by Canadian standards
were fairly modest, but they included leaseholds on HiHium
Lake on which log cabins were built and leased back from
the Province for $1 per year. In the first years, from about
1925 to 1930, these cabins, four in all, were nothing but log
walls with tent roofs, mainly for the use of elk hunters who

packed in on horseback from the Circle W Ranch on Deadman Creek some twenty miles distant and three thousand feet below. As the popularity of these cabins increased and the phenomenal fishing became more publicized, five more cabins were built and saddle horses were transporting guests and their gear up a steep and arduous trail to the lake.

Through the 1930's and in the depth of the depression, only the wealthy could afford the long train trip up the Fraser River from Vancouver and hire motor transportation from Ashcroft to Circle W. But there were such people, and HiHium and other remote lakes like it became the vacation spots of the rich and famous.

The Hollywood crowd soon discovered HiHium and as the primitive road into the lake from Circle W became more traveled, authentic street signs nailed to trees along the rutted road appeared, like: *Hollywood*, *Vine* and *Wilshire Blvd*. Guests from the LA area occupied several Circle W cabins at the same time every year, making for some notorious parties.

It was rumored that Clark Gable and Carol Lombard spent a few days of their honeymoon in one of the Circle W cabins. There was 'clear evidence' of their staying at the Eagle Point cabin. For example, the initials "C G + C L '40 was rumored to have been carved into one of the logs of the original cabin, but removed by souvenir hunters many years later. If one knew where to look, the spot could still be seen where a six by ten-inch piece of the log was split off to secure the initials in one piece.

Dicky's first stay, his raffle winnings, was for three nights at Home Cabin. It was neither the best of the nine cabins of Circle W, nor was it the best time of the season for fishing. Home Cabin was located at the near end of the lake next to the boathouse and caretaker's cabin, so there was a lot of activity. Its doorway was exactly five feet ten inches high, and at five ten and one-half, it was hit and miss for Dicky, depending on his stride. At the end of three days his baldhead looked like a sack of walnuts.

The lake at the near end was shallow and weedy, so to fish, one had to motor out a quarter mile to the end of the weeds. Early in the season, the weather was often wet, cold, stormy, and blustery, as was the case for Dicky's first stay.

In spite of the negatives, those three short days in 1974 were wonderful. Pat's marketing ploy paid off because Dicky returned every year thereafter.

Fishing at HiHium was better in the early years, but the consistency of everything else kept bringing him back. The BC Government placed a ban on any new waterfront construction and prohibited logging within sight of the lake, so from year to year, nothing visually changed—nothing except for the numbers of people. As the road-accessible lakes around Merritt and Kamloops became increasingly inhabited, people would endure bad roads to get to fishing otherwise lost to urbanization. Condos on previously remote lakes such as Peterhope and Hatheume turned people to even more remote places.

As with all things, change happens, and with HiHium, it was the fishing. In a valiant attempt to maintain quality fishing to more fishers, BC Wildlife changed the limits and the means of fishing, but still more fishers came. And with more, the roads became easier. Fish camp owners attempted to keep the roads they controlled as bad as possible, but the logging companies worked at cross-purposes by making their roads better and finally it became possible to drive to within a mile of HiHium on quality roads, needing only to endure a mile of ruts and mud to get to what was once a very distant destination. Even HiHium succumbed to the encroachment of civilization.

46   Eagle Point

Your oncologist leaves a voice mail to call his office. Not hearing from him, and thinking there was no further need to do so, you wonder....

Of all the cabins on HiHium, the one at Eagle Point was special to Dicky: One of four original cabins, it was sited on top of a promontory on the end of a long peninsula in the shape of a long fishhook. It commanded a view of the entire lake, and was accessible from either of two docks that were placed on opposite sides of the hook's bend. It was a two-room arrangement whose kitchen was the original log structure. As in the other eight Circle W cabins, its walls were a combination of log and lap boards that supported a simple shed roof covered with rust-colored tarpaper. In 1987, a third room was added that opened views through floor to ceiling corner windows, so that even in dark and rainy days, one could sit in relative warmth by the woodstove and view the bay in back of the cabin. Over the years of returning to this view, Dicky named this bay Eagle Cove. Appropriately, and sometime later, a pair of bald eagles built a nest on a great broken-top fir overlooking the cove.

So returning to Eagle Point was always the year's high point. A fishing report written for the Washington Fly Fishing Club's *Creel Notes* encapsulated Dicky's feelings about this special place:

"I guess what keeps bringing us back to HiHium each year is its consistency. The hospitality of the owners, the Benzaks, the rustic isolation—always anticipated, always received. The only thing that seems to be unpredictable is the weather, and this year it was great.

Cool, crisp nights and warm, clear days. The aspen trees were bright golden and the sunsets/sunrises spectacular. The fishing? Slower and more challenging than in July, but there's no doubt the lake's Kamloops trout were still plentiful. If we wanted to bear down and seriously fish instead of photographing autumn colors or gathering mushrooms, we were good for about a fish an hour from twelve to twenty inches. Every one mint bright and combative, feeding mainly on freshwater shrimp and leeches, making for luscious smoking.

This was a wonderful trip, but the last evening was particularly memorable:

The lake was calm as glass, and to the west the last vestige of sunset left reflections of reds and pinks on a shimmering stripe from boat to distant shore. To the east, the sky and lake met in a confluence of indigo. The brightest of stars had already made their appearance.

The fish suddenly were surfacing for small cinnamon sedges that were emerging near the rocky shoals. A single rod was available for such an occasion—a number six, eight-foot cane instrument built by Peter McVey, owner and chef extraordinaire of Corbett Lake Lodge, but strung not with a floating, but rather an intermediate line. Not enough time to change, so a liberal coating of floatant was applied. A four pound tippet and number twelve elk hair caddis quickly replaced the size six Doc Spratley found to be most productive during the afternoon.

The twilight reflection had now narrowed to a few degrees, making it necessary to maneuver the boat to see the rises. Only enough light remaining for a few more casts. Fish seemed very active now. A long cast to cover a large fish working in the shallows. A take!

Strike! Missed! Cast again—another take! Nothing! Refusal? Getting too dark to tell. Keep trying. Finally, a large boil and heavy connection—for two seconds. Broke it off!! Damn—!

Although I probably could have tied on more tippets and continue to fish by flashlight, I didn't. It seemed fitting to end this trip with the memory of that beautiful twilight and the rush of adrenaline brought on by that last strike. I returned to Eagle Point feeling satisfied and very much at peace."

47   Al

"I was just following up on your condition," said Dr Tovler, "I didn't mean for you to worry, but I just like to have my 'survivors' visit on occasion so I can see how you're doing"

You schedule a visit the next time you're in Seattle, grateful after seven years, to be on his list of 'survivors'

One of Dicky's favorite people was a member of the WFFC who, next to the charter president Enos Bradner, was one of the most recognized and a favorite of all who had the pleasure of knowing him. Where Enos was considered the father and founder of the club, Alan Pratt was probably the club's character and soul. During Al's forty years of membership, he never held office, probably turned down offers to be president several times, but probably did more to define the WFFC than any other member. And nowhere was it more evident than in the club's logo: It was the unmistakable artwork of the same Alan Pratt who for years was the senior cartoonist for the *Seattle Times*. Anything and everything the club published contained something he donated from his pallet of skill and humor, with emphasis on the humor.

Dicky first heard, or rather, read of Al from a treasured copy of *The Wretched Mess News* he acquired while still working at the Satellite Control Facility in California. Al had teamed with another humorist by the pseudonym of Milford Poltroon to write a tongue-in-cheek, and in their words: "A yellow-journalistic rag on fly-fishing in and around West Yellowstone Montana—wherever that is." The *WMN* caught on big in San Francisco, and Dicky phoned in a request for a subscription when he heard about it on an AM radio broadcast of the *Cal Dunbar Show*. From Al's self-description as *WMN's* "Litter and Pollution Editor," Dicky knew he had to meet Al, and at his first introductory dinner meeting at the WFFC, he sought him out and shook his hand.

"I thought your picture of the entrance of the Corps of Engineers Seattle Office was priceless," Dicky said after they established their conversation around the *Wretched Mess News*.

Dicky's reference was to a hand-railed set of stairs that abruptly faced a door-less cinder block wall.

"Oh yes," Al replied with a grin. "And do you know the Corps has a blown-up copy of it in the District Commander's office? They're one of our biggest subscribers."

Years later, Al called Dicky late one evening at his Normandy Park residence in Seattle's south suburbs. Another of Al's many contributions to the club was his almost permanent chairmanship of the nominating committee for club officers. Each November, a committee was elected to name a slate of candidates to run the club for the next year, and Al was calling to ask Dicky a question:

"We were wondering if you would be available to head up the club as president next year," he asked

Dicky, of course, was honored and said so as he accepted the nomination, which, by tradition was tantamount to being elected. To formalize the process, however, Al proceeded to draw life-sized caricatures of each nominee on butcher paper, unroll them ceremoniously and scotch-tape them to the wall before the assembled membership at the November dinner meeting. Dicky's likeness, complete with king's robe, crown and scepter was unrolled last to a faux drum roll provided by Bill Rundall, the outgoing, and soon-to-be-past-president. Dicky had been Bill's treasurer that year and apparently did a sufficiently good job to be elevated past the next logical office of vice-president. During his tenure, Bill and Dicky engaged in a running joke about absconding with the club's funds and disappearing to Mexico to fish with Pat. With Al and Bill, Dicky experienced some of his more enjoyable fishing trips.

48   Clever Ideas

After not seeing your oncologist for over seven years, you are relieved he's not worn down from having so many ex-patients no longer on his list of 'survivors'. You conclude that this breed of professionals is indeed very special.

Al's artistic creativity extended to his fishing implements as well. Starting with his boat, a twelve-foot jon boat with freeboard of questionable margin for his nine horsepower outboard, he adorned its sides with a parade of trout caricatures, each with mouth agape in pursuit of the next fish. Not stopping there, the periphery of his lime-green Chevrolet van also sported the same parade of fish. He outfitted its inside with the rudiments of camping: stove, ice box, porta-potti, and bed. On the hood, a plaque replaced the Chevy emblem, naming the vehicle simply as: Fishwagon. As a final touch, on the back door he mounted a carved fish with a moose-horn protruding from his head. A plaque beneath proclaimed its taxonomy: Carpoose.

On any given Friday afternoon, Dicky might meet Al in the Seattle Times parking lot where they would depart for a weekend of fishing. On the Olympic Peninsula, Dabob Bay was their favorite destination for searun cutthroat. There, they made friends with an octogenarian widow who owned waterfront acreage on a small, oyster-laden estuary. Audrey, in her run-down two-story home, resembled a character out of central casting of the *Egg and I*. Pet chickens roamed her kitchen, and narrow pathways among decades of accumulated possessions allowed the only movement between rooms. A cluttered front porch of her home faced a horse pasture bordering the water where she invited them to camp whenever they came to visit. After they fished for the day, she delighted in joining them in campfire conversation punctuated with a tip or two of Jack Daniels. For protection, she kept a large Great Dane, Duke, whose only danger to visitors was its huge appetite. After their first visit, in which Dicky's camper was invaded by Duke who made off with a loaf of bread, fortunately the only food left in the open, they subsequently brought a fifty pound bag of dog food to keep Duke well fed and otherwise occupied during their stay.

They experienced some of their best cutthroat fishing in front of Audrey's place. Sometimes a bonus steelhead might be caught, and in the Fall when the big leaf maple trees bordering the shoreline turned bright yellow, silver salmon appeared, sometimes in great numbers. Whenever the silvers came, fishing took on a new dimension: Heftier rods strung, bigger flies attached to stronger leaders and casts longer and more repetitive. Some days only a few fish might be caught, their bite quite unpredictable; yet when they were there, Al and Dicky kept casting in hopes things would change. Maybe the tide flow was important, or the weather, but sometimes their fortunes would improve and every other cast might yield a strike from a salmon ranging from five to twelve pounds. These were times to which they looked forward, but even fishless outings, were memorable.

A trip to the Lower Stillaguamish River was such an outing. It was to be a day trip for searun cutthroat. Dicky met Al at his place in Woodinville on a fall Saturday morning where they stacked their boats on the Fishwagon.

"This year there ought to be a pretty good run of humpies," Al said as he steered onto the northbound lane of State Route 9. "We can launch at the Florence Bridge and drift with the incoming tide—half way to Sylvana if we're lucky. By the time the tide peaks we can motor back to the launch, re-load our boats and get home before dark."

"Sounds like a good plan," Dicky said, trying to remember when any fishing trip went exactly as planned.

They launched their boats, and indeed the incoming tide took them far upriver. Fishing was slow, and by the time long shadows were forming from the west, they had caught and released only a few ten-inch cutthroat for their efforts. Al had drifted in his boat farther upriver, so he started his outboard and headed downriver toward Dicky who was ready to call it a day.

"I'm going to try it below the launch before I quit," Al hollered as he motored downriver past Dicky. Before he reached the first bend, he opened the throttle on the Mercury and sped downriver, but just a few minutes later the sound of his motor suddenly increased, then—nothing.

To Dicky, this sound, and sudden lack thereof, was ominous. Quickly, he started his own outboard and raced downriver. Rounding the bend where he thought the sound stopped, he came upon a scene of flotsam: first a covered diaper pail which Al prudently used to pack cameras and other valuables was bobbing down the river, then a half-full bottle of Jack Daniels, a down jacket, an oar and barely recognizable, the bow of Al's jon boat. The rest of the boat was submerged, upside down, motor holding it in place. Seeing this apparent scene of a serious accident, Dicky became fearful for Al.

Just as he was about to dive in search of his friend who might be drowning, unconscious, or both, he happened to glance to a spot on the far shore where a dark figure was huddled half way up the bank and under some overhanging alders.

"Are you alright?" Dicky yelled as he steered his skiff toward Al who was wet and shivering, knees pulled up to his chest. Dicky removed his own down jacket and pulled it over Al's shoulders.

"I...I must have run up on that log," he said, pointing upstream at a partially submerged snag that protruded downstream and upward at a shallow angle. "The last thing I remember is rounding the corner at a pretty good clip, then I was under water, looking up at the inside of my boat."

Dicky retrieved the bottle of Jack Daniels that had floated ashore and gave it to Al who promptly took a long swig. Then, together they pulled the jon boat ashore, dumped the water out and chased down the remaining floating debris. Taking a quick inventory of his equipment, Al figured he lost a Hardy reel and his landing net. The motor was clearly drowned, so they towed his boat behind Dicky's skiff and arrived at the boat launch just as the sun was setting.

They were both silent, reflecting inwardly at what could have been. After Al changed into dry clothes, they loaded his boat on the Fishwagon. Then, struggling with Dicky's skiff, tried to remember why it was easier to load when they left Al's place earlier in the day. Finally, after tying it down and loading motors, rods and other stuff, they sat in the Fishwagon, finished off the rest of Jack and snacked on pepperoni, cheese and taco chips. In no shape to drive, they went to sleep, Al on his bed and Dicky on the floor, legs curled around motors and equipment hastily thrown in.

Al was first to wake, at around midnight.

"I think I'm going to be sick," he said, as he stepped over Dicky and rolled open the van door.

Maybe Dicky was already awake. A spitting headache prompted a search for aspirin and a Pepsi, and

Dicky couldn't remember if he went back to sleep or not. But alerted by Al's prompt exit, he wondered if Al's malady was caused by a good portion of the liter of Jack, or by the trauma of the Stilly.

They sat in the Fishwagon for another hour and drank coffee, finally deciding to drive to Al's place where they would transfer Dicky's boat to his camper and then reevaluate whether he should continue home in his still diminished condition. Al figured he could drive OK, but as he steered the Fishwagon toward Sylvana and the freeway beyond, he failed to negotiate the first right-angle turn and drove straight into a cornfield. As they sat there, twenty rows deep, Dicky suggested that he ought to drive.

49   Goofus

Dr Tovler looks at your chart and notes the last PSA reading taken by Dr Rand six months ago. "While you're here, we might just as well have our lab take some of your blood, so we can calibrate Dr. Rand's readings," he says.

Episodes such as those on the Stilly prompted Al to create awards for members who screwed up in memorable ways. Presented at the club's Christmas party, he would embellish their stories, relish their humor, but always stop short of embarrassing the recipient. Made of materials from his basement clutter, he made use of his talent for the comical to devise some of the most Rube-Goldbergish awards, complete with dedication plaque and hook for hanging. Receiving members usually faked embarrassment, but considered these awards as badges of honor and displayed them proudly in dens or studies. They were after all, Al Pratt originals, called "Goofus" Awards.

Dicky had several such awards. One was presented for fishing too close to a Washington State Ferry, causing his fly line to twist irreparably in the wake of its prop. Another presentation, called the Grand Combined Chopaka and Chinese Boat Drill Award, required a two-paragraph explanation.

Chopaka Lake was venue to most Goofus Awards, mainly because more members gathered there, but also because the environment: wind, rain and sometimes-severe fishing conditions tested their skills, or lack thereof. One award was for stepping through the bottom of a member's boat, another for forgetting to bring rods but not their cases, and yet another for driving off without first pulling up camper jacks. All these screw-ups were documented in Al's offbeat way of entertainment, and except for a few recipients, everyone agreed his Goofus Awards were the best part of the annual WFFC Christmas Party. One recipient decided he would get even with Al.   Bill Karban, one of Seattle's Finest, faked giving Al a special award. It was supposedly in a large metal garbage can, and before anyone knew what was going on, Al was handcuffed to the empty can and had to deliver the rest of his presentations so handicapped. Bill claimed the key was lost until late in the evening when it curiously appeared in Al's hip pocket.

These hi-jinks were common at most of the earlier Christmas parties. One club member, Howard Grey, was a producer of outdoor related films and, with the club's charter president Enos Bradner as principal actor, produced a film entitled *The Nymph of the Stilly*. The plot was simple: 'Brad, who was a bachelor all of his life, encountered the Nymph while fishing his favorite drift on the Stillaguamish River. The Nymph, played by a stripper from one of Seattle's topless clubs on First Avenue, wore only a pair of hip boots and miniscule panties. The footage could well have been a trailer for the *Benny Hill* series, but it ended with Brad's camper rocking merrily as the scene faded to the credits.

Reruns of The Nymph of the Stilly were played for years, usually at Christmas parties, and on some occasions, a live nymph was again recruited, wearing only her hip boots and G-string. A wicker creel bounced on her hip from which she dispensed party favors as she pranced among the appreciative members. Sadly, the film was lost, or perhaps destroyed by a disgruntled wife of whoever was charged with its safeguard. It might still be out there in someone's attic though, and once a year a reminder is put in the club's newsletter for members to take another look.

50   WETBUNS

More good news: "Your PSA is zero point zero",
Dr Tovler exclaims with a smile. You are grateful
for this news, of course, but worry about the
effects of radiation spillover. You discuss this, and
he suggests a colonoscopy.

From his early childhood on Richter Hill, the cutthroat
was Dicky's favorite trout. Before joining the WFFC, he
fished for searun cutthroat in the Toutle River with Uncle
Ralph who called them Harvest Trout. He and Gerry fished
tidewater tributaries to Willapa Bay and caught bright
cutthroat still with sea lice, but there they called them
Bluebacks. He knew they were one and the same. After his
introduction into the WFFC, he soon learned they could be
caught in saltwater, not necessarily in the large and
daunting open sea, but along shorelines of sounds and bays
and in the mouths of rivers and creeks—estuaries. The
club, in fact, was actively participating with the Washington
Department of Fish and Wildlife to study, propagate and
protect them. Members, Dick Thompson and Ed Foss were
instrumental in setting up work parties with the Department,
and it was on one of these activities Dicky learned how
important these fish were to the club.

"Could you help us move some nets tomorrow?" Ed
asked.

The year after Dicky came into the club, Ed was
WFFC president and wielded his authority to get some of
his favorite projects completed. Calling from his Union
Carbide office in Tacoma on a Friday afternoon, he was
hastily setting up a work party.

"The folks over at Domsea Farms have some spare net pens for us if we can move them tomorrow. They'll be great rearing pens for the searun brood stock we caught at Belfair and Dabob, and all we need to do is move them to the National Marine Fisheries Lab across Rich Passage," he said. "It'll be hard, dirty work, so bring your waders and gloves."

For a little added incentive he added:

"Maybe if we get finished early, we can do a little fishing for searuns, so bring your fly rod."

Domsea Farms was a commercial salmon enterprise located off the south shore of Bainbridge Island. It was a subsidiary of Ed's company and was partially owned by heirs of Charles Lindberg. Dicky remembered seeing their net pens from the Seattle-Bremerton ferry, and as Ed spoke, he started to make the connection. Ed continued:

"We'll meet at 9:30 at the Fisheries Labs in Manchester. Thompson sometimes works there and he's arranged for a tug and barge to haul the nets."

Dick Thompson's borrowed tug looked like a working model of the much larger Foss tugs that plied the waterways of Puget Sound. There was only room for Thompson in its small wheelhouse, and, coupled to its much larger barge, it was apparent the journey across Rich Passage might take some time. Dicky was the only one who brought a rod that day, and he wondered if Ed was just optimistic about having time to fish afterward. Not to forego a chance to fish however, he took his rod on the barge and payed out line as it slowly made way to the other side.

Halfway across, Dicky had payed out several hundred feet of line and backing in order to troll at a depth where Thompson assured there would be a salmon.

"What kind of sinking line are you using?" Thompson yelled over the increasing single-cylinder din of the tug. Laboring against the incoming tide, they were making little headway so he increased the tug's RPMs.

As the Seattle-bound ferry rounded Point Glover and picked up speed, it must have been a curious sight for its passengers and crew: Directly in their path was a miniature tug connected to a barge loaded with a dozen passengers wearing waders. One of them had a fishing rod on which he was frantically reeling.

This was Dicky's first labor of love for the searun cutthroat. With work parties such as these, he could now do something to help My Trout, and over the years, he became as involved as his job at Boeing would allow. First he helped in Game Department projects to collect creel census information: querying fishers as to numbers, sizes and hours fished. Then he fished for and tagged fish to be released and perhaps caught again by fishers who would report where and when they were caught. He participated in fin clipping parties at hatcheries where a specific fin was removed from small fingerlings to identify their stream of origin. It was difficult work grasping the small and slippery smolts that were first immersed in something to calm them. There would be fifty thousand or more fish to clip, and at best, one worker could clip maybe a thousand before his eyes started crossing and he had to quit for the day. Ed Foss was such a clipper, but being left handed, it wasn't until the second day someone discovered his error. This, of course warranted a brilliantly illustrated Goofus Award entitled: *How to tell your right pectoral from your left.*

But work parties were also gatherings of kindred spirits who, after bestowing their efforts, liked to gather afterwards, either at favorite watering holes or at a special outing. One favorite watering hole was Harold's Tavern. It was located on the North shore of Hood Canal and because of its proximity to the searun cutthroat's habitat, became a logical place to stop for a hamburger and beer after a long day of collecting brood stock or tagging fish. Less than a mile away, Belfair State Park became a convenient place to camp, which many did instead of driving to Seattle and back the next day. As these fish-outs became more organized, so did the camp-outs, and soon assignments were made: bring and pitch the club awning, provide wood for the bonfire, bring food, and most important: cook.

Dicky volunteered to cook. He didn't pride himself as particularly talented in that regard, but felt he could perhaps contribute something unique. He had read about a recipe in *Grey's Sporting Journal* and decided to give it a try. He experimented first at home, plying guests with cocktails before serving up his masterpiece along with plenty of French bread and wine. It turned out to be 'pretty good', according to the guests, and so buoyed, announced to the club that the November outing at Belfair State Park would feature bouillabaisse as the main course.

"What the hell is bouillabaisse?" came several shouts, almost in unison.

Now Dicky had to perform. He saved backs, heads and tails from the remnants of salmon he and Gerry caught and filleted for smoking. These he boiled in chicken broth until he had several quarts of thick strained liquid, which he froze. The rest of the main ingredients: halibut, cod, shrimp, Dungeness crab, clams and mussels he purchased fresh at the Pike Place Market. Fresh vegetables: celery, onions, potatoes and garlic—lots of garlic—he purchased at Safeway, along with a quart of olive oil and six loaves of French bread. Finally, he went to his garage and selected a case of his best wine: a homemade vintage of '77 Barbera. He figured if the stew was a bust, there would be at least the wine and bread.

But apparently it *was* acceptable, because even though he purchased ingredients for 30, and only 20 showed up, the pot was completely emptied the next morning for members to take home. One member, Bob Graham, ladled several pints into a bowl he covered with foil and placed in the refrigerator of his camp trailer. Unfortunately, in hitting a rather severe bump on the way back to Seattle, the refrigerator door popped open and his dinner-to-be and a dozen eggs fell out, spilling on the carpeted floor. The tragedy wasn't discovered until several days later. Bob's trailer was never the same and he finally abandoned it on a lot he owned on the Skykomish River.

So acceptable was Dicky's bouillabaisse, that he continued hosting this outing for the next twenty-five years. Some years tested the resolve of some members, however, as the November weather could be miserable. On many outings they stood at the edge of a sputtering fire with rain drenching any who strayed from under the club awning. It wasn't too many of these outings before Dicky or Al—I forget which—decided to give it a name, or rather an acronym: WETBUNS. Appropriately enough, it stood for: Winter Event to Taste Bouillabaisse Under Nocturnal Skies.

51   Homemade Wine

Now you have another specialist on your case, this time an internist who specializes in gastrointestinal disorders. Your colonoscopy results are negative, meaning there were polyps that are borderline cancerous. You're back to watching and waiting...

Dicky now had the time and resources to pursue My Trout and engage in other hobbies such as reel collecting and wine making. Even though he and Gerry still made fruit wines with their simplistic labels: elderberry (E), raspberry (RA) and now and then a mean blackberry (B); he felt he needed to get more technical. Joining the Boeing Winemaking Club helped. There, different aspects of winemaking could be learned, and after a few forays into grape concentrates with marginal results, he was introduced to Tony Picardo and the Rainier Valley Grape Train.

About 3 miles south of Seattle's Chinatown District, the Rainier Valley, like Chinatown, became an ethnic enclave in the early 1900s. About 80 Italian families settled there and brought with them their talent for gardening and winemaking. Since grapes didn't fare too well in their sun-deficient gardens, they were imported from California's Imperial Valley and shipped via train, usually in one or two boxcars. As others became aware of this bounty, more grapes on more boxcars came, until it was necessary to place orders months ahead with Tony Picardo, Rainier Valley's self-appointed grape buyer. Tony knew grapes, and if one placed an order for some vintages that may not have had the right sugar content, he'd set them straight. This advice hadn't always set well with some members of the Boeing Wine Club who thought they knew better.

Dicky called Tony and placed an order for 200 pounds of zinfandel and was steered instead to Barbara. This advice resulted in one of his best wines. Unfortunately, 200 pounds only made four cases, one of which he donated to the WFFC Christmas raffle. Because it was so well received, Al suggested he ought to take a bottle back to his *Seattle Times* office to give to Tom Stockley. Tom was the Time's wine columnist, and to Dicky's surprise and delight, several weeks later an article appeared in his Wednesday column:

"The market has been flooded lately with new releases, particularly from great chateau estates of the world. Here's one of the best I tasted recently:

The magnificent Chateau St.Earns, in medieval times a Chrysler Agency and Arco station, has been the home since 1969, of the famed St. Earns label, where Friar Stearns so lovingly has squeezed his grapes and other things to produce superlative wines, rivaling all competitors—or nearly all, anyway. The good friar takes pride in never turning loose a wine until properly aged at least a couple weeks and the sediment is pretty much settled (except one Elderberry back in '71 that was a real dog; never did clear). St Earns wines are known for their bouquet, body and freedom from side effects (other than mild lower-tract distress) throughout the Northwest and as far afield as Oso, Mattawa, Two Dot, Montana and Felt, Idaho. Few other vintners dare make these claims, or care to..."

Early the next morning, Dicky received an urgent call from the regional wine buyer for Safeway who requested an immediate shipment of fifty cases. It took several minutes for Dicky to convince the disappointed manager his wine wasn't commercially available, and certainly not in these quantities.

After this request, and encouraged by Stockly's column, the notion of getting into the wine business was discussed at a later fishing trip with Al. They had completed a successful day's fishing on Dabob Bay and were mellowing by a driftwood bonfire on Mrs. Eldridge's beach.

"It *could* be a profitable business," said Al as he poked at the glowing coals. "After all, what the world needs right now is an executive pop wine. It should even have a screw cap. The important thing is the label. I'll bet we could sell every bottle if we used the famous Saint Earns label."

"Well, it's your artwork and clever prose," Dicky replied. "It's hard work making a decent wine, though. Maybe we could just buy a bunch of cheap bulk wine and rebottle it."

That was as far as the notion ever progressed, however, and after another glass of wine, a few more pokes at the fire, conversation turned to the next day's fishing.

52 Photography and Fly Casting

A return visit to your internist for another colonoscopy reveals no further polyps, and no indication of cancer. Another load off your shoulders, but you start visiting your specialists more often, and with renewed attention.

Dicky's desire to be close to My Trout extended to all aspects of fly-fishing. Under the tutelage of experts within the WFFC, he studied entomology, took advanced fly tying lessons, and learned to cast. Al was a good caster, and through their relationship, Dicky learned a lot just by watching. Al called one day and asked if he wanted to help Jimmy Green teach some of his Fenwick employees how to cast. Jimmy was Fenwick Rod Company's chief designer and not coincidentally, the current world champion caster. This was the beginning of a dimension of fly-fishing, above all others, that fascinated Dicky. After watching the effortless poetry of Jimmy's casting demonstration, he knew he had much to learn, but after a lot of practice, he did learn.

One learning vehicle he and Al used was the camera. Al had several Olympus Single Lens Reflex cameras he liked because of their simplicity and ruggedness. They were tossed loose in a waterproof diaper pail he carried in his jon boat, and often, when Dicky's casting was particularly bad—or good—he would notice Al taking his picture.

"Here's a couple we could send to Field and Stream," he kidded, after bringing a stack of glossies to their next meeting.

Al had access to the *Seattle Time's* photo lab and all the film he wanted, so it wasn't unusual for him to bring a stack of action shots of Dicky's casting. There wasn't a lot of instructional value in stills, other than to show form, or lack thereof. Dicky needed continuous action feedback, so he bought a used BetaCam and tripod. Now he could self-critique his casting, and set about perfecting his ability to cast far, and with accuracy.

On a fall outing to Dabob Bay with Al, Jimmy, and his wife Carol in pursuit of salmon, Dicky's casting apparently was noticed, because when Mel Kreiger called Jimmy for some assistance in a Fenwick-sponsored fly-fishing school he was sponsoring, Dicky's name was offered. Mel lived in San Francisco and had a long and fast friendship with Jimmy. They both were members of the prestigious Golden Gate Casting Club, and where Jimmy excelled in tournament casting, Mel was a natural teacher. Needing resident instructors in regions where he wanted to conduct his Fenwick schools, Mel called Dicky to teach at a school he had organized to run over a weekend at Quinault Lodge on the Olympic Peninsula.

It was shortly after the eruption of Mt. St. Helens and ash from a second eruption was evident as far north as Olympia. One group of students to enroll consisted of six dentists' wives. From Yakima, they had been housebound for weeks by a foot of ash from the first eruption and were glad, indeed giddy, to get away and leave their dentist husbands to their own devices.

"When you instruct the casting stroke, it's sometimes helpful to grasp the student's rod hand and give them a feel how power is applied," Mel said to Dicky as they prepared for the first class.

"This involves some diplomacy, as some men don't like their hand touched by another man, and it can also make women nervous. Once you establish their permission, stand behind them with your left hand on their shoulder, and grasp their rod hand with yours while applying your own casting stroke."

Dicky quickly learned the dentists' wives were anything but nervous. One took a fancy to him and delighted in leaning back into his groin and wiggling her butt seductively in time to the casting stroke. Frustrated, he moved to the next wife who made similar moves, only less flagrantly. Clearly, they were on the make, and at dinner that night, it was difficult to keep the conversation, instructor to student, on fly-fishing, as per Mel's instructions.

Dicky's thoughts regressed twenty-five years to another wife who, equally aggressive, managed to bed him with ease. Now a similar opportunity seemed imminent, and although tempted, he was now more in control of his hormones and could even be diplomatic in declining the invitation:

"Y'know, I'd like to," he said to wiggly wife as they found themselves alone at the salad bar. "You're very sexy, and under any other circumstances I might be tempted, but..."—and his words came in a whisper—"...I'm married."

This response wasn't received well, and Dicky returned with his salad to a very quiet dinner partner. Over desert, he tried to reestablish conversation around fishing, but finally she threw down her napkin and retired to the bar. She didn't show up for the post dinner movie and fishing knot practice, so he assumed she was successful in bedding someone else.

Dicky continued teaching for Mel in other Fenwick classes around the Northwest, and when Mel established his own school through his business, *Club Pacific*, he was invited to other venues in California. Mel chose only the finest places for his classes, charging his willing students accordingly, and rewarding his instructors with plush accommodations and great places to fish. One of Dicky's favorite places was Hat Creek Ranch below Mt Shasta in Northern California. Then, Dicky was commuting weekly to San Francisco to manage a Boeing subcontract, so it was a matter of driving a rental car back to Seattle and stopping en route to instruct, and to fly fish a premier trout stream. This gave him an excuse to buy yet another rod: a seven-piece Hardy 'Smuggler' he could keep in his briefcase along with a reel, extra spool and a box of flies. Just in case.

53   What Hath We Wrought?

You religiously return to have your PSAs and colonoscopies taken at the recommended intervals suggested by your specialists. Before you were fatalistic about your survival, but after fifteen years, watching and waiting turns to hope.

Back in Seattle, Dicky became one of the WFFC's most ardent instructors. In the winter, he held fly tying classes for thirty or more students, and just before opening day in the spring, he and several other instructors could be found at the Green Lake Casting Pier with up to fifty students. When Norman Maclean's autobiography: *A River Runs Through It* became a movie, the sport of fly-fishing took off like a rocket. Soon there weren't enough instructors to go around, and new fishing tackle companies clamored for anyone with skills to teach and promote their products. Schools were established at fishing lodges, new products were introduced into a suddenly burgeoning market, and 'how to' videos and books appeared almost overnight, where before there were none.

Dicky looked back at the crucial decision he made in 1975. Then he said to himself, not totally with conviction: *There isn't enough interest in fly-fishing to establish a business, so go back to the aerospace industry where you can make enough money to support your fishing hobby.*

The aerospace industry *was* good to Dicky. Little did he suspect the value of high-level contacts he made while in the NRO. Just as valuable, were his security clearances, which were becoming harder and more expensive to obtain. Previously, the FBI had been responsible to conduct background investigations at government expense, but now, private contractors took over and the costs were borne by companies needing cleared personnel. Every five years, background checks had to be revisited and for many, polygraph tests were required. Polygraph tests posed problems for many of the '60s generation because marijuana had been a subject to be abridged by interrogators. Anyone failing a test, by regulation, had their clearance suspended until further investigations could be completed. These presented additional costs, also borne by the contractor, so it was tacitly agreed that the subject of pot would be asked in such a way as to allow a former transgressor to pass his or her test.

Passing his polygraph tests, Dicky worked as a consultant on several challenging jobs during the years before he totally retired from the aerospace business. These were for the most part, related to early 'Star Wars' programs for which the Reagan Administration seemed to have unlimited funds. One particularly outlandish program, called Brilliant Pebbles, would consist of thousands of basketball-sized satellites placed into orbit, each autonomously targeting any missile entering its target trajectory, and flying destructively into its path.

To Dicky, these programs were nothing more than huge, blue-sky boondoggles with hundreds of contractors all claiming to be experts, and all hiring former 'experts' from other defunct programs. He attended one technical review meeting where it seemed every hanger-on in the entire Military-Industrial Complex descended. Held at the Lawrence-Livermore Labs in California, no fewer than two hundred highly salaried engineers, scientists and managers crowded into the main auditorium for two days to hear how Brilliant Pebbles was supposed to work. Using his pocket calculator, Dicky estimated meetings such as these alone would cost taxpayers millions of dollars.

In the 80's and early 90's, the numbers of such programs seemed to grow exponentially, making Dicky wonder how any could possibly be funded, given the huge software challenges involved. Armed with cost estimation algorithms he developed, he presented his questions to program managers, government and industry alike, but they were dismissed as something that could be 'worked out later'. He wondered if these programs made the country safer than those he worked on when dedicated career military officers were more involved in their management. Now, companies whose names he never heard of seemed to be running the show. He wondered how his former associates still working at the NRO felt about this trend.

He wondered if everyone's efforts in promoting fly-fishing had similarly gotten out of hand.

He wondered if My Trout could elude those hordes of fly-fishing enthusiasts he helped to educate.

He wondered if, in spite of relentless logging by the WTCo, My River could survive.

54   HiHium

"I'm afraid your PSA is continuing to rise," said your oncologist. "The bone scan confirms...."

Time is somewhere into the future. How far isn't important. Dicky's return to HiHium isn't important either, but probably he will go. It's September or October, his favorite months to anchor over a shoal he knew well. The aspens behind Moose Point will be brilliant yellow. He'll probably be with a woman or with several younger women. Maybe he'll be with a young man he should have fished with more.

Afterward

My River was the South Fork of the Chehalis.

Because I was born a few feet above her floodwaters, I claimed her as mine. Mom tried to get to the hospital, but on the way to town, the flood of '36 stopped us a mile past the Curtis store. Five years later when I learned to fish, I was fortunate to live near her.

My River flowed gracefully down the Boistfort Valley and once contained native and searun cutthroat—My Trout. Also there were once rainbow and steelhead, four runs of salmon and an assortment of chub, sucker, eel and shiner. Her gravel shoals and riffles were once dotted with flat pebbles of soapstone eroded from large seams of riparian limestone that formed underwater ledges. Competing for a place in the bottom of riffles and drifts were once hoards of caddis larva, mayfly nymphs and fresh water mussels. Along the shoreline, crayfish once scooted under clumps of waterlogged wood, and dried shucks of huge stonefly nymphs could once be found stuck to boulders on her gravel bars.

This was My River, where I swam, fished, trapped, hunted, and grew up thinking she would always be there, not in her pristine condition perhaps, because winter floods eroded her banks and summer irrigators sapped her strength. But still the salmon and steelhead returned, and My Trout could still be caught from her riffles.

Now My River is beyond recognition.

In December 2007, a perfect storm of melting snow and torrential rain loosened a huge mudslide that dammed up one of her tributaries that later broke loose and unleashed an unprecedented flood. People, property and animals were the first noticeable casualties of the maelstrom; but within the banks of My River, the progeny of aquatic creatures that existed before, were swept away or will be forever covered with the mud that oozes from perpetual scars on BawFaw whenever it rains. In past floods and droughts, their diminution was gradual and people who lived nearby hardly noticed. This time, their demise may well be irreversible.

If I'm wrong, I probably won't be around to find out.

Acknowledgements

Danielle Panush-Gamiz for her encouragement when this was just a scribble of personal recollections of my days on Richter Hill.

Priscilla Tiller for her book: *The Wooden Bench,* within which I was able to confirm places and names in the Boistfort Valley I had long forgotten.

Gerry Keller who endured several truncated and recalled versions while the vetting process took place.

Cheryl Rogers-Barnett for exposing the girl I met at PlayQuato to be an imposter. Had I read her memoir *Cowboy Princess* first, I would have realized it couldn't have been her. She *was* curious as to who would go to such lengths to keep me on a string. Me too.

R. Cargill Hall, NRO Historian Emeritus, for his helpful recommendations and reviews above and beyond his charter.

Brenda Holland who kept encouraging me to keep it light, even though she knows me to be overly introspective.

Louis Perrinello, a writer and cancer survivor himself, who urged me to keep on writing.

Mark Pratt, who, as his father, saw the humor, albeit sometimes poignant.

Pete Baird, Chuck Ballard and Bill Rundall: trusted friends who assured I wouldn't be banned from the club by writing this.

Linda Hathaway and her NRO Information Access and Release Team: for bird-dogging this through several bureaucratic national organizations.

Daughters Candy and CaraMia for putting the idea in my head for writing this in the first place.

And for DeVonne, who, as my favorite and first reader, kept her perspective. As I wrote, I often wondered what she would think when she read *this* part, but she didn't judge. For that, and for many other reasons, I love her dearly.

Dedication

This book is dedicated to the kind folks of the Boistfort Valley. They have suffered much from the December 2007 flood and will continue to struggle for years to get their lives together.

Individual donations can be directed to:

http://www.boistfortvalley.com/

899252

Made in the USA